Longman

E

ACTIVITY

M R Luckas

*Formerly Head of the Geography
Department, Goldsmiths' College
University of London*

Longman
London and New York

Longman Group UK Limited
Longman House, Burnt Mill, Harlow, Essex,
CM20 2JE, England and Associated Companies
throughout the World.

© Longman Group UK Limited 1991

First published 1991
ISBN 0 582 355842

Set in 10/12pt Times Roman, Linotron 202
Produced by Longman Group (F.E.) Limited
Printed in Singapore

British Library Cataloguing in Publication Data
Luckas, M. R. (Michael Rawson)
  Economic activity. – (Longman modular
  geography series).
  1. Economic geography
  I. Title
  330.9

  ISBN 0-582-35584-2

Library of Congress Cataloging-in-Publication Data
Luckas, M. R. (Michael Rawson)
  Economic activity / M. R. Luckas.
      p.   cm. — (Longman modular geography
  series)
  Includes bibliographical references and index.
  1. Economic geography. I. Title. II. Series.
HF1025.L78   1991   91-17332
330.9—dc20   CIP

Contents

Preface

This modular series of nine separate but inter-locking geography texts is designed primarily for sixth form students in the 1990s in the UK. The series is written by a team of authors who, with the Joint Editors, are Chief Examiners and Moderators for a number of GCE Examining Boards, and have been actively involved with sixth form teaching of geography for GCE 'A', and now 'A/S' examinations, as well as at college and university level.

In any modular system, self-standing parts are complementary to each other and to the series as a whole which caters, in its full range of systematic studies, for the needs of any conventional UK geography 'A' Level syllabus. In this series, there are nine texts: three physical and three human, together with three which focus on the interfaces (a) within physical geography, (b) within human geography and (c) between physical and human geography. Thus, the traditional compartmentalisation of the subject is challenged and new interdisciplinary syllabus and educational developments antici-pated. Moreover, real case-studies on global and local scales abound throughout, providing a continuing, but ordered and necessary, real-world perspective. Assignments of varying types are to be found in each chapter, providing stimulating work at the sixth form level as well as maintaining the spirit and approaches of GCSE.

Above all, this series offers a representative range of geography books, covering most of the subject, from which individuals may select their own combination for study. A combination of selected physical, human or interface texts can be tailored to suit any teaching programme and designed to meet the special requirements of a specific 'A' or 'A/S' examination syllabus, in-cluding those 'A/S' syllabuses which concen-trate on physical or human topics alone. Again, the available expertise and preferences in any given sixth form centre could govern the selec-tion of texts adopted for study. Such selections could favour specialisation (either in physical or human geography) or the interdisciplinary approach (based primarily on the interface volumes). This choice is yours.

Geography is a changing academic subject in a changing world, a changing society and a changing environment, creating great interest and new challenges at all educational levels. The inquisitive and illustrative style of these texts will provide sixth formers with the oppor-tunities to learn, by self-discovery, how theory matches practice and how the local, or distant, geographies can come alive in the classroom. Geography is in a unique position, straddling the humanities and the sciences, yet maintaining a strong academic and professional identity of its own. This series of texts serves to promote and advance that identity, in both the pure and applied senses, providing a contribution to training for good citizenship, and environmental awareness, as well as perspectives on human opportunities and environmental issues the world over.

B P Price
J A Taylor
(Joint Editors)

1

Economic Systems and Resources

ECONOMIC SYSTEMS

Everyone in society is a consumer of goods and services. Many people, either as individuals or working together in firms, are involved with producing the goods required. This production and consumption requires a great deal of human effort and organisation, referred to as *economic activity*. Obviously, the goods that are demanded cannot be made without an input of resources into the production system, for example energy and raw materials. Society has become increasingly concerned about the consequences of the ways in which these resources are exploited and, especially, at the rates of consumption of the world's available amount of

non-renewable resources, that is, those resources which are not naturally replenished on a human time-scale. There is also great concern about the degree to which economic activities harm the physical environment.

Characteristics of economies

The exploitation of resources is affected by their uneven world distribution, with some countries being richly endowed while others are impoverished. Deficiencies can, of course, be overcome by a movement of materials and goods from one country to another. As a result, the world economic system is characterised by a high degree of interdependence between coun-

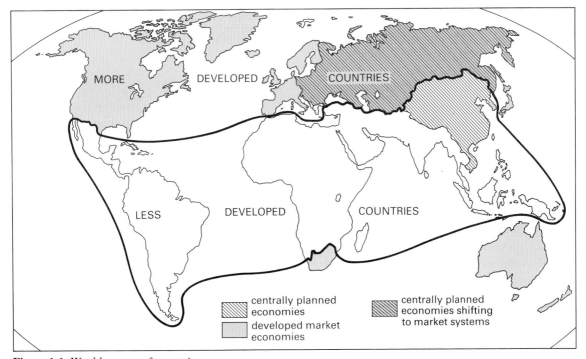

Figure 1.1 *World groups of countries*

	GNP per capita		Population		Contribution to GDP by				Consumption per capita			Cars	TV
	Total $US 1988	Change 1987–88 per cent	Total million 1988	Change 1987–88 per cent	Agriculture	Industry (Manufacture percentage in 1987)		Services	Protein gm/day 1980	Energy kg 1987	Steel kg 1987	per thousand people 1985	per thousand people 1985
Low income LDCs													
Zaire	146	−2.2	33	2.9	32	33	(na)	35	33	73	2	6	0
Bangladesh	151	0.4	109	2.6	47	13	(7)	39	42	47	5	1	1
Kenya	283	1.9	23	4.2	31	19	(11)	50	56	99	13	13	4
India	287	1.8	813	2.0	30	30	(20)	40	47	208	17	3	3
Ghana	346	−1.7	14	2.9	51	16	(10)	33	44	129	2	7	6
Newly industrialising countries													
Mexico	1 880	2.6	84	2.0	9	34	(25)	57	74	1 299	105	100	111
Brazil	2 022	8.2	150	2.4	11	38	(28)	51	61	825	70	86	127
S. Korea	3 327	10.0	43	1.3	11	43	(30)	46	82	1 475	413	23	175
Hong Kong	7 447	6.2	6	1.1	0	29	(22)	71	91	1 525	306	50	na
Singapore	8 433	7.6	3	1.1	1	38	(29)	61	80	4 436	658	141	188
Oil exporting countries													
Iran	1 582	1.3	51	3.2	26	36	(na)	38	77	955	95	49	55
Iraq	2 168	−5.0	18	3.5	18	46	(na)	36	68	732	70	34	55
Venezuela	2 790	0.4	19	2.6	6	38	(22)	56	75	2 394	186	130	124
Libya	5 333	0.0	4	3.1	5	63	(na)	32	87	2 674	174	203	66
S. Arabia	5 838	4.0	16	4.2	4	50	(9)	46	80	3 292	324	272	254
More developed countries													
UK	10 556	4.0	57	0.2	2	38	(25)	60	92	3 805	254	338	479
France	11 248	2.8	56	0.4	4	31	(22)	66	105	3 729	258	439	375
W. Germany	18 923	2.5	61	0.0	2	38	(33)	60	91	4 531	481	441	360
USA	18 951	3.0	246	0.9	2	30	(20)	68	106	7 265	448	714	790
Japan	23 616	4.3	123	0.5	3	41	(29)	57	89	3 232	553	371	253

Table 1.1 *Measures of the economy of selected countries*

tries. This is to be seen, for example, in the movement of raw materials from *less developed countries* (LDCs) to *more developed countries* (MDCs) and a contra-movement of manufactured goods. This division into LDCs and MDCs is one commonly used to group together countries on a world scale (Fig. 1.1). Other divisions are possible.

In Table 1.1, selected countries are placed into one of four groups according to population and economic variables, each group being arranged in rank order of *gross national product* (GNP) per capita. GNP is a convenient way of comparing the wealth of countries. It is the value of all the goods and services produced within a country plus net income from abroad. The GDP measure in the table, *gross domestic product*, is the total value produced by the domestic economy, that is, it excludes net

foreign earnings. (Note that where the dollar sign, $, is used in the text or tables it stands for the US dollar unless otherwise stated.)

The first group of countries in the table includes low income LDCs which are simply identified on the basis of low GNP/capita, but they are also characterised by high population growth rates, by the importance of *primary production* (e.g. agriculture and mining) in the economy and by low consumption rates per capita of food, energy and goods. The *newly industrialising countries* (NICs) are notable for their high rates of economic growth as measured by change in GNP. They have higher levels of consumption of goods and of materials, for example of energy and steel, than the LDCs.

The oil-rich countries show varying economic characteristics, depending in part on population size. Despite their oil income, measures of

GNP/capita for Iraq and Iran are not excessively high because national wealth is shared by so many people. In contrast, the high GNP/capita values of Libya and Saudi Arabia are linked to the benefits coming from the export of crude oil and petroleum products relative to population size.

The MDCs are wealthy countries with high levels of output from industries, and with significant contributions from service activities. They consume large amounts of materials and goods. Basic materials like steel, for example, are used by manufacturers to make *producer goods*, industrial tools and equipment, as well as *consumer goods* such as cars and washing machines.

Other ways of grouping countries are used in the text. Reference is made to the *developed market economies* (DMEs) and the *centrally planned economies* (CPEs). The DMEs are those developed countries with freely-elected representative governments and with economies managed through market forces of the kind described in this chapter. The CPEs are command economies in which the state directly controls the economy, using targets and quotas to guide levels of production and consumption.

There are many changes taking place in the economies of countries in different parts of the world. In several of the long-established industrial economies, employment in service activities is becoming more important at the expense of that in manufacturing, thus the shift to what has been called *post-industrial society*. In other countries, especially the NICs, industrial development is proceeding at a fast pace and they are emerging as important world manufacturers and suppliers of goods. This is the process of *industrialisation* (Fig. 1.2). Not all countries, however, are sharing in the world's more desirable social and economic changes and a number of the poorer LDCs are experiencing little economic growth.

Regional economies within countries are also

Figure 1.2 *Shipbuilding at Ulsan, South Korea. Shipbuilding typifies the country's early phase of industrial growth.*

Figure 1.3 *Steelworks, Pittsburgh, USA in 1968*

changing. Older industrial regions (Fig. 1.3) are experiencing decline as firms close down or move, as for example, in the USA, from old production centres in states such as Pennsylvania and Ohio to new locations in Texas and Florida: the move from *frostbelt* to *sunbelt*.

In short, the study of economic activity is not a static or routine matter, but one in which keeping up with rapid economic change and attempting to explain it and to understand its consequences is a challenging but rewarding task.

The working of the economy

The basic driving force of economic activity is the demand created by people for goods and services. Everyone needs at least a survival level of essentials such as food, shelter and medical care. Many people in wealthy industrialised countries also want luxury goods and the opportunity to use a wide range of services.

This demand from consumers is satisfied by producers, that is those firms which use resources to make and supply goods and services. The ways in which the main groups in an economy relate to each other are shown in the simple model in Figure 1.4. Note that the interchanges between the parts of the economy result from the actions of four decision-making groups: consumers, producers, resource owners and government. The *consumers* are regarded as the most fundamental group since they generate demand. Secondly come the *producers*, that is firms which have built factories for processing raw materials into useful goods, or businesses set up to provide services. The third group consists of the *resource owners* who provide the raw materials and other inputs that are needed at places of production. These resource inputs are referred to as the *factors of production* and include labour and capital, as well as natural resource inputs such as those from forestry, mining and agriculture. Finally, *government* exerts a powerful intervening, or controlling, force on the ways in which the economic system as a whole operates.

Governments in DMEs might intervene by imposing high taxes so that the amount of money people have left for personal spending is limited and consumption is curbed. Low taxes, on the other hand, let people retain more spending money and consumption is stimulated. Intervention can be more direct as in the state ownership of activities, for example, of health services or of utilities like electrical power supply. In contrast to this kind of mixed economic system within a democracy, for many decades in CPEs such as the USSR and those in Eastern Europe, the state has controlled the means of production and the levels of consumption. Now, in the early 1990s, many of these economies are being organised to become more like the market economies.

Omitted from Figure 1.4 is the important link between the economic system and the physical environment. Along with the production and consumption of goods come waste materials which can pollute the natural environment. This pollution imposes extra costs on society because of damage to the environment. These are *social costs* which can affect both people and the environment a long way from the source of the pollution. For example, the Chernobyl disaster of 1986, resulting from a fire at a nuclear power plant in the western USSR, caused radioactive fall-out in places as far away as Lapland, where reindeer had to be slaughtered, and North Wales, where sales of sheep were banned.

Price and the market system

The economy in Figure 1.4 is controlled by market forces. Raw materials and energy are exchanged in a market which links resource owners with producers, while consumers buy their requirements in the goods and services market. Money flows back into the system as spending on direct purchases. Money from the government and from the savings and profits of the private sector also returns as capital investment into resources and production. Stability in the market is reached when demand and supply move towards the balanced relationship shown in Figure 1.5, that is when the supply line is steeper than the demand line. When the price is low, demand is high because more people can afford to buy low-priced goods. Note that the demand line slopes downwards to the right in reflection of this. Producers, on the other hand, have an incentive to supply goods when prices are high and hence the supply line rises from lower left to upper right across the graph. Equilibrium is reached through adjustments shown by the figure. The initial quantity, Q_1, supplied

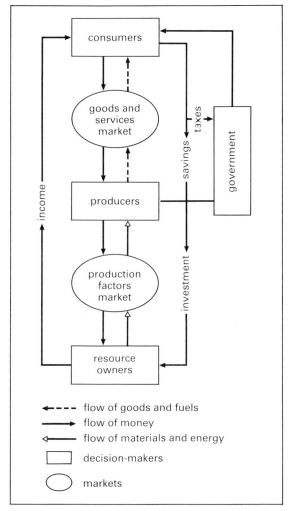

Figure 1.4 *Decision-making groups and markets in the economy*

to the market is short of that demanded and the price rises from P_1 to P_2. At this level there is surplus production, Q_2, and the price falls. This sequence of adjustments continues until a final point of balance, or *equilibrium*, is reached when supplies match the quantity demanded, Q_e, at a price P_e. No unwanted goods are left unsold, and both consumers and suppliers are satisfied. Price in effect is the arbiter of supply willingness and demand eagerness, so that in economies of the kind shown here, prices act to signal how resources are to be allocated to production in order to satisfy the demand for goods.

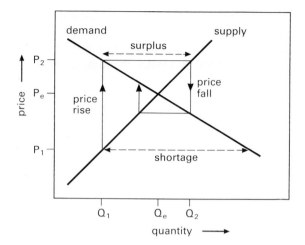

Figure 1.5 *Supply and demand adjustments towards equilibrium*

ASSIGNMENTS

1 Study Table 1.1.
   a. State three differences between LDCs and NICs.
   b. Suggest why energy consumption per capita is so much higher in the NICs compared with the LDCs.
   c. For the LDCs and NICs, plot the percentage GDP figures for agriculture against those for manufacturing, and comment on the pattern produced.
2 a. What kinds of environmental pollution are possibly caused by your school or college?
   b. Name two kinds of pollution caused by an industry such as iron and steel or chemicals.
   c. Suggest two ways in which this pollution might be controlled.
3 a. Choosing data from Table 1.1, draw compound column diagrams for one LDC and one MDC to contrast the proportion of GDP contributed by agriculture, manufacturing and services.
   b. Describe and attempt to explain these differences.
4 With the aid of Figures 1.4 and 1.5, explain how the market for goods and services works.
5 a. Use data from Table 1.1 to plot GNP per capita against cars in use per thousand people.
   b. Work out the Spearman Rank Coefficient of correlation, and comment on the relationship shown by your graph.
   c. Give reasons for the variation in the cars in use amongst the MDCs.

TYPES OF NATURAL RESOURCES

Natural resources mean water and air, and raw materials won from the land as mineral ores, energy and *biotic products*. Land itself is a resource not only when used for growing crops and grazing animals, that is the production of biotic products, but also as the space which is occupied by domestic and commercial buildings. Natural resources can be divided into *non-renewable*, *renewable* and *other* resources (Fig. 1.6).

Non-renewable resources

The non-renewable group, also called finite, capital or stock resources, have finite limits and will ultimately be depleted. One group, the fossil fuels, are totally destroyed by use, and the world's reserves are therefore depleted at the rate of consumption. Present rates of consumption thus have implications for future availability; simply, if more is used now less is available later.

Non-metallic resources such as stone, gravel, sand and clay are recoverable from a variety of

Figure 1.6 *Classification of resource types*

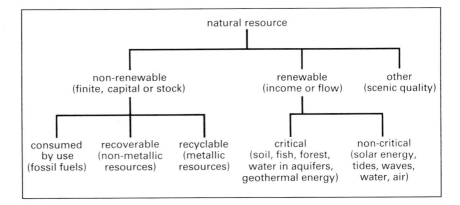

geological deposits. These resources are widely distributed and are relatively abundant.

Metallic minerals are referred to as *recyclable* because they can be reclaimed from end products when they are scrapped. Complete recycling would greatly reduce the need to mine new metal ores, but in practice total recovery is not possible for the simple reason that the costs of collecting the scattered scrapped items are high. The discarded materials from households, for example, are so spread around that, despite efforts to collect them, many are lost to future use. It is, however, feasible to recover waste metal from industry because of the greater concentrations involved. Metal refining industries themselves use scrap because of the energy savings that can be made. Recycling rates in the USA, for example, are around 15 per cent for aluminium and 50 per cent for iron.

The significance of a resource can change with time, for example, the large-scale exploitation of bauxite awaited both the industrial technology and the demands of the nineteenth and twentieth centuries. More recently, uranium ores have become identified as resources, having gained economic significance since the development of nuclear fission and its application to the generation of nuclear power.

Resources and reserves It is necessary to distinguish between resources and reserves of finite raw materials. *Resources* are materials that are of use to societies at a particular time. *Reserves* are the proportion of resources that can be mined under prevailing technical and socio-

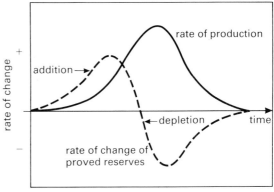

Figure 1.7 *Theoretical production cycle and changes in reserves of a non-renewable resource*

economic conditions. At any one time, reserves are simply the economically usable portion of total resources. Based on the known reserve, a prediction can be made about the life-time availability, or *production cycle*, of a raw material. As shown in Figure 1.7, production rises sharply at first, drawing on reserves which are still being proved, but is then followed by a period of falling production as the available reserves are used up.

The question, 'How long will a finite resource last?' cannot be answered with precision. The ultimate size of the world's stock of resources is not known. The situation is like a complex interconnected web in which a change in one part alters the shape of the whole. For example, if rates of demand start to fall, the production cycle will be pushed to the right and the peak of the curve in Figure 1.7 will be less pronounced; a given amount of reserve will last longer. At these lower levels of demand, prices will fall and the incentive to find additional reserves will also fall. After a time production will use up reserves, supplies will get short and prices will be adjusted upwards, giving an incentive to search for more reserves, possibly by applying new technology to do so. A new cycle of changing relationships between reserve size and demand will be set in motion. What happens, therefore, is that over a period of time there are changes in the rate at which the finite resources are unlocked from the world's total stock and set aside as reserves for current use.

Renewable resources

Renewable resources are not limited to certain time periods. One group, the *non-critical*, will always be available because of its recurrent nature, for example, water power or solar energy. The *critical* group, however, could be destroyed unless properly managed. This group includes resources such as soil, fish and forests.

A predicted production cycle for a critical type of renewable resource is given in Figure 1.8. In the initial stages, the yield rises as the rate of extraction is less than the rate of reproduction or replacement, for example, as new fish stocks or new stands of timber. At the *maximum sustainable yield*, rates of reproduction and extraction are in balance, but if more effort is applied to exploit more of the resource, yields fall and the stock becomes unbalanced as the mature stock declines. Continued exploitation accelerates the decline until the critical

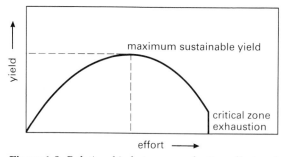

Figure 1.8 *Relationship between production effort and sustainable yield*

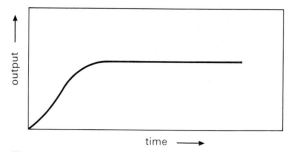

Figure 1.9 *Production of a continuously available renewable resource*

threshold is reached, at which stage extinction threatens. It would make sense, therefore, to manage these renewable resources at the maximum sustainable yield. Natural environmental and economic conditions make this difficult, and as discussed in Chapter 2, some seas, such as the North Sea, have been depleted of stock as a result of over-fishing.

The non-critical renewable resources are naturally occurring materials which are continuously available and indestructible (Fig. 1.9). Their use often depends on a great deal of human effort and ingenuity, as in the attempts to develop techniques to tap solar energy. Harnessing these resources can be costly where sites are remote from industrial production centres and from markets, for example, the water power developments at Churchill Falls, Canada, and at Itaipu on the River Paranà between Brazil and Paraguay.

Other resources

Placed in a final group of other resources (Fig. 1.6) are intangibles such as the perceived value of the landscape. In recognition of the importance of preserving natural features, selected areas are protected by designating them as national parks, forest parks or game parks. The world's first national parks were established by the USA at the end of the nineteenth century, for example, Yellowstone in Wyoming, Yosemite Valley (Fig. 1.10), King's Canyon and Sequoia in California and Mount Rainer in Washington. Many other countries have followed with their own allocation of parks and other natural envi-

Figure 1.10 *Yosemite Park: scenic grandeur as a natural resource for recreation and tourism*

ronmental areas. In African countries management objectives are often directed at protecting wildlife, whilst at the same time providing for tourism, as at Tsavo Park in Kenya and Serengeti Park in Tanzania.

ASSIGNMENTS
---

6 a. What waste materials are collected at your school or college?

  b. Suggest ways in which you would encourage the recycling of waste.

  c. Why is scrap recovery from industrial users much easier to organise than from domestic users?

7 a. What is the difference between a resource and a reserve?

  b. What are the factors which influence our knowledge of amounts of reserves?

8 a. With reference to Figure 1.6, give three reasons for classifying resources into non-renewable and renewable groups.

  b. Describe the form of the curve in Figure 1.8, and explain what is meant by a critical renewable resource.

  c. Use Figure 1.10 to note three features of this national park.

THE USE OF NATURAL RESOURCES

Of the total stock of natural materials in the world, only a part can be counted as the resource base at any one time. Despite its physical existence, a natural material is not regarded as a resource until there is both a demand for it and the technology to extract and utilise it at an economic price. Costs are involved in using resources, for example, the inputs of labour and capital in mining and processing. These two inputs are discussed more fully in Chapter 6, but for the moment, labour can be considered as the size of the workforce, its skills and the skills of management, and capital, either as money or as investment in machinery and buildings.

Demand for natural resources

Increases in the demand for natural resources are brought about by four closely interrelated factors: population growth, rising standards of living, industrial development and technology. In the mid-1980s, with the world population growing annually at 1.7 per cent, there were demands for extra natural resources. Note though that this average percentage change disguises the fact that population is increasing in some countries at more than twice this rate. High rates of population increase are part of the cause of an under-supply of essentials like food in some LDCs. Adequate food supply is an especially acute problem in some African countries, where home food production per capita has fallen in the 1980s (see Chapter 2). Even in countries where the rate of population increase has slowed down, the sheer magnitude of the additional number of people to be fed each year imposes immense pressure on the ability to supply sufficient food. China and India, for example, each had an average annual population increment of about 13 million in the period 1985–90.

Although the per capita demand for many goods in the LDCs is low (see Table 1.1), the total consumption can be large because of the sheer number of people involved. Total steel consumption in India, for instance, is some 14 million tonnes, which is not far short of that in the UK. If in the future the LDCs shifted to higher levels of per capita consumption of goods, the impact on the demand for world resources would be substantial.

Increased demand for resources in the DMEs

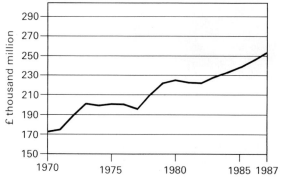

Figure 1.11 *Changes in total disposable income in the UK at constant 1985 prices, 1970–1987*

is more to do with rising standards of living than with population growth. People have more money to spend because *disposable income*, the amount left over from gross income after deductions for taxes and pensions, has gone up in the DMEs as shown by the example for the UK (Fig. 1.11). As people become more prosperous they spend increasing amounts on luxury goods. The high rates of consumption of goods contribute in turn to high standards of living. Car ownership and the use of electronic equipment have greatly increased over the twenty-five years to 1985 (Fig. 1.12), while most householders expect to use a range of domestic equipment like refrigerators, washing machines

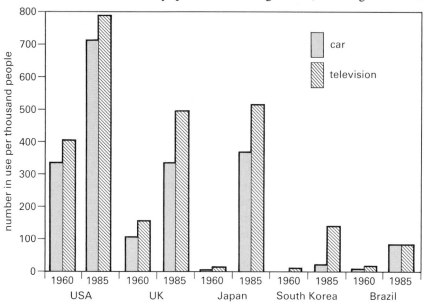

Figure 1.12 *Changes in use of selected goods, 1960–85*

14

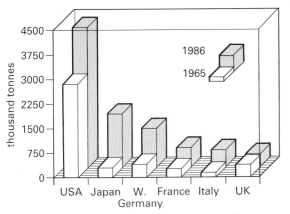

Figure 1.13 *Changes in aluminium consumption, 1965–86*

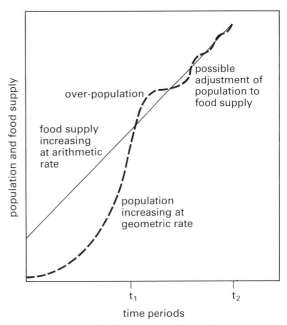

Figure 1.14 *The Malthus model of population increase and food supply*

and other electrical appliances. Many of these items are replaced, not only when they wear out, but also when new versions are marketed. All this adds up to a sizeable demand, and imposes a corresponding demand on the materials, metals like aluminium (Fig. 1.13) and plastics, needed to make such consumer goods.

Technological change boosts demand even further. Innovations lead to the introduction of new products. The market for television sets expanded very rapidly in the USA and in Europe in the early 1950s and that for computers from the 1980s. With the introduction of new goods there is a ratchet effect on consumption, that is, new demand is built upon the previous demand, pushing up total consumption to ever higher levels over a period of time. Demand for entirely new materials can be created, as with silicon chips, for example.

The situation of the NICs is interesting. Compared with MDCs, their demand for consumer goods, like cars and television, is not especially high, although as shown in Figure 1.12 for Brazil and South Korea, these demands are increasing. Already, however, the NICs are important consumers of energy and of industrial materials like steel (Table 1.1).

Depletion of resources

From time to time, when the rate of consumption accelerates, there is concern about the depletion of resources. Nearly two hundred years ago, fears about population outstripping food resources were expressed by Thomas Malthus. His argument, summarised in Figure 1.14, was that in a subsistence type of economy, a crisis of supply would result if population was gaining at a geometric rate, but food supply only at an arithmetic rate. In the absence of increases in the rate of food production, checks on population through starvation, disease and war would enforce a balance between the size of population and the resources available to it.

More recently, in the early 1970s, fast economic growth and high demand for resources led to studies of the complex interrelationships between population growth, resource consumption, manufacturing output and environmental pollution. Figure 1.15, taken from *Limits to Growth*, a report for the Club of Rome in 1972, shows one example of several models of the world based on the computer analysis of several variables. This version suggests that a continuing population increase accompanied by greater industrial production would gravely deplete existing resources and overwhelm the world's

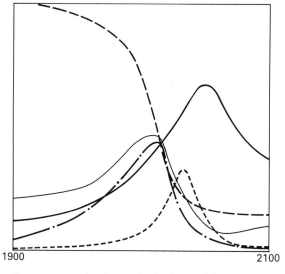

Assumes no major changes in physical, social or economic relationships.

——————————— population
— — — — — resources
——————————— food/capita
—— · —— · —— industrial prod./ capita
- - - - - - - pollution

(from Meadows: *Limits to Growth*)

Figure 1.15 *Constraints to population and economic growth at a world scale*

9 a. State, and briefly comment, on three factors which affect demand for resources.

   b. Suggest two ways in which the rate of depletion of resources might be slowed down.

10 Study Figure 1.15.

   a. Describe the relationship between (i) population and resources and (ii) population and industrial production per capita.

   b. Attempt to explain these relationships.

11 a. What is meant by the term 'disposable income'?

   b. For the UK and Japan, use Figure 1.12 to compare the changes in the use of goods.

   c. Explain why people in wealthy countries spend more of their disposable income on non-essentials than on essentials.

12 Refer to Table 1.1.

   a. For both energy and steel, estimate for each LDC the total quantities demanded if per capita consumption rose to four times the present amounts.

   b. Compare these figures with those already found in the MDCs.

   c. Comment on the implications for world resources if consumption in the LDCs rose by such an amount.

delicately balanced natural ecosystem through pollution damage. The resulting resource and environmental crises would be followed by a dramatic reversal in the population trend.

However, resource consumption changes would be more complicated than the model suggests. If the supply of a resource became short, its price would go up, some people would no longer be able to afford it and demand would drop back. Furthermore, high prices would act to limit the rate of depletion by encouraging conservation and technical innovation leading to alternatives. Many people in society are now willing to conserve resources and to be more resolute in dealing with pollution, as for example by the introduction of lead-free petrol and controls on acid gas emissions at coal-fired power stations.

THE DEVELOPMENT PROCESS

The concept of development is a complex one. It involves the quality of life as well as economic conditions. Thus conditions related to nutrition, medical care, literacy and political stability need to be considered in addition to income, consumption and trade. Furthermore, development also implies change, hopefully as a process of improvement in social, economic and political activities. Development is thus a more comprehensive change that just economic growth.

Stages in economic development

People employed in the production activities of a country may be placed in one of four employment sectors: *primary, secondary, tertiary* and *quaternary*. People in the primary sector are involved in the exploitation of natural resources, as in agriculture, forestry, fishing and mining, while those in the secondary sector take the raw materials from the primary sector and manufacture them into useful products. This transformation adds value to the end product in comparison with the lower values of the raw materials used. The commercial and trading functions of a society are covered by the tertiary sector. In this sector are wholesaling, retailing and transport activities, together with businesses that perform services. The quaternary sector involves high levels of decision-making in administration, financial management, information processing and research and development.

The balance between these various sectors provides a clue to the level of economic development of a country. The sector model of development (Fig. 1.16) describes the way in which employment changes with the economic development of the economy. As time goes by, people move from primary tasks, especially from agriculture, into manufacturing. This industrialisation adds to a country's economic prosperity with an increasing range of goods being produced, consumed and exported. To support these industries, transport, financial and other services are needed and so the tertiary sector expands. Eventually, highly innovative economic change takes place, with a growth of communication and management functions concerned with information handling within the quaternary sector. As the tertiary and quaternary activities grow in importance, secondary activities diminish in relative importance as shown in Figure 1.16. This contemporary change, the emergence of *post-industrial society*, is due partly to the need for more people in the tertiary and quaternary sectors and partly to improvements in industrial productivity so that fewer people are required to manufacture an increasing amount of goods.

Economic growth

Economic growth is the capacity of a country to increase industrial output and hence GNP per capita. There is accompanying growth in the consumption of commodities, goods and services, and an expansion of trade and savings. An important implication arising from the information in Figure 1.16 and Table 1.1 is that a possible way for LDCs to secure economic growth is by industrialisation. This is what the high-GNP MDCs appear to have done. A well-known model which suggests such a growth sequence is that of American economist W. W. Rostow, 1967. The five stages of the *Rostow economic growth model*, based on the modern

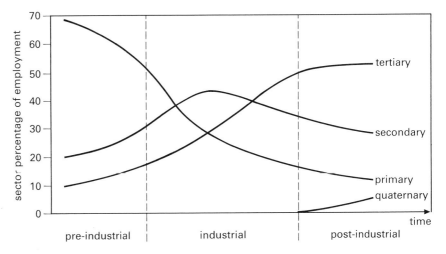

Figure 1.16 *Sector model of economic development*

Figure 1.17 *Rostow's Stages of Economic Growth model*

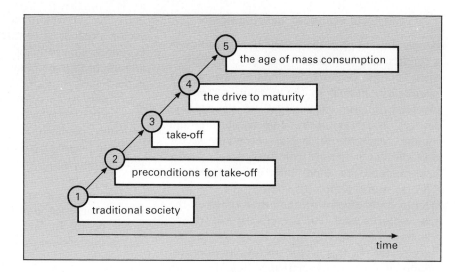

history of development observed for advanced countries, are given in Figure 1.17. Stage 1, the *traditional society*, is an agricultural society in which farming is largely carried out at a subsistence level, with no opportunity for increasing the output per person. By the second stage, industry as well as agriculture has developed. There is rising investment, at around 5 per cent of GNP, and a major improvement of transport.

The *take-off stage* is crucial; here the mechanisms for self-sustaining growth of the economy emerge. What seems to be critical is that there is investment at a higher rate, over 10 per cent, into one or two fast-growing industries so that the momentum of manufacturing growth is sustained, as happened in the case of the textile industries in nineteenth-century Britain (Fig. 1.18). The earnings, from both home and abroad, generated by such industries provide capital for the necessary investment into the economy at large, giving impetus for new activities like machine manufacturing and for improvements to transport. As growth spreads to all sectors of the economy, the *drive to maturity stage* is entered. Technological improvements widen the product range and create demands for higher labour skills in manufacturing. The tertiary sector expands as more services, especially transport services, are demanded. In the last phase, the *age of mass consumption*, the increasingly affluent society is

dominated by the production and consumption of durable goods.

Although from the model it is not entirely clear how the economic processes cause linkage from one stage to another, the key ingredient appears to be the build-up of capital into productive activity. It should be borne in mind that the Rostow model is based on the sequence followed by the western industrial economies. It is not necessarily a suitable model for present day LDCs for others to follow at a much later date. A quite different set of economic circumstances exists, especially on account of the global scale of modern industrial production. This makes it difficult for LDCs to compete in world markets for manufactured goods.

Although, the world can be considered as an interdependent economic system as suggested at the start of this chapter, dependence remains one-sided. Imbalances of resource consumption are commonplace, with the world's wealthy industrial nations being the dominant consumers. In 1985, for example, the five DMEs given in Table 1.1 used 46 per cent of the world's six main metal minerals and 42 per cent of all the crude oil. Much of the flow of capital is towards the DMEs, whilst many LDCs have fallen increasingly into debt. The gap between the two broad groups of countries, in terms of wealth and standards of living as measured by the consumption of goods, is large and shows

Figure 1.18 *Textile mills at Preston, Lancashire, in 1920: a legacy of nineteenth century industrial development*

little sign of reducing. So far as other needs, such as education, medical care and housing, are concerned, some LDCs are gravely under-provided. For the most impoverished of them, and especially for those afflicted by environmental disasters such as drought and human disasters brought about by war, even famine has yet to be eradicated.

ASSIGNMENTS

---

13 a. Study Figure 1.16.
   (i) At the start of each stage, what was the percentage employment in each of the sectors?
   (ii) Suggest why secondary employment peaked half-way along the industrial stage.

b. For any one LDC, find out about its primary sector and why it is important.

14 With reference to the Rostow model:
   a. what are the features of stage 2?
   b. suggest why stage 3 is such an important one;
   c. why is there some doubt that LDCs should follow the model as a route to economic development?

15 a. For the NICs and MDCs (Table 1.1), on some graph paper, plot GNP per capita along the horizontal axis against steel consumption along the vertical axis.
   b. Sketch a best-fit line through the array of points.
   c. Which two countries are furthest from your line?
   d. Suggest why they consume more steel than expected.

2

The Non-Fuel Renewable Resources

LAND AND WATER RESOURCES

Human survival depends upon the produce obtained from land and water resources. These are the renewable or flow resources noted in Chapter 1 and shown in Figure 1.6. The soil is the resource base of crops and livestock, and is a renewable resource as it can be maintained, and its fertility even enhanced, for the benefit of future generations. However, over-intensive use of the land can cause soil erosion as Figure 2.1 shows for an area in central Mali, West

Africa. Because soil can be misused, it is classified as a critical sub-set of resources in Figure 1.6. Biotic resources from forests and seas are also critical as they can be depleted as a result of mismanagement.

In contrast, water appears to be a perfect example of a sustainable flow resource since it is naturally recycled as part of the geophysical chain. Nevertheless, in places, water is limited and shortages occur. There are problems of access to water for some people simply because nature does not deliver water where it is needed. Periodically, some places are so gravely

Figure 2.1 *Soil erosion through over-intensive land use, Central Mali, West Africa*

under-supplied with water that natural life-support systems fail the people. These are the tragedies that strike in semi-arid areas such as the Sahel zone of the south Sahara margin.

Although there is great variety in the use of land, agriculture and forestry predominate. Of the world's land surface, 35 per cent is arable and pasture land, and 30 per cent is forest. People also value land because of its scenic quality, and gain satisfaction from recreation based in areas of particular landscape merit such as coasts, mountains and lakelands (see Chapter 7). Finally, a small proportion of the world's land has a very high value as space occupied by houses, shops, factories and offices.

Competition for land

Because land is fixed in location and supply, there is often fierce competition for it. An increase in demand from one user has to be met by a transfer from one type of use to another. There is great pressure for such transfers in the more urbanised parts of the world, and, in the MDCs, it is common to attempt to limit change from rural to urban use. Intervention like this influences the economics of land resources as in the case of the UK's Green Belt policies.

The idea of *economic rent* helps explain how the competition for land is resolved. This concept was used by J. H. von Thünen in his study of agricultural location published as *The Isolated State* in 1826. In his analysis of the spatial organisation of farming, von Thünen simplified the real-world conditions by limiting the number of factors, such as soil, slope and drainage, that had to be taken into account. He imagined that a town, the sole market-place, was supplied with food and other needs from a surrounding featureless plain of uniform soil fertility. On this *isotropic surface* (a surface equal in all directions) farmers worked to maximise profits. Under these conditions, the economic rent, or net income, which a farmer gains from growing a particular crop can be expressed by a simple equation:

Economic rent = yield (market price – production cost) – (yield × transport rate × distance from market)

Table 2.1 shows how the economic rent at a place is calculated assuming that for any one crop, market price, yield, production cost and transport rate are constant no matter where it is grown. As is shown in Figure 2.2(a), economic rent depends on the distance of the place of production from the market. Very simply, it is the price a farmer in a more distant location would be prepared to pay to occupy a better position nearer the market.

Patterns of land use

A pattern for three crops is shown in Figure 2.2(b), drawn from the hypothetical data given in Table 2.1. Note that each crop has a different price, yield, production and transport cost. A farmer at the market-place gains the greatest economic rent by growing high-value vegetable crops, but they are costly to transport to market because they need careful handling and suffer wastage. A farmer's revenue from growing these crops falls rapidly with distance and at 10 km it is worth switching to dairying,

Crop/ produce	Price £/t	Yield t/ha	Production cost £/ha	Transport rate £/t/km	Econ/Rent at market* £/ha	Economic limit** km
vegetables	220	10	1200	5.00	1000	20
dairy	180	8	840	1.25	600	60
wheat	100	5	200	0.60	300	100

Table 2.1 *Hypothetical data for crop production around a central market*

*   economic rent/ha = price × yield – (production cost + transport cost)

** economic limit = economic rent at market (transport rate × yield)

t   tonne

because it costs less to transport dairy products. By similar reasoning, just beyond 40 km farmers are better off growing wheat. Although wheat commands the lowest market price, the cost of delivering it to market is low and hence even at this distance wheat can still be sold profitably. The limit of cultivation is ultimately reached at 100 km, beyond which limit transport charges cancel out all the money earned by selling wheat into this particular market.

Von Thünen's original work showed a pattern of farming which reflected the market needs and agricultural methods of the early nineteenth century (Fig. 2.3(a)). The narrow belt of forestry in the second ring arose from the importance of wood for fuel and building, as well as its high costs of movement. Further

from the market, declining intensity of use is shown by arable with fallow, and finally ranching. Von Thunen was alert to ways in which the land-use patterns would be modified by actual situations. Figure 2.3(b) shows that if river transport were used, the lower transport costs allow an outward extension of each zone along the river.

Several studies have used the von Thunen model as a framework for examining modern patterns of agriculture (Fig. 2.3). These patterns broadly indicate declining intensity of land use with distance from a market. Some simple types of system, like that at Soba village, Nigeria (Fig. 2.3(c)), are strongly influenced by distance factors. Within the village are garden plots used for vegetable crops. These plots are

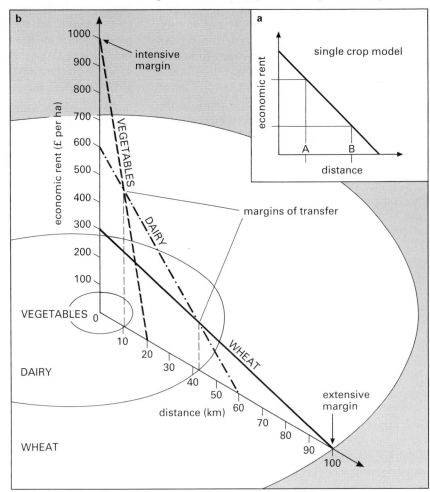

Figure 2.2 *Economic rent models, showing the resulting pattern of land use in b*

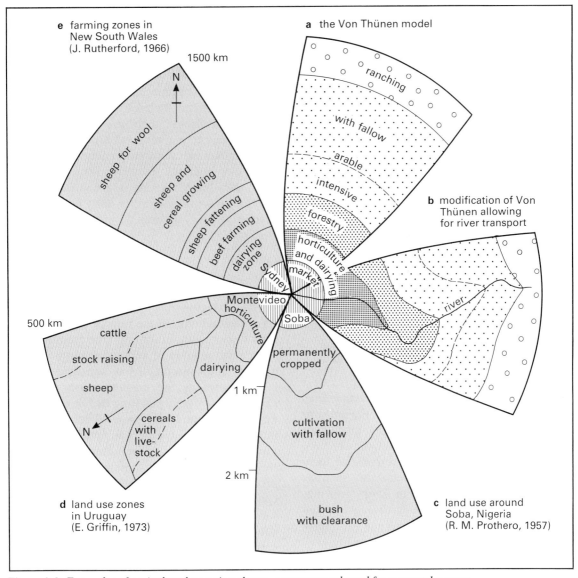

e farming zones in New South Wales (J. Rutherford, 1966)

1500 km

sheep for wool

sheep and cereal growing

sheep fattening

beef farming

dairying zone

a the Von Thünen model

ranching

with fallow

arable

intensive

forestry

horticulture and dairying

market

Sydney

b modification of Von Thünen allowing for river transport

river

Montevideo

horticulture

Soba

500 km

cattle

stock raising

sheep

dairying

cereals with live-stock

1 km

permanently cropped

2 km

cultivation with fallow

d land use zones in Uruguay (E. Griffin, 1973)

bush with clearance

c land use around Soba, Nigeria (R. M. Prothero, 1957)

Figure 2.3 *Examples of agricultural zonation shown as transects adapted from several sources*

intensively used and are manured to keep them fertile. Fertility is also maintained on the permanently cropped zone, but more extensive methods are used beyond 1 km with the introduction of fallow land. A study by E. Griffin of agriculture in Uruguay (Fig. 2.3(d)), suggests elements of von Thünen's concentric pattern near Montevideo, modified by an extensive stock-raising zone related to relatively poor soils in the east of the country. In the highly simpli-

fied version of agricultural patterns in New South Wales, Australia given in Figure 2.3(e), the intensity of activity decreases with distance from Sydney. However, other important influences on the patterns related to relief and climate are not revealed in the diagram.

Economic rent also measures the intensity of use. A farmer at an inner location commanding higher economic rent at A (Fig. 2.2(a)) can afford to improve the land by fertilising or draining. Such extra expense cannot be afforded further away from the market at B, where economic rent is less, and here *intensive production* gives way to *extensive production*, with the inputs into farming being reduced. Complications occur near large urban areas where there is greater competition for land. At the *rural-urban fringe* the value of land for agricultural purposes is often lower than its speculative value for building purposes. A farmer's willingness to maintain inputs on the farm is affected by the possibility of selling out to property developers. Farming at the city margin also suffers from the effects of trespass, thefts and livestock worrying which reduce agricultural land value.

FACTORS AFFECTING FARMING ACTIVITY

Physical factors

Models of land use like von Thünen's provide a framework. The real world is more complex, as suggested in Figure 2.3. For a start, the uniform physical conditions assumed in the model are uncommon since soil, terrain and climate vary from place to place. Farmers respond to local conditions by undertaking activities, such as dairying, livestock rearing or crop growing, deemed to be most suitable in the light of the prevailing physical conditions. Thus in Britain farmers engage in crop production in the lowlands of the drier east of the country and in dairying and livestock rearing in the hilly and wetter west. A response to the vagaries of weather is for farmers to use combinations of crops, or of crops and livestock, rather than to rely on single crop production. This gives rise to the complex patterns of farming which are common over much of Western Europe.

Economic factors

Economic factors are also more complicated than the economic rent model assumes. Transport costs, for example, are not just a function of distance, but depend on particular routeways, a fact recognised by von Thünen himself as already shown in Figure 2.3(b). Today, efficient road transport permits long-distance movement of produce so that the producer's distance from market is of less significance than in the past. In any event, farmers themselves do not necessarily sell, nor transport their produce directly to market; marketing may be arranged through co-operatives or special governmental organisations. For example, for over fifty years after 1933, the Milk Marketing Board in Britain provided a collection system for dairy farmers, thus permitting dairying even in areas remote from markets.

Political factors

In the developed world, farming is greatly affected by government action. The Common Agricultural Policy of the European Community aims to restructure farming. One measure is to reduce the number of very small farms. This is done by the *consolidation* of scattered plots of land (known as the *remembrement* policy in France), or by amalgamating two or three small farms into one larger farm. There is also a policy on prices which was introduced when food supplies were short. This policy works through a system of *guaranteed prices* so that production is underwritten and farmers are encouraged to intensify the use of land, leading to a surfeit of foodstuffs which have to be stored at considerable cost. People are increasingly concerned about the wisdom of producing large surpluses and about the financial and environmental costs involved. A different set of land management objectives is seen to be desirable. These are aimed at reducing output by taking land out of production, referred to as *set-aside schemes*, and by promoting alternative rural activities in forestry, recreation and small-scale industry.

Behavioural factors

Success in farming depends upon the management skills of the farmer. The farmer has to decide what crops to grow, or what animals to keep, and what *inputs* to use for profitable production. Uncertainties are therefore introduced by the behaviour of individual farmers. They may not want to achieve maximum profits, but enjoy a livelihood with less money, but better quality of work. For this and other reasons of management, farm income is likely to vary, rather than fit a maximum as described in von Thünen's model.

The inputs are the factors of production of land, labour and capital. *Land* is a relatively fixed commodity for a farmer, though he may buy more of it, or improve its quality by adding fertilisers to it or by draining it. *Labour* on small farms is often just the farmer and his family, plus occasional hired help and contractors. Large farms may have a farm manager plus skilled and semi-skilled workers, and also make use of contracted labour. The trend is for large commercial farms to reduce the workforce per unit area, but to apply more *capital* in the form of equipment, on the assumption that more tractors, drilling machines, spreaders and harvesters lead to greater productivity. This seems the case from evidence in the USA, where over the twenty years from 1950, labour use in farming halved, power and machinery use increased by a factor of 2.5 and output rose fourfold.

Farmers make complex decisions about how much of each of the various inputs are used to produce saleable products. Look at Figure 2.4 which shows how two inputs, labour and capital, might be used. The diagonal lines show how each input can be varied; a little more capital results in less labour so that the total cost traced by an isocost line remains constant. At X, the total of 20 is made up of 15 units of labour and 5 units of capital, a balance of inputs which might describe a small farm with a little equipment. It is assumed that this is the most efficient combination for the farmer's output target of 500 tonnes. Other combinations of inputs along the 20-line do not reach this target production. Note that to produce 500 tonnes at point K on the graph would involve a total cost above 20 units. The combination of labour and capital, just where the output curve touches the

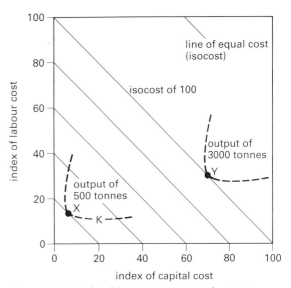

Figure 2.4 *Idealised farm input costs and output targets*

isocost line, is the best for this scale of production. The farm at Y is operating at a much larger scale, needing 100 units of input to produce 3 000 tonnes. It is highly capitalised in terms of equipment as shown by the balance of inputs, 30 of labour and 70 of capital, and has a higher output per unit of input compared with X, that is, it is gaining *scale economies*.

ASSIGNMENTS

1 a. Make a list of physical environmental factors which affect farming.
  b. For two of your factors describe how farming is affected.
  c. Comment on two advantages and two disadvantages of government intervention in farming.
2 Study Figure 2.2(b).
  a. What would be the economic rent at the market if the price of vegetables went up by £10/tonne?
  b. Explain why vegetable crops are grown near the market.
  c. If production costs of wheat were reduced by £60/ha, where would the new limit of cultivation be?
  d. Suggest how a farmer might reduce his costs of production.

3 a. Make a copy of Figure 2.4 and mark on it a farm with 20 units of capital and 60 units of labour.

  b. What type of agriculture might be associated with these intensive labour methods in MDCs?

  c. What are the consequences of intensifying agriculture in MDCs?

AGRICULTURAL SYSTEMS

The idea of inputs and outputs can be used to make a classification of agricultural systems. A particularly instructive approach is that based on *agro-ecosystems*, that is 'agriculture viewed as an ecological system with inputs and outputs of energy and matter' (I. G. Simmons, 1980). Simmons suggests that agriculture can be considered as composed simply of four *food chains*: crops used as human foodstuffs; crops fed to house livestock; grassland feeding of livestock, with year-long grazing; grassland feeding of livestock with winter housing and crops as feed.

The output from these food chains in terms of the effort needed to produce them can be measured by comparing the energy value of the input against that of the end product or simply, an *energy input/output ratio*. The inputs are solar energy plus fossil fuels in a variety of guises such as machinery, fertilisers, pesticides and fuels. Figure 2.5 shows that maize produced by intensive commercial methods needs large amounts of energy so that for each unit of energy used in production the energy output is relatively low at 2.58. Agriculture for animal products is even more energy intensive and an output as low as 0.5 is not uncommon per unit of energy input. A high energy cost has to be paid to produce protein in the form of meat. Apart from energy, plants and animals must have nutrients. Flows of nutrients are referred to as 'closed' when they return to the land as compost or manure, or as 'open' when they are lost as runoff. By combining the energy inputs and nutrient flows, a classification of agricultural systems can be devised. Table 2.2, adapted from Simmons's classification, gives just five types of farming system for discussion here.

Extensive livestock farming

This activity is typified by low inputs per unit area. Extensive grazing lands are needed to support the system; at a subsistence level for survival and at a commercial level to make a profit. At a subsistence level, *nomadic herding* fits the idea of low intensity use of the land, with only some 0.5 persons/km² commonly supported. Animals are fed on natural grasslands,

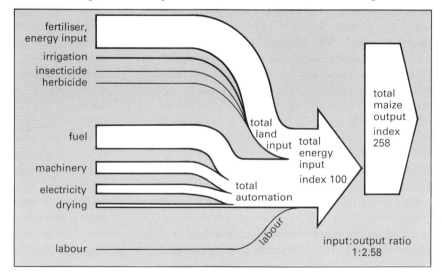

Figure 2.5 *Energy budget for a maize crop in an industrialised country*

Table 2.2 *Farming types as agro-systems*

Farming type	Energy density GJ/ha	Energy ratio input:output	Nutrient cycle
Extensive livestock	0.6 to 5.0	na	closed
Shifting cultivation	2.0	1:20 to 1:65	open
Extensive arable	4.0	1:30 to 1:40	closed
Mixed farming	12 to 15	1:15	closed
Intensive agriculture	15 to 40	1:0.15 to 1:3.5	open

GJ = giga joule (1000 million joules), or approximately 22kg oil equivalent

for example those of the arid and semi-arid regions stretching from the Sahara to Mongolia. Finding sufficient pasture for animals involves seasonal movement by peoples like the Tuareg, Masai and Kazak. There is a general decline, though, in nomadism; population pressure and environmental limitations such as drought are forcing a shift of people from these areas.

Extensive *commercial livestock ranching* operates on a very large scale. Sheep ranches in Australia, for example, are up to 8000 ha and cattle ranches in northern Australia even larger at 600 000 ha. The large scale of operation on these cattle ranches is a response to water deficiencies and pasture shortages in the dry season between September and December. Only 15 per cent of the cattle are fattened on the ranches, most being sent out to coastal pastures in Queensland which are near to meat packing and export facilities at ports such as Cairns, Townsville and Gladstone.

Extensive cattle ranching often takes place in zones which are, because of environmental conditions are marginal for crops, as on the western plains of the USA, the Karoo of South Africa and the south-east pampas of Argentina. Very low inputs are involved, for example 1 man hour/ha. Outputs are correspondingly low, at 0.2 kg/ha on poor pasture and up to 2 kg/ha on better quality grass.

Shifting cultivation

Shifting cultivation features: the rotation of land plots, low population densities, low inputs, and low yield per ha. Although returns from shifting cultivation are low per ha, they are high per man-hour of effort and per unit of energy input. The energy ratio for cassava in West Africa is 1:23, which compares very favourably with mixed farming ratios in many MDCs.

Shifting cultivation is based on felling forest trees, and then burning the felled wood and ground vegetation. The burning checks weeds and releases potash from the felled biomass. Crops are grown in the clearings for two to three years after which time weed infestation and loss of soil fertility force the cultivators to move and clear another patch. The abandoned plot reverts to secondary forest, and if left long enough recovers soil fertility. Where population density is low, 20- to 30-year cycles of plot rotation are feasible. With greater population pressure, the system adjusts to shorter fallow periods, those in Africa (Fig. 2.6) being described as rotational bush fallow.

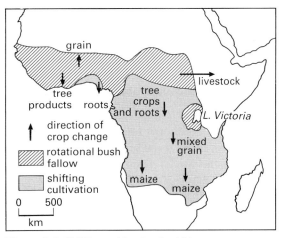

Figure 2.6 *Shifting cultivation in Africa*

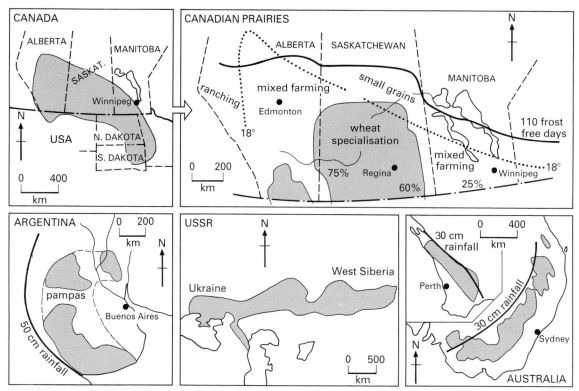

Figure 2.7 *World wheat producing regions*

Shifting cultivation is distributed patchily across the tropical zones of South America, Africa and Asia. There are different explanations for the present distribution, either that it is a remnant, left after the land needs of permanent farming are satisfied, yet where land is plentiful; or that the method of cultivation survives where the skills long practised by the cultivators have produced a system well adapted to the exacting environment.

Extensive arable farming

Extensive arable farming is associated with low inputs and outputs per unit area. Large units of production characterise grain farming, with state farms in the Soviet Union of up to 6 000 ha, and wheat farms in the North American prairies and in the Argentinian pampas averaging 500 ha, although a few are many times bigger.

Five areas of extensive wheat farming are shown in Figure 2.7. The areas in the USSR extending from the core region in the Ukraine to Kazakstan and West Siberia were opened up as new wheat growing areas in the 1950s. Some 40 million ha of wheat were planted in these steppe grasslands where rainfall is variable, frequently being less than 250 mm per annum. Wheat from the highly mechanised state farms (*Sovkhozy*) in these regions has added a potential 100 million tonnes a year to Soviet production, although in drought years output might fall by as much as 25 per cent.

North American wheat farms are highly capitalised and are farmed with the aid of large-scale machinery working across extensive areas (Fig. 2.8). Fossil fuel inputs are high, with machinery and fuel accounting for about one-third of the total input. In order to reduce capital outlay on equipment, especially expensive items such as combine harvesters, and to deal with such large acreages at harvest time, farmers often engage teams of contract harvesters, who work their way through the wheatlands. Canadian wheat production (Fig. 2.7) is concentrated in Saskatchewan. Other areas of the prairies have become more diversified and grow a range of small grains and oil-seed crops. There is a programme of fallowing the land throughout the prairies in order to reduce wheat output. This resting of the land also contributes to soil conservation.

Tropical plantation agriculture is another example of large-scale agriculture. This system of cash-crop production was introduced by west European countries during the colonisation of tropical lands in the eighteenth and nineteenth centuries. In several parts of the world, LDC governments have now taken control of plantations, and have set up state farms or have subdivided the land into smallholdings for peasant farmers. Even so, large foreign-owned estates are still involved in the production of rubber and palm oils in Malaysia and Indonesia; bananas in Ecuador, Costa Rica, Panama and the Philippines, and tea in India and Sri Lanka. Some estates are operated as private farms, as are the coffee haciendas in Brazil, but often the high capital investment needed to set up such large-scale production has come from companies. The rubber plantations in Liberia, for example, covering some 40 000 ha, were set up

Figure 2.8 *Wheat harvest at Clyde, Washington State, USA. Large scale methods suited to open level terrain.*

Figure 2.9 *Sugar cane estate and processing plant in Malawi*

by the American Firestone Company. Figure 2.9 shows a sugar cane estate and associated processing plant operated in Malawi by the Lonrho company.

Mixed farming

Crop production combined with livestock on family-run *mixed farms* is common in western Europe and North America. Both grass and crops (wheat, barley and roots in Europe, corn and small grains in the USA) are used for feeding. Inputs are high, especially of energy and fertiliser. Where heavy applications of fertiliser are used, grain yields up to 4000 kg/ha are achieved. Such high inputs can cause environmental problems, particularly when surplus fertiliser is flushed into rivers.

Family farms tend to be small, between 40 and 100 ha in the USA corn belt, but much smaller in western Europe. Many farms in western Germany are smallholdings run as part-time operations. Generally, such small farms

are inefficient, and European Community policy is aimed at a restructuring of such units. On mixed farms, income is mainly from the sale of livestock products: animals sold for slaughter or from milk products. Some crops are sold, but most are used for feeding animals. The mix of enterprises, crops and livestock gives rise to a complex pattern of activities.

In some places, mixed farming has given way to greater crop specialisation, with farmers getting more income from the sale of crops such as wheat, barley, potatoes, sugar beet and vegetables than from livestock. Vegetable crops are often grown under contract to processing firms. This specialisation is not only altering the diversity of farming, but also the landscape as a result of the removal of hedgerows when fields are enlarged.

Intensive agriculture

Concentrated energy inputs of up to 40 GJ/ha (Table 2.2) are associated with some types of *intensive farming*. There is heavy capital investment in specialised buildings and equipment. Daily energy inputs are high because of the amounts of foodstuff, fuels and fertilisers used. High gross outputs result, though, from horticulture, intensive livestock feeding and battery methods of feeding poultry. However, because of the high inputs, the energy input/output ratio is low, averaging 2.

Industrialised *feed-lots* of the Midwest, USA, are highly intensive systems, based on the buying-in of feed, corn and grain to fatten livestock for nearby meat-packing and processing centres such as Chicago. However, so many feed-lot units have been located in former cattle ranching areas that Texas and Nebraska are now more important for cattle feeding than Iowa in the Midwest.

A distinctive type of intensive cultivation, especially in parts of Asia, is that of *wet-rice cultivation* (Fig. 2.10). This system's ecological stability and long-term success in supporting a high-density rural population is due to the skilful management of the ecosystem. The flooded paddy fields provide an environment which naturally supplies nutrients and minimises their loss. Additional small inputs of dissolved nutrients flow in with the irrigation water. The waterlogged conditions slow down decomposition and nitrate loss, at the same time providing an environment for algae growth which fixes nitrogen. The processes operating in the ecosystem restore fertility and maintain crop yields even when two crops a year are grown. This intensive production, yielding 4 000 kg/ha, requires a large labour force for repairing canals and field bunds, preparing paddy fields, planting nursery rice and transplanting seedlings and the final harvesting using knife or sickle.

Figure 2.10 *Wet rice cultivation, Northern Thailand*

THE WORLD FOOD ECONOMY

The world's food production system is capable of supplying global needs; the glaring anomaly is the great over-supply in many DMEs and shortages in several LDCs. These shortages occur despite the importance of agriculture to their economies (Fig. 2.11) and the large numbers employed in this activity.

Food supply and needs in less developed countries

As was explained in Chapter 1, the problems of food supply are partly related to population growth rates. Where the increase in domestic food production falls behind the population increase, countries become less self-sufficient in food supplies. This is not serious if the country can afford to import foodstuffs, but low-income LDCs lack the finance to do so. A situation of declining per capita food production prevails in many African countries (Table 2.3). Take care, though, in drawing conclusions (other than about general trends) from this data, which is selective of countries and time periods.

An indication of a country's capacity to produce food from its own resources is given in column 2 of the table which shows that within each region there are wide variations in self-sufficiency. Improvements in crop yields are common to most countries with the exception of some in Africa (columns 3 and 4). Changes in food output per capita (column 5) show that six of the African countries listed had falling per capita production; population increases are outstripping those of food supply. In fact, out of 45 African countries for which data are available no less than 30 experienced a drop in food output per capita between 1965 and 1985. In contrast, lower rates of population change, accompanied by big gains in food output, led to a positive change in the Asian group, apart from Bangladesh. However, despite these improvements, the amount of total food supply in Asia is still limited and undernourishment is not uncommon. What then are the prospects for agricultural improvement in the LDCs?

Increasing food supply in less developed countries

There are three main routes towards increasing food production: to bring more land resources into agricultural use; to increase yields; to shift production from cash crops for export to food crops for human consumption. The issues involved are more complex, of course, than just those of increasing food supplies. Farming also

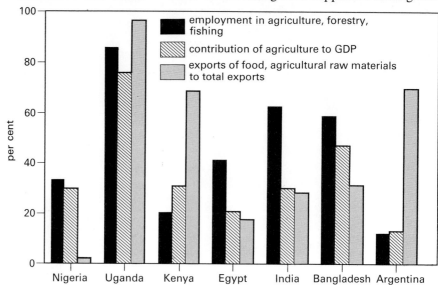

Figure 2.11 *Agriculture and primary activity contributions to selected less developed countries in mid-1980s*

Table 2.3 *Some aspects of food resources for selected less developed countries*

Country	Calories domestically produced % of supplies	Percentage change in crop yields 1975–85 Cereals	Roots and tubers	Food output change per capita 1965–85 (per cent)
AFRICA				
Botswana	52	−62	22	−36
Gabon	72	2	10	−9
Lesotho	73	−11	17	−29
Angola	86	−37	7	−28
Ivory Coast	106	10	32	36
Gambia	112	17	−8	−28
Zimbabwe	114	−23	19	−8
Swaziland	151	13	−34	53
ASIA				
South Korea	78	33	22	34
Sri Lanka	83	57	170	29
Bhutan	84	−1	3	9
Bangladesh	95	20	7	−18
Burma	105	68	65	21
Philippines	112	34	18	18
Malaysia	132	−1	−7	70
Thailand	133	11	14	34
C. and S. AMERICA				
Venezuela	70	34	11	2
Trinidad	76	8	2	−6
Jamaica	81	6	2	13
Chile	82	59	26	−1
Dom. Republic	121	27	9	12
Guyana	135	35	14	−20
Cuba	139	35	14	54
Argentina	153	22	19	10

Countries arranged in order of calories produced, showing the four lowest and the four highest region by region.

needs reorganisation through *land reform*, that is a fairer land distribution amongst people. To be effective, such changes need to be integrated into wider programmes of rural development in order to promote other social and economic improvements particularly in health care, education, marketing and transport. Nevertheless, despite problems in some African countries, other continents show improved food production since 1966 (Fig. 2.12).

Extension of the cultivated area Agricultural land is scarce in many LDCs; unused land is likely to have environmental limitations, being too steep, wet, arid or subject to pests. For these reasons, making use of what is at present unproductive land in Africa is particularly difficult. In some countries, agricultural land is being prepared at the expense of the tropical rain forests. Large areas of these forests are being converted to agricultural and other uses, espe-

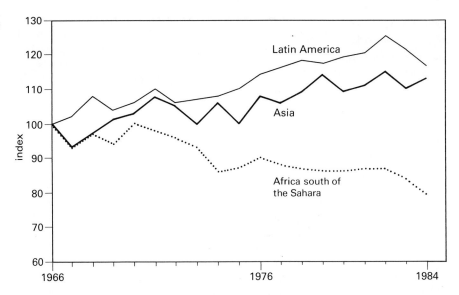

Figure 2.12 *Changes in food production by continental regions*

cially in Latin America and Asia (see below: *Forest Resources*).

Another possibility is to irrigate arid and semi-arid areas. Irrigation is expensive, with the reclamation of land costing up to £20 000/ha. It is often more effective to irrigate existing cultivated areas to increase yields, a practice closely linked to agriculture improvements of the *green revolution*.

Intensifying production Improvements to crop yields have already been achieved by many LDCs (Table 2.3). To an extent, these improvements are as the result of the green revolution, brought about since 1960 by the introduction of high yielding varieties (HYVs) of crops, accompanied by large inputs of fertiliser, pesticides and irrigation. Generally, these high-input methods have had more success in Central America and south-east Asia than in Africa. Yields of wheat in the states of Hayrana, Bihar and Punjab in India increased by between 20 and 40 per cent following the adoption of HYVs. Rice yields have increased by a spectacular 90 per cent in areas of the Punjab where water control allows new dwarf varieties of rice to be grown. Water is a key to success in growing these new varieties. Peasant farmers working small plots of land and without their own wells have lost out on these improvements.

The green revolution involves changes to traditional farming methods, but for some rural communities it is difficult to adopt new techniques. This is especially the case in tenant systems where there are few rights of land ownership. Understandably, tenant farmers are reluctant to adopt new methods if the future is insecure. If the green revolution is to spread more widely across peasant systems of farming, re-allocation of land through land reform is one of the necessary changes. A final obstacle to the adoption of the green revolution is its cost. Many peasant farmers do not generate enough revenue to pay for the fertilisers and other inputs needed to sustain the high yielding strains.

Despite the benefit of increased production, the green revolution has not been a universal success. Alternatively, solutions to agricultural problems might be based on lower level technology, for example, *alley-cropping* which involves alternating rows of crops with rows of nitrogen-fixing shade trees and shrubs (Fig. 2.13). Higher crop yields are gained, while the hedgerow prunings provide a valuable source of small roundwood for use as fuel.

Food crops for cash crops LDCs grow both food and non-food cash crops for export. These earnings are an important source of foreign

Figure 2.13 *Alley cropping: a Nigerian farmer builds a ridge for planting yams between rows of fast-growing hedgerow trees*

currency to low income countries. If commodity prices fall, they are trapped into trying to keep up their earnings by producing even more for export at the expense of food crops. To shift from non-food crop production will be difficult, not only because of local problems of distributing, storing and marketing food crops if more are grown, but also because of vested interests, including foreign interests, in maintaining cash crop output.

ASSIGNMENTS

4 For mixed farming in DMEs, discuss the effects of the following factors on agricultural production:
  a. farm size
  b. guaranteed prices
  c. intensification of methods.

5 a. What is meant by intensive farming?
  b. Describe the characteristics of any one form of intensive farming, commenting on its merits and disadvantages.

6 a. Comment on the problems of applying high-input methods in an attempt to increase agricultural production in LDCs.
  b. Describe alternative ways of trying to increase agricultural output and assess their success.

7 For the countries with low self-sufficiency of domestically produced calories (Table 2.3):
  a. find out about their GDP per capita;
  b. plot a graph to show the relationship between these two measures;
  c. use the Spearman Rank method to test for a significant result and comment on your analysis.

FOREST RESOURCES

The distribution of forests

The *closed forests*, forests with a continuous tree canopy, are the most extensive of these resources (Table 2.4). They occur in two major vegetation zones (Fig. 2.14): the *coniferous forests* and the *tropical rain forests*, each of about 1000 million ha extent. Coniferous forests are stands of needleleaf trees; these stretch widely across the USSR, Fennoscandia and North America. They are the most important commercial sources of wood in the MDCs. The *tropical forests* are characterised by a variety of tree species growing together. This mix of trees, difficulties of access and extreme environmental conditions create problems for commercial exploitation.

Other world wood resources are the cool temperature broadleaved *deciduous forests* and the warm temperature *evergreen forests*. Over many centuries, deciduous forest has been reduced in extent by clearing for agriculture and now includes stretches of *open forest* where the tree canopy is discontinuous and the tree density low. On a continental basis, Africa has a high proportion of open forest, reflecting the extent of forest degradation as a result of clearing for cultivation and of fuelwood collection.

Production and use of wood

The production of timber in the MDCs is mainly for industrial purposes, that is for making planks and veneers, paper and wood-based products. The USA, USSR and Canada dominate industrial wood production, followed by Sweden and Finland. Levels of production in the USA and European countries reflect the market demand, the accessibility of forests for these markets and the intensity of commercial use of planted timber. Canada, Sweden, Finland and the USSR take the principal share of net world exports. No less than 65 per cent of Canadian production is exported and it dominates the world trade of newsprint and wood pulp for paper-making.

World demand for paper and board products has increased by 100 million tonnes since 1970

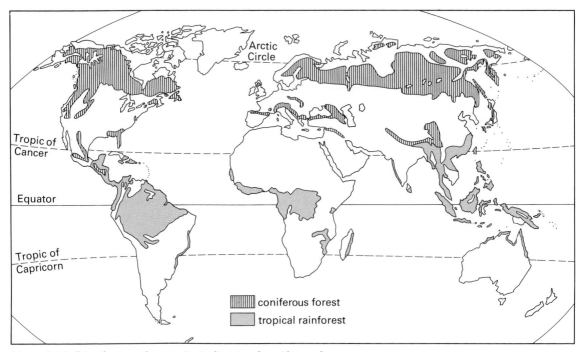

Figure 2.14 *Distribution of tropical rain forest and coniferous forest*

Table 2.4 *Forest resources and wood production*

REGION Country	Area of forest and woodland 1980 (million ha)		Deforestation of closed forest average annual amount 1981–85 (thous ha)	Average annual production 1982–84 (million cubic metre)	
	Open	Closed		Industrial Wood	Fuelwood
AFRICA	498	221	1 268	53	361
Angola	51	3	34	1	8
Ethiopia	23	4	6	2	29
Kenya	1	1	11	1	28
Nigeria	9	6	300	7	82
Zaire	72	107	160	2	29
C. and S. AMERICA	240	693	3 924	91	254
Bolivia	23	44	87		1
Brazil	157	358	1 360	58	161
Colombia	5	46	820	3	14
Peru	1	70	260	1	7
ASIA	95	457	1 762	231	703
China	45	125	*	82	155
India	5	52	132	19	215
Indonesia	3	114	600	28	117
Japan	1	24	*	32	1
Malaysia	0	21	255	33	7
EUROPE	22	137	*	284	55
N. AMERICA	275	459	*	465	108
Canada	172	264	*	143	6
USA	103	195	*	322	102
USSR	137	791	*	274	81
Australia	65	42	*	15	3
WORLD	1 338	2 845	*	1 426	1 570

Country is given when total forest exceeds 50 million hectares, or when production of either industrial wood or fuelwood exceeds 25 million cubic metres, except for Europe
* data not available

when the total was 125 million tonnes. The use of these materials for packaging has seen particularly rapid growth. Pulp and paper production is dominated by DMEs (Fig. 2.15), a reflection of market opportunities and also of the high capital costs of building large-scale paper mills. However, Asian countries, principally Japan, are becoming increasingly important as world paper producers. Forest resources for making pulp are now being managed by planting fast-growing eucalyptus trees and radiata pine trees. Plantations in South America, Africa and the Iberian Peninsula have the potential to supply up to 15 per cent of the world's need of pulp fibre. Conservation of natural forest resources is also achieved by using waste paper.

Several LDCs, particularly Indonesia, Malaysia and the Ivory Coast, are major exporters of hardwoods such as mahogany and teak, and earn foreign currency from these exports. South-east Asian countries exported 21 million cubic metres of logs in 1986, with Japan taking over 50 per cent. Attempts are being made by Asian timber producers to increase the

Figure 2.15 *World pulp and paper production, 1988*

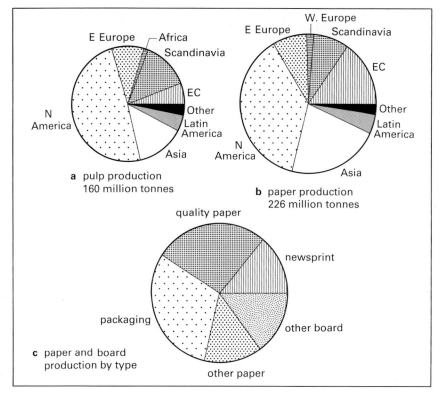

a pulp production
160 million tonnes

b paper production
226 million tonnes

c paper and board production by type

home processing of timber so that items of greater value, such as sawn planks, plywood and veneers, are exported.

More than half the world's total wood production is from the LDCs, most of which is used by them as fuelwood. As Table 2.4 shows, African countries in particular use large amounts of fuelwood relative to forest resources. The time and effort taken in the collection of wood is increasingly demanding as supplies dwindle. It is a task which is often done by the women in village communities (Fig. 2.16), and which unwittingly contributes to woodland degradation.

Deforestation

The large-scale removal of tropical forests was an all too common feature of environmental change in many tropical countries in the 1980s. Estimated average annual rates of deforestation of tropical forests during the early 1980s in South America, Africa and Asia were 4 million, 2 million and 1 million ha respectively. Thus in

South America an area the size of Switzerland is cleared of forest each year. In contrast, *reafforestation* and the reversion of agricultural land to woodland is adding to the amount of forest cover in many MDCs.

In some tropical lands, sheer population pressure is forcing the conversion of forests to agricultural use. Clearance of parts of the Amazonian rain forest has been accelerated by commercial farming and land speculation fostered by government tax and land policies. An estimated 8 million hectares of forest were replaced by cattle ranches between 1966 and 1978, while in just one state, Rondonia, the area cleared of forest went from 1 million ha to 3 million ha between 1982 and 1985. Here, as elsewhere in Amazonia, there is a close correlation between deforestation and lumbering with its associated road construction. In southeast Asia, more specifically Indonesia, the depletion of forests is associated with the planned resettlement of people (Fig. 2.17), plus colonisers who penetrate formerly inaccessible

Figure 2.16 *Women collecting firewood, Kalsaka village, Yatenga province, Burkina Faso*

Figure 2.17 *Clearing tropical rainforest for transmigrant's colony, Kalimantan, Indonesia*

places by following logging roads. Peasant farmers gain access to formerly remote tracts of forests, and after the extraction of selected trees by the lumber companies, set about burning off the vegetation to prepare land for cultivation. In some of the more accessible areas of Malaysia, Indonesia, the Ivory Coast and Nigeria, timber extraction is so concentrated that the forest is being depleted as a resource. World-wide it is estimated that 40 to 60 per cent of tropical forest clearance is due to colonisation by landless people, 10 per cent to commercial logging and another 10 per cent to fuelwood gathering.

The environmental consequences of deforestation are not only a loss in the diversity of flora and fauna, but also increased flooding and soil erosion resulting from the destruction of watershed vegetation. The scale of forest clearing in Amazonia is so great that there is even concern about the possible effect on world climate. Is there, then, a solution to deforestation by means of forestry management?

Forestry management

A transition to sustained timber production was achieved in some areas of the USA as long ago as 1900, with forests being managed by selective cutting. This maintains maximum growth from vigorously growing trees, rather than allowing them to reach beyond maturity when there is no net growth amongst the stands of old trees. By matching timber extraction to the growth rate, depletion is eliminated.

If these techniques were applied to natural tropical forests, it might be possible to slow the rate of deforestation. More intensive management is possible on plantations. Plantation forests are becoming more important in tropical areas, with new areas being planted up at the rate of 500 000 ha per annum. Unfortunately, present rates of deforestation are faster than the gains from new plantations. One problem is that although plantations add to timber supply they do nothing to curb deforestation caused by clearing for agriculture.

The objectives of forestry management are wider than just timber production; they concern tree maintenance, watershed protection, flood control, water supply and provision for recreation. In the MDCs such multiple uses are closely tied to conservation objectives. When the US Forestry Service was set up in 1905, for example, one of its tasks was the management of national forests for public welfare. Today there are 75 million ha of national forest in the USA, with a further 30 million ha of managed forest in the national parks. In the USSR, 20 million ha of forest are included in national parks and a further 300 million ha have protected status. Since 1970 in the LDCs an estimated 86 million ha of tropical forest have gained this status. Much woodland is also included in national parks, particularly in Africa.

ASSIGNMENTS

8 a. Suggest why USA, Canada and the USSR dominate world production of industrial timber.
  b. Comment on three main uses of industrial timber.
  c. Find out about and comment on the supply and use of hardwood timber from Asian countries.
9 a. Use the data in Table 2.4 to work out the percentage rate of deforestation in terms of total forested area for the African and Central/South American countries.
  b. Give a comparative assessment of the scale of the deforestation problem in these two regions.
  c. What are the main causes of deforestation?
  d. Comment on two consequences of deforestation.

WATER RESOURCES

The water resources of a region are made up of several contributions. The largest is *run-off*, which is mostly discharged into rivers and lakes. Run-off is precipitation minus losses due to *evapotranspiration* and to *infiltration* into the soil and bedrock. Water is also available from

Table 2.5 *Water resources for selected countries*

Country	Water resource available (thousand million cubic metres per year)	Water abstracted	Water abstracted per capita (cubic metres per year)	Percentage abstracted by sectors		
				public	ind.	agric.
LDCs						
Ghana	53	*	35	44	3	54
Venezuela	856	4	387	37	4	59
China	2 800	460	462	6	7	87
India	1 850	380	612	3	4	93
Argentina	694	28	1 059	9	18	73
Sudan	130	19	1 089	1	0	99
Egypt	58	56	1 202	7	5	88
MDCs						
UK	120	28	507	21	79	1
France	185	33	606	17	71	12
Italy	187	46	811	15	16	69
Australia	343	18	1 306	16	6	77
USSR	4 684	353	1 330	6	31	64
Canada	2 901	36	1 501	18	70	11
USA	2 478	467	2 162	12	46	42

Available resources = internal resources plus river flows from other countries. Note Egypt's own resource is only 2 thousand million cu m per year. Year of per capita amount is not the same for all countries and varies from 1970 to 1985
Public abstraction is for domestic, commercial, industrial users
Industrial abstraction is that made by industries themselves
* The amount for Ghana is 0.3

rivers which flow in from adjoining regions, or from bore holes drilled to tap underground resources. Run-off is greatest in Asia and South America and least in Australia. However, within continents there are great variations in water balance, that is between precipitation received and water lost as evapotranspiration. Most of Australia with the exception of the eastern zone, the south-west of the USA, much of the Middle East, and Africa outside of the tropical rain forests all suffer water deficiency to differing degrees. As a natural flow, run-off fluctuates from season to season, and might be at its lowest when demand is highest, especially if a region uses water for irrigation. However, by interrupting run-off and storing the water in reservoirs, supplies are enhanced and made more secure.

Water supply and demand

For selected countries, the relationship between water resources and needs, as measured by the amounts *abstracted*, that is water drawn from rivers and underground sources as water supplies, is given in Table 2.5. Ghana, Venezuela and Canada have exceptionally large resources relative to the amount of water abstracted; the USA, UK and France have reasonably wide margins. Egypt, on the other hand, has insufficient supplies of its own and relies on water brought in from other countries by the River Nile. This inflow is controlled by the reservoirs behind the Aswan High Dam and other dams.

On the supply side, the response to demand comes in the engineering work which is carried out. Most regions of settlement concentration need more water than can be provided locally.

Where population and commercial activities are concentrated, as for example, in south-east England, water has to be imported into the region. To keep costs down in Britain, the Thames and other rivers are used to convey water, but large storage reservoirs are needed to safeguard supplies and accommodate fluctuations in demand. Some of these reservoirs occupy valuable land along the Thames valley, upstream from Teddington. They are part of the complex supply and treatment network required to bring a regular flow of water to consumers.

Water fulfils a wide range of functions: as supplies to domestic and industrial users; for irrigation; in hydro-electric power generation; for waste disposal and as a basis for recreation.

Domestic uses So far as the LDCs are concerned most of the domestic demand for water (included in the public sector column, Table 2.5), is for drinking and cooking purposes. Water use is greatly restricted in many LDCs because of poor access to supplies, people in rural areas having to walk to collect drinking water from stand-pipes and wells, or low quality water from rivers. Less than 20 per cent of the population in parts of south-east Asia and tropical Africa have access to safe water supplies. In contrast, domestic water consumption

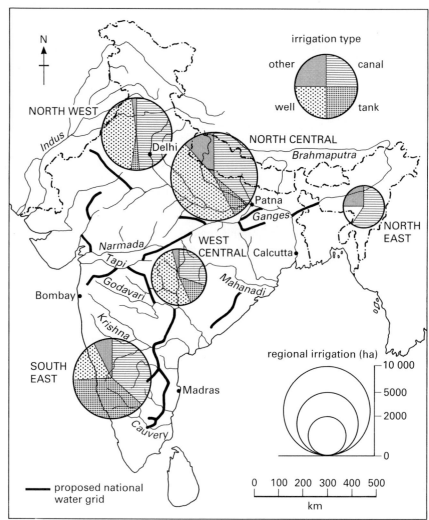

Figure 2.18 *Types of irrigation in India by regions*

Figure 2.19 *Irrigation system, Saudi Arabia*

in MDCs, at up to 300 litres per capita per day, is as much as fifty times that in the LDCs. The comparatively low cost of water in MDCs encourages extravagant use by householders. North Americans and West Europeans use copious amounts of water for personal hygiene, in domestic appliances such as washing machines, and for washing cars and watering gardens.

Irrigation   Nearly 20 per cent of the world's cropped area is irrigated. In a number of LDCs, over 90 per cent of the water abstracted is for irrigation, other demands being tiny by comparison, as for example in Egypt and the Sudan (Table 2.5). As irrigation is needed in areas deficient in water, supply difficulties have to be overcome. The solution is often based on a combination of methods involving storage of water received in a wet season, transfer from other regions and pumping from underground sources. In India, for example, water is supplied from small earth-bunded reservoirs referred to as tanks, from wells and from canals used to transfer water from rivers and reservoirs. Regional variations in the methods of supply are shown in Figure 2.18, together with the proposed national water grid for transferring water to areas of water need in the west and south. In many districts, wells, pumped by electric or diesel engines, have made more water available from deeper sources, but at the same time have lowered water tables.

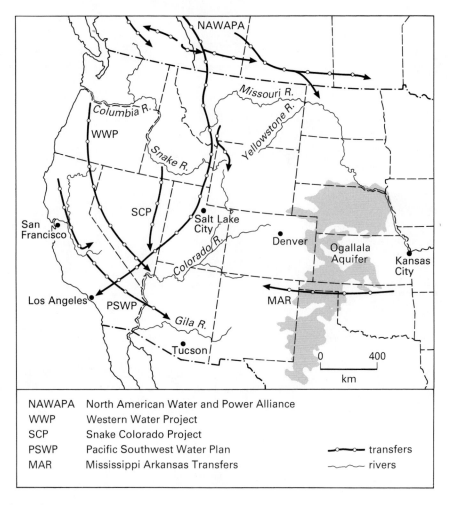

Figure 2.20 *Proposals for water transfers in the western United States and location of the Ogallala aquifer*

NAWAPA	North American Water and Power Alliance
WWP	Western Water Project
SCP	Snake Colorado Project
PSWP	Pacific Southwest Water Plan
MAR	Mississippi Arkansas Transfers

transfers
rivers

A problem in some irrigated areas is *salinisation*. This is caused when water evaporates from the soil and brings salts to the surface. This can happen when there are high rates of evaporation from land which is over-watered or becomes saturated when feeder canals leak. Parts of the Indus Plain, Pakistan, are so seriously affected that they have been lost to agricultural use. In India 15 per cent of a total 60 million hectares of irrigated land is affected by salinisation, while on a world scale possibly some 7 per cent of irrigated land is affected. Careful control of rates of irrigation or use of overhead spray methods as in the new, but expensive, irrigation techniques of *circle farming*, can help solve this problem. Circle farming is served by water which is pumped

from a central supply spigot to sprinklers along a rotating arm, allowing the amount of water delivered to crops to be very closely controlled. This method is used in semi-arid areas in the USA. Saudi Arabia has transformed desert into grain and animal production units but at very high cost and by using up underground resources of *fossil water* (Fig. 2.19).

Depletion of such *natural aquifers* is a matter of concern as the water resource can no longer be regarded as renewable. Consider the case of the Ogallala aquifer (Fig. 2.20) which is tapped to serve some 20 per cent of the irrigated cropland of the High Plains, USA. Water abstraction, 90 per cent of it for irrigation, is at a rate which is depleting southern parts of this vast store of water (3 700 million million cubic metres in 1977). Alternative supplies are not readily available in this region, nor generally in the south-west USA where population and economic growth is greatly adding to demand for water. Rivers are already intensively used. The Colorado River is yielding water to capacity limits from existing reservoirs at Lake Powell, Lake Mead and Lake Havasu. There is concern about a possible water crisis at the end of the 20th century. Various schemes to divert water southwards from the Columbia-Snake River basins and, more ambitiously, from rivers in Alaska and Canada have been investigated. Quite apart from the technical difficulties and environmental issues that this would entail, the political climate is against the transfer of a precious commodity like water across state boundaries, let alone international ones. Finding new sources of water for the rapidly growing economy of the south-west USA will not be easy.

Industrial use The industrial sector is a major water consumer in MDCs (Table 2.5). The metal processing, power and oil refining industries, paper and pulp, textile and chemical manufacturers and the food and drink processing industries are all major users of water. In the chemical and food processing industries, supplies of high quality water are needed as water is part of the end product. Some industries, like beer brewing at Burton-on-Trent, developed because of the quality of water available at the site. Much larger quantities of water are abstracted by some activities for cooling purposes. In these cases the water is not consumed, although it is likely to be degraded, being returned with a low oxygen content and possibly with some contaminates. Power stations, for example, return some 90 per cent of the water abstracted. The disposal of spent water by industry gives rise to concern about the extent to which these effluents are polluted.

Waste disposal Rivers, lakes and seas are used as carriers of waste water. Polluted waste water is an outcome of many processing activities,

particularly with the making of wood pulp, chemical manufacturing and oil refining. Where there are industrial concentrations along rivers, estuaries or seas, there is often severe pollution, as for example at Merseyside and Teesside, south of Lake Michigan, the northern Adriatic Sea and parts of Japan's Inland Sea. Industry is required in most DMEs to conform with anti-pollution laws. In Britain, firms are inspected and are licensed to discharge effluent. Until 1989 regulation was through the Water Authorities, but of 20 000 cases of inland waterway pollution in 1987 legal action was taken in only 288 of them. There are often technical problems in cleaning up polluted water and the costs are high. The Water Authorities themselves had responsibility for sewage disposal. New installations and improvement of old treatment works are needed for British standards to reach those set by the EC environmental directives. Regulation of these standards passed from the Water Authorities in 1989 as noted in the next section on water management.

Dispersed forms of pollution, such as waste disposal to streams by local industries and run-off from heavily fertilised agricultural land, are especially difficult to control. Nitrate and pesticide pollution of drinking water is a widespread problem in agricultural regions in the EC. Serious incidents of pollution also occur through accidents, as for example when chemicals were discharged into the Rhine from a manufacturing plant in Switzerland. This had international consequences as many communities down river in West Germany were affected.

Water management

Water's varied functions and the universal demand for it mean that broad schemes of management are necessary. Multiple functions are often involved like those at the Kielder reservoir in Northumberland which supplies water to north-east England, and is also used as a recreational resource. Schemes along the Volga River in the USSR are directed not only at hydro-electric power development, but also at flood control and irrigation. Hydro-electric power developments and the recreational uses of water are discussed in Chapters 4 and 7.

Small units of organisation, even those based on natural hydrological units like river basins, are not large enough for effective management. In Britain in 1974 ten regional authorities were set up to undertake water regulation and supply, and river management in place of the former 1600 separate water boards. Following the 1989 Water Act, these authorities were privatised and replaced by ten water companies with responsibilities for water supply and sewage disposal, plus a separate body, the National Rivers Authority, with responsibility for environmental regulation.

Rapid increases in demand for water add to the need for efficient management. Problems of supply are not necessarily best solved by simply building more capacity. More appropriately, approaches based on *water conservation* could be used to limit the amount of new engineering work needed. However, if water is cheap, people see little need to save it. One route to conservation, therefore, might be to charge people more for the amounts of water used. In Britain this would involve a major change to metered supplies. In general, a charge system based on actual amounts used is considered essential in order to encourage water saving.

Marine resources

The world's oceans provide a rich and varied set of resources. As well as possessing fish resources, the oceans are the habitat of some of the world's largest creatures, are a medium for transport, have a potential for energy development, possess minerals and contribute to the recreational value of coastal areas. Sadly, they also act as sinks for the dumping of waste.

The oceans are reckoned to have a combined sustainable yield of around 90 million tonnes of fish a year. Fishing rights are given to coastal nations under the terms of the Law of the Sea (1982). Within a 370 km (200 nautical mile) offshore zone, designated as the *Exclusive Economic Zone*, maritime states have sovereign rights to marine resources, including seabed resources. Foreign vessels may fish these waters provided that the rights of the maritime country are safeguarded.

World fishing is concentrated in parts of oceans. The largest catches are from fisheries in the north-east Atlantic and the north-west and south-east Pacific (Fig. 2.21). These locations reflect favourable physical environments. Off the west coast of the British Isles, for example, there is the productive marine environment associated with the North Atlantic Drift and the *continental shelf*, the submerged gently sloping margin of the continent. Enriched plankton

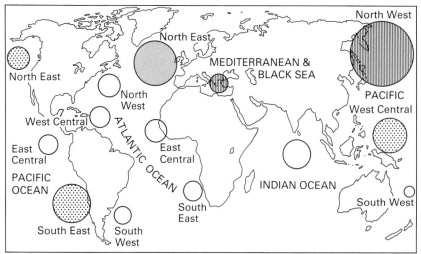
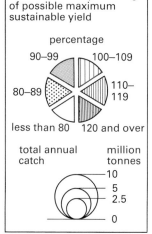

Figure 2.21 *Ocean fisheries and fish catches in relation to sustainable yields, 1984*

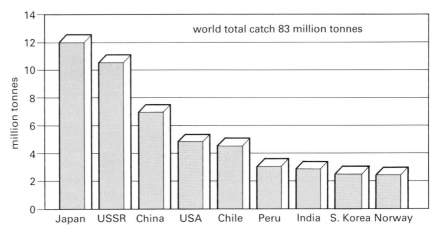

Figure 2.22 *Major fishing nations by tonnage caught, 1984*

supplies occur where warm and cold ocean currents mix offshore from Japan, and in the upwelling waters of the Peruvian coast. The largest fishing nations in the world are Japan and the USSR (Fig. 2.22), which together accounted for some 30 per cent of the world's total catch of around 80 million tonnes in 1985. Both countries have deep-sea fishing fleets served by processing vessels.

As shown in Figure 2.21, two fishing regions, the north-west Pacific and the Mediterranean and Black Seas, were showing signs of over-fishing in relation to maximum sustainable yields in 1984. As discussed in Chapter 1 and shown in Figure 1.8, fish resources can give a sustained yield, but if fish are regarded as a common property, with no controls such as quota agreements, there is nothing to stop the continual arrival of newcomers who want to have a share. The result is the depletion of the stock of fish. For example, overfishing of cod and herring in the Atlantic depleted stocks to such an extent that by the 1970s catches dropped sharply. To assist recovery of these stocks, fishing was banned in the North Sea and quotas were set elsewhere. The North Sea and Atlantic fishing grounds are subject to intense competition from European Community countries. The management and allocation of fishing rights in these waters were formulated in 1983 with an agreement based on a system of quotas and specified fishing zones within 20 km of the coast.

ASSIGNMENTS

10 a. From Table 2.5 calculate water abstraction as a percentage of water available.

    b. Attempt to explain the circumstances of those countries where the percentage is high.

    c. For a country of your choice, examine ways in which water supplies are developed.

11 a. Use the data in Table 2.5 to draw diagrams to compare the sector use in one LDC with that in one MDC.

    b. Suggest reasons for differences between your two countries.

    c. With reference to Figure 2.17 comment on the main uses of water supplied to the domestic market.

    d. Suggest ways for conserving water in the domestic sector.

12 a. Why is irrigation often a key component in the successful adoption of the green revolution?

    b. Outline two major problems in applying irrigation in LDCs.

    c. Find out about any one irrigation scheme in an LDC and comment on how it has benefited the country.

13 a. Why does overfishing occur?

    b. Which oceans are overfished?

    c. What can be done to control excessive ocean fishing?

    d. Find out more information about the Law of the Sea and examine the difficulties in reaching international agreement about fishing rights in water beyond the 370 km limit.

3

Minerals and Mining Activity

FACTORS AFFECTING MINING ACTIVITY

Minerals are in demand as the raw material inputs of the production system, being sold by resource owners to producers through the production factors market (Fig. 1.4). In this chapter, discussion is focused on the two non-renewable groups of minerals, classified as the *recyclable* (metallic) and the *recoverable* (non-metallic) minerals. Recyclable ores are of high value and are traded on world markets, whilst many recoverable ores are of low value and are worked near to local markets. Mining of metallic ores is unevenly spread because deposits are concentrated in certain areas of the world. The presence of a mineral at a place does not necessarily mean that it will be mined: whether a mineral deposit is economic to mine depends upon the cost of producing it and transporting it to market relative to the price it fetches at the market.

Mining development and production costs

Historically, the mining of metal ores was greatly affected by their quality as measured by the amount of associated impurities and the actual metal content of the ore body. Prior to the invention of the basic iron-making process

Figure 3.1 *Mechanised underground mining of copper ore at the Carolusberg mine, Okiep Copper Company, South Africa*

Figure 3.2 *Open pit mine for copper and gold, Queensland, Australia*

by Thomas and Gilchrist in 1878, for example, iron ores that were free from phosphoric contamination were used. The adoption of the basic process allowed the use of phosphoric ores, including the extensive deposits in Lorraine, France, and Kiruna, Sweden. Copper ores were worked in the late 1800s at rich deposits like those in Cornwall, England, and northern Minnesota, USA. Many rich ores have since been worked out in old established areas or are only workable at depth and hence at high cost. Underground mining requires a sizeable labour force, and, unless wage rates are low, as in some African and Latin American countries, labour cost as a proportion of total cost is high. Deep mining involves further expense in hauling the ore to the surface and water pumping, costs which greatly increase as mining probes deeper

underground. Some modern underground mining (Fig. 3.1), however, is large scale and highly mechanised. Other examples are the Kiruna iron ore mines in Sweden and the Mantos Blancos copper mine in the Atacama Desert, Chile.

In the 20th century, improvements in mining methods and in mineral processing have allowed deposits of low grade ores to be exploited. A disadvantage of working ores of low metal content is that great quantities of rock material have to be cut. For a copper ore of 0.5 per cent metal content, for example, as much as 200 tonnes of ore material and 400 tonnes of *country rock* (the surrounding rock) might have to be excavated to recover 1 tonne of copper. By using open-pit methods of mining (Fig. 3.2) the costs can be kept low enough to justify the exploitation of such deposits. An additional

Figure 3.3 *Location and production of selected minerals in West Africa, 1986*

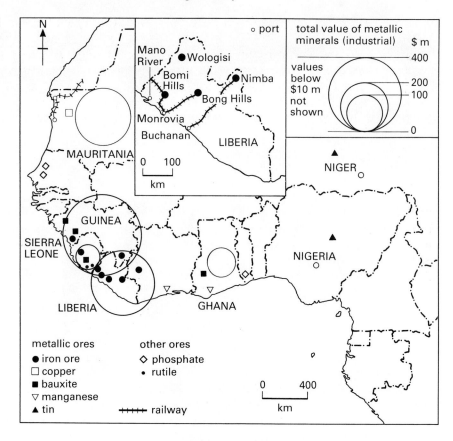

problem is that the cost of transporting low grade ores to market is high because of the *loss in weight* on processing. The alternative to transporting raw ores is to upgrade them at the mine, the extra cost of bringing in fuel to process the ores being offset by reduced costs of transporting the upgraded ores.

Development costs at opencast mines which work low grade ores include the removal of overburden and the construction of mining and processing installations. When minerals are discovered in remote areas, development costs are increased because of the need to build access roads, railways and ports, houses and service facilities; for example, 50 per cent of the cost of the Lamco iron ore project at the Nimba mine in Liberia was for the railway and harbour construction work. Features of the Liberian developments are shown in Figure 3.3 along with other West African mineral locations. At Pilbara, Australia (Fig. 3.4), rail links of

250 km were built to connect ports at Dampier and Port Hedland to mines at Mount Tom Price and Mount Whaleback. Mining townships and service facilities also had to be established. The

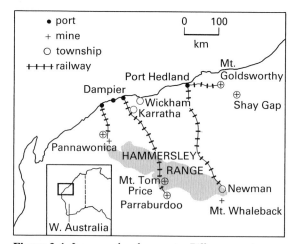

Figure 3.4 *Iron ore developments, Pilbara, western Australia*

opening up of mining operations in formerly undeveloped regions is thus costly in terms of building the infrastructure; offsetting these costs are the economies of scale associated with working the large ore reserves at such locations.

The high costs of exploration and development explain the involvement of *transnational companies* (TNCs) in mining. Not only do these companies have the resources to finance such large investment, they can also offset risks by operating in several countries. Furthermore, they profit by participating in all the stages of mineral activities: from mining and processing right through to metal fabrication and marketing. However, since the mid-1960s, the role of the TNCs has changed, with several of the LDC mineral-producing countries taking greater control of their mineral industries.

The combined effect of price and cost on mining location

The location of mining activity is affected by the interrelationships between the price of the mineral at the market, the production costs at the mine and the transport costs of delivering the mineral to the market. These relationships are shown in Figure 3.5 which is based on the work of A. M. Hay, 1976. The left-hand axis of the graph gives the price of the mineral at the market. Production costs per tonne are shown

by the scale on the right-hand axis and vary at each of five mine locations, M to Q, as shown by the height of the columns. The locations of market and mines is shown projected on the surface below the graph. Mine costs are taken to be generally higher in the core region, nearest to the market, and lower in the peripheral region furthest from the market.

The two diagonal lines across the diagram are revenue lines, calculated by taking the transport cost per tonne per km away from the market price per tonne. Thus at the market revenue is equal to price, but falls away steadily with distance as transport costs rise. Line A describes a situation in which there are high prices for the mineral, £400 per tonne, and high transport charges at £5 per tonne/km. Mines with production costs below line A are profitable, that is M, O and P. The balance of costs at each of these locations is very different. At M, revenue is sufficient to pay for the high production costs. The lower production costs at O, combined with intermediate transport charges, result in a small profit. The extremely low production costs at P just offset the high transport costs which are incurred at this distant location.

Given a different set of conditions, line B, in which both price and freight charges are lower, at £200/tonne and £1/tonne/km respectively, the mines in the core region are uneconomic. The mine at O is no longer profitable largely on

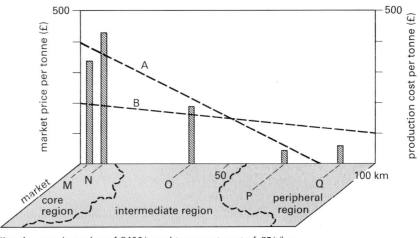

Figure 3.5 *The location of mining activity in relation to market*

line A = market price of £400/t and transport cost of £5/t/km
line B = market price of £200/t and transport cost of £1/t/km

account of the reduction in price. For the low cost mines in the peripheral region, their distance from the market is no longer such a serious penalty, and the mines at P and Q are profitable.

The different economic conditions shown in Figure 3.5 can be related to real world situations. A shift of mining to more remote, but lower cost, regions, has been encouraged by the lowering of sea transport costs following the use of large mineral ore carriers. These reductions in transport costs partly explain the growth of Australia as a major iron ore exporter. The mines P and Q could be said to represent the Australian conditions in relation to distant markets in Japan and Europe. The opening up of such resource frontiers, on the other hand, has contributed to a reduction or closure of more costly mining in the core areas such as Lorraine, France.

Environmental factors

The increased scale of mining operations has led to greater environmental concern in many areas. Environmental damage is clearly evident in the form of the massive pits, piled up wastes and polluted ecosystems often associated with mining. Copper and iron ore mining in the USA produces 750 million tonnes of waste rock annually. In the UK china clay extraction produces waste on a ratio of 7:1 to useable clay. Great quantities of quartz and mica waste are produced which are piled up to form obtrusive

Figure 3.6 *China clay workings and waste tips, St Austell area, Cornwall*

landscape features in the St. Austell area, Cornwall (Fig. 3.6), where some 2500 ha of land are affected by china clay workings.

Water and air pollution produce different kinds of problems. The *tailings* (waste materials) from metal-concentrator works are highly acidic. The natural hydrological system can be polluted by water draining from waste tips. Table 3.1 shows the levels of lake pollution near the Copper Cliff nickel smelter, Sudbury, Ontario. Acidity is twice as high near the smelter as it is 86 km away. Sulphur dioxide emission into the atmosphere is a serious problem, as it can cause total destruction of vegetation in the vicinity of a smelter as for example at Trail, British Columbia. However, following the building of an acid reclamation plant, vegetation in the valley at Trail has recovered.

In many countries, public concern about the environment has led to much closer scrutiny of proposals for mine development. In the USA, the National Environmental Development Act requires that Environmental Impact Assessment (EIA) is made if new projects affect Federal interests. Thus the public is made aware of the possible consequences of new projects. In other countries, planning legislation establishes con-trols over development. Measures to protect or to restore sites can be imposed, with companies required to reinstate the land after quarrying for minerals. Such environmental protection can be costly, as in the USA where pollution control in the copper industry is reckoned to add 10 per cent to costs.

ASSIGNMENTS

1 a. Outline the main factors which affect mining costs and the delivery of mineral raw materials to markets.

   b. Make a copy of the graph in Figure 3.5. What would be the effect on mining activities if freight rates for line B were £2/t/km up to 50 km and £1/t/km from 50 km?

2 Using Figure 3.3 and your atlas:

   a. estimate the value of minerals produced in Guinea and in Liberia;

   b. describe the distribution of minerals in West Africa;

   c. suggest the problems that might have affected the building of the railways between mines and ports in Liberia.

3 a. Put the data from Table 3.1 into two columns by rank order.

   b. Apply the Spearman Rank correlation method to analyse the relationship between distance from the smelting plant and lake pollution as measured by acidity.

   c. Comment on your analysis.

4 To what extent should economic needs override environmental considerations in the development of minerals?

Distance of lake from smelter (km)	Acidity (pH)
4	3.4
5	3.2
10	4.2
13	3.5
20	3.3
39	5.7
47	4.2
50	5.8
57	4.4
63	6.7
74	6.4
86	6.8

Note: Low pH values indicate high acidity

Table 3.1 *Acidity in lakes near Copper Cliff nickel smelter, Sudbury, Ontario*

MINERAL PRODUCTION AND USE

Industrial metallic minerals

Metals are essential to manufacturing industries and hence to modern economies. Although more than twenty metallic minerals make up the main inputs into the industrial system,

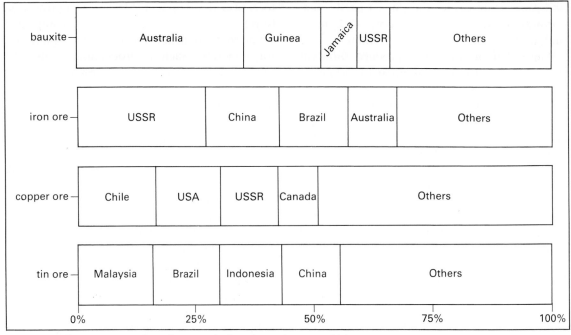

Figure 3.7 *Concentration of production of selected metal ores in 1986*

	MDC PRODUCERS				LDC PRODUCERS		
	Bauxite	**Iron ore**	**Copper ore (metal)**		**Bauxite**	**Iron ore**	**Copper ore (metal)**
	(thousand tonnes)				(thousand tonnes)		
WORLD	91 000	916 000	8 400				
USSR	6 275	250 000	1 030	China		142 480	
Australia	32 432	94 015	248	Brazil	6 000	132 000	
USA		39 614	1 147	Chile			1 400
Canada		36 167	699	Peru			397
S. Africa		24 482		Zaire			503
Poland			435	India	2 338	48 821	
Sweden		20 490		Zambia			513
Yugoslavia	3 459			Indonesia			
Hungary	3 022			Philippines			217
Greece	2 230			Venezuela		17 396	
				Guinea	14 656		
				Jamaica	6 964		
				Surinam	3 731		
				Guyana			

Table 3.2 *Leading producers of three industrial metallic minerals, 1986*

	Percentage of World Total						
	MDC PRODUCERS				LDC PRODUCERS		
	50	53	42		38	28	37

Information is given for the leading producers of each mineral seven of them can be counted as the key ones entering into world trade: bauxite and the ores of iron, copper, nickel, tin, lead, zinc.

Mineral ore production is characterised by concentration in a small number of countries, as shown for selected minerals in Figure 3.7 and Table 3.2. Four countries account for 45 per cent of the world output of copper ores, whilst just two, Australia and Guinea, produce 50 per cent of the bauxite. The leading world producers of seven major industrial metallic minerals are the USSR, Australia, Canada and the USA (Fig. 3.8). The USSR and USA are both major producers and consumers, while Australia and Canada, with large surplus production over needs, are major exporters. LDC production is largely for export, although in the case of iron ore, China, Brazil and India also use large quantities in their own iron and steel industries.

Iron Of the metal minerals, iron ore is the most important in terms of the amount mined

and traded. Iron ore is used to make steel which is an *alloy* of iron with manganese and other metals, such as chromium, nickel and tungsten, depending on the properties wanted in the steel. The iron ore is first reduced to iron metal, *pig iron*, in a blast furnace charged with iron, limestone and coke. Impurities are then burnt off in a steel furnace by blowing oxygen through a molten charge of pig-iron and scrap iron, alloying metals being added to produce steels of the required qualities. The steel is finally rolled out as sheets and bars for dispatch to manufacturers. In an *integrated iron and steel works*, blast furnace operations, steel making and rolling are all combined on the one site, with transfers of molten and hot metal between the plant. This arrangement is energy efficient, while the size of such works, with capacities of 10 million tonnes a year, gives scale economies. Most of the world's steel-making capacity is located in market areas. The EC and Japan rely on imported iron ore which has led, (Fig. 3.9),

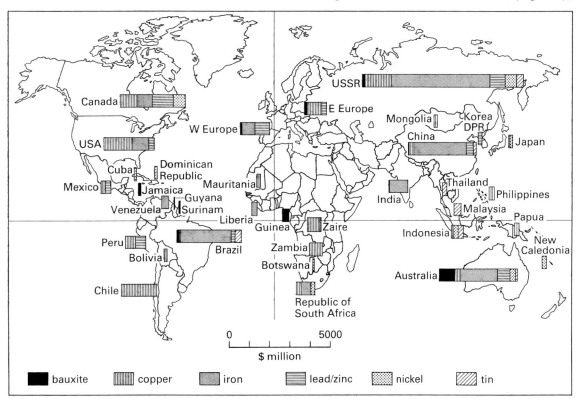

Figure 3.8 *Major metallic mineral producers, 1986*

Figure 3.9 *Steelworks and oil refineries, Llanwern*

to the selection of coastal locations for steel works.

There are ample reserves of iron ore in the world from which to supply the iron and steel industries. The present reserves which are economic to exploit exceed 150 000 million tonnes, or about 90 000 million tonnes of contained iron; enough to last 200 years. Although iron ore resources are concentrated in certain countries, as shown in Figure 3.8, smaller deposits are widely distributed throughout the world. Each of the broad groups – the CPEs, MDCs and LDCs – has about one-third of the known reserves.

The USSR is the largest single mineral producer in the world, with an impressive scale of output and range of minerals (Fig. 3.10). Production of iron ore outstrips that of other minerals. The richer ores from Krivoi Rog in the Ukraine and Magnitogorsk in the Urals are being depleted, with the result that more extensive low grade deposits are gaining in importance, especially the vast resources of the Kursk Magnetic Anomaly to the north of Donbass. The Urals are intensively worked for a large number of minerals as well as iron ore. Demand for iron ore in the major metallurgical districts of the USSR means that, on occasions, ore is transported over long distances as, for example, from the deposits near Bratsk to the Kuzbass region.

The distribution of metallic ores in North America is shown in Figure 3.11. Extensive deposits of iron ore occur to the west of Lake Superior and in Labrador. The Lake Superior area includes the long-established iron ore workings along the Mesabi Range. Reserves here were greatly extended in the 1960s by

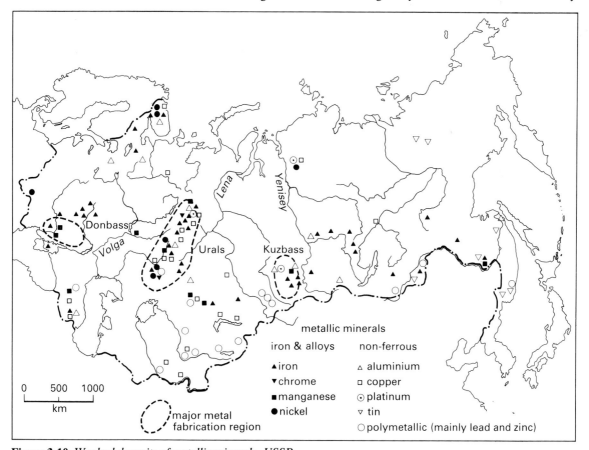

Figure 3.10 *Worked deposits of metallic minerals, USSR*

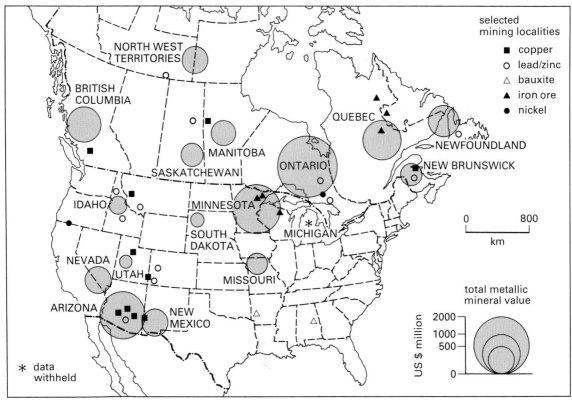

Figure 3.11 *Principal metal mining locations and production in North America, 1985*

applying new mining and processing methods to win the hard taconite ores which are abundant. The mining area in Labrador is an example of development of a *frontier resource*. It is relatively remote from markets and mining operations have to cope with extreme environmental conditions in an area of permafrost.

Australian iron ore mining is concentrated in western Australia (Fig. 3.12) and is a major reason why this state is Australia's most important metal producer by value. Production of iron ore was expanded rapidly after 1960 following evaluation of the extensive deposits in the Pilbara district of western Australia. These developments were encouraged by market opportunities in Japan, with long-term export contracts agreed between the mining companies and Japanese steel companies. Although in terms of value iron ore was the most important mineral produced in 1987, Australia is a major world producer of a wide range of minerals,

with resources distributed across the continent (Fig. 3.12).

Of LDC producers, Brazil, India, Liberia and Venezuela are principal exporters of iron ore (Fig. 3.13). Brazil is the leading exporter of iron ore in the world. Although ores from the deposits in Minas Gerais are used by the Brazilian steel industry, large amounts are also exported, especially from the Itabira mines via the deep water terminal at Tubarao. Serra dos Carajas in the state of Para has the world's largest single iron ore deposit (Fig. 3.14). A mining township at Carajas and a railway link to a new exporting terminal at Itaqui are associated with this major resource.

Aluminium Aluminium is used to serve special industrial applications where durability coupled with lightness is required; for example, aluminium is essential to the aircraft and aerospace industries and is increasingly important in con-

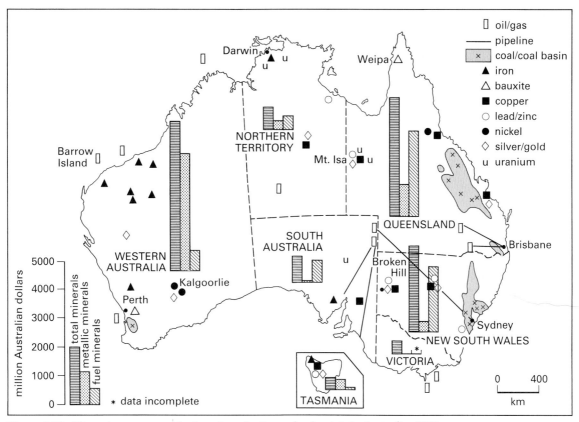

Figure 3.12 *Mineral resources and mineral production value by state in Australia, 1987*

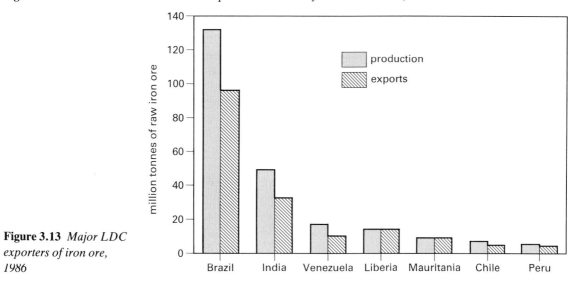

Figure 3.13 *Major LDC exporters of iron ore, 1986*

structional applications and as a proportion of the metal content in cars and household goods. Electrical cable is made from it when lightness combined with good electrical conductivity is required, and it substitutes for copper in this application when copper prices are high.

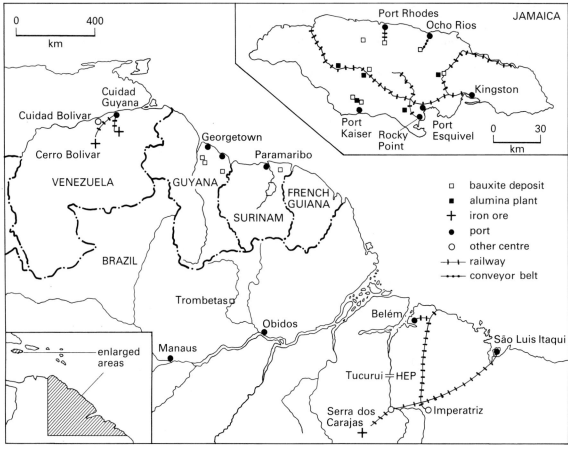

Figure 3.14 *Major metallic minerals in part of South America and Jamaica*

The raw material of aluminium is bauxite, a clay containing *alumina* (aluminium hydroxides) which occurs in surface deposits, permitting low-cost mining operations. World reserves are abundant at 22 000 million tonnes. About 70 per cent of these reserves are in LDCs, with most in Brazil (30 per cent). Australia has the bulk of the remaining reserves at around 20 per cent. Australia was the dominant producer of bauxite in 1986, with large amounts being excavated from the deposits along the Weipa Peninsula, Queensland (Fig. 3.12). Guinea, Jamaica and Brazil are the main bauxite producers of the LDC group (Fig. 3.14 and Table 3.2).

Aluminium is made in two stages. The first stage, carried out at a refinery, is the conversion of bauxite to alumina. This is followed by the smelting of alumina to produce aluminium metal. Alumina works are located in both resource and market areas. Several LDCs have established alumina production and are exporters of both bauxite and alumina. Very large quantities of electricity, 14 000 kWh per tonne of aluminium, are needed for the smelting of aluminium metal from alumina. These energy requirements account for 65 per cent of the costs of producing the metal. Smelting takes place in areas possessing low cost power supplies as in Canada at the Kitimat plant in British Columbia and at works along the margin of the Canadian Shield with the St. Lawrence valley. Major industrial nations such as Japan and West Germany are also substantial aluminium producers. Apart from Brazil and Venezuela, the LDCs remain unimportant producers of the metal.

Copper Copper is used to make electrical cable and tube, and is also alloyed with other metals: with tin to make bronze and with zinc to make brass. Copper metal is made by smelting the ore in a furnace followed by electrolytic refining to produce pure copper. World reserves of copper ore are estimated at 500 million tonnes, about half of which is in the LDCs, mostly in Chile (20 per cent). North America has the bulk of MDC reserves (20 per cent of the world total), and there is a further 10 per cent or so in the USSR. Production is concentrated in the four countries shown in Figure 3.7, but Zaire and Zambia are also major LDC producers and exporters. World trade in copper is not usually of the ore because of the waste material involved. The ores are smelted in mining areas to produce *Blister Copper* of 65 per cent copper content.

The final processing, *copper refining*, is carried out in resource areas when electrical power supplies are available, as in Zambia, and also in market areas. For example in the USA where low grade copper is mined in the mountain states of Montana, Utah, Idaho and Arizona (Fig. 3.11). The ore is concentrated and smelted near the mines, but the majority of the refining is carried out near industrial markets. In these market locations refineries have access to scrap copper which comes from engineering firms; this close association between the copper metal consumers and producers is cost-saving.

Tin Compared with the metal minerals discussed so far, the amount of tin produced and consumed is small. Its principal use is in the plating of steel sheet for use by the container-making industry. Greatly improved plating techniques based on electrolysis have meant that the demand for tin as an industrial metal has increased at a slower pace than the demand for tin plate itself. Furthermore, demand for tin cans for packaging by the drink and food industries has been affected by the increased use of aluminium cans. Overall, technical changes have limited growth in the market for tin.

However, tin is a high value commodity ($12 500 per tonne in 1986) and of considerable

Figure 3.15 *Tin mining in west Malaysia*

economic significance to Malaysia, Indonesia and Brazil, where a large part of the world's reserves of 10 million tonnes is concentrated. These countries, along with the USSR, are the chief producers (Fig. 3.8). Much of the tin in Malaysia comes from alluvial deposits washed down into river beds from *lodes* higher up the valleys. Large-scale excavation of the deposits is carried out using dredgers. Smaller-scale methods use high pressure water jets to wash out the ore from valley sides, the technique being similar to that used in china clay workings in Cornwall. Tin mining is located along the west coast of West Malaysia (Fig. 3.15). As the cost of smelting tin ores is relatively low, the LDC ore producers also produce tin metal for export. The south-east Asian producers, Malaysia, Indonesia and Thailand, account for 40 per cent of the world's output of the metal.

Nickel, lead and zinc The market for nickel is dominated by the steel industry, where it is used as one of the main metal alloys, particularly in making stainless steel. Nickel reserves are of the order of 60 million tonnes and are widespread. Three MDCs – the USSR, Canada and Australia – dominate world production, accounting for 50 per cent of the total of 770 000 tonnes in 1986. Taken as a group, LDC reserves are considerable, with production from two countries, New Caledonia and Indonesia, accounting for 20 per cent of the world total.

With reductions in the use of lead in petrol and paints, the main demand for lead is for making batteries. The principal uses of zinc metal are in galvanising steel and in making brass. The compound zinc oxide is used in the manufacture of white paint. Ores of lead and zinc ores are frequently found in association and are widely distributed in world terms (Fig. 3.8). Three MDCs – Australia, the USSR and the USA – accounted for 40 per cent of the 3 million tonnes of lead produced world-wide in 1986. Because zinc and lead are found together in ore deposits, these three MDCs, plus Canada, are also major producers of zinc. These four countries produced 40 per cent of the world total of 7 million tonnes. Amongst a number of LDC producers of these metals, Mexico and Peru are important for both.

Consumption of industrial metals

As the major manufacturing industries require large inputs of refined metal, consumption of these materials is concentrated in the MDCs. The seven countries quoted in Table 3.3 account for over 60 per cent of the world's total consumption of three key refined metals, aluminium, steel and copper. Some countries are heavily dependent upon imports of minerals to support their metal refining industries. Japan and the EC members import 90 per cent of the principal minerals needed. Home supplies are greater in the case of the USA, with the exception of the strategic minerals noted below.

The consumption of non-ferrous metals, aluminium, copper and nickel, has increased in

	Aluminium 1986	Steel 1984/85	Copper 1986
	(thousand tonnes)		
USSR	1 885	159 945	1 300
USA	4 268	103 779	2 102
Japan	1 624	76 638	1 219
W. Germany	1 186	31 920	771
Italy	510	22 402	395
France	593	15 945	401
UK	389	14 667	340
WORLD	16 396	714 970	10 073
Percentage of world total consumed by listed countries:	64	59	65

Table 3.3 *Selected major consumers of three industrial metals*

most industrialised DMEs in the period 1965–86. Significant increases in demand for aluminium have occurred as shown in Figure 1.13, with the USA the dominant consumer, even though its use of aluminium has increased at a slower rate than many other countries. There is a contrasting situation for steel in that several DMEs show falling or stagnating consumption (Fig. 3.16). Japan is the clear exception with consumption doubled over the period.

Strategic and precious metallic minerals

There are some metal minerals, notably chromium, cobalt, manganese and platinum, which are not produced in any quantity, if at all, in the United States, the European Community or even in otherwise mineral rich Australia. Just two countries, the USSR and South Africa, mine 70 per cent of the world's supplies of chromium, 60 per cent of the manganese and 90 per cent of the platinum. It is because of this extreme geographical concentration, with the associated risk of dislocation of supplies to western industrialised nations, that these minerals are classified as *strategic*.

These metals have special uses in metallurgy and in chemical manufacturing for which it would be difficult to find substitutes. High quality steels for engines, turbine blades and bearings are made from alloys with manganese, cobalt and chromium. Platinum has a special application as a *catalyst*, that is it triggers or speeds up chemical reactions, in oil refining and in chemical manufacturing. Without platinum it would be more difficult to make the lead-free high quality petrol needed by modern internal combustion engines. A new use which will increase demand for platinum is in catalytic convertors for car exhausts.

Several of the western industrial nations, especially the USA, have investigated the possibility of obtaining strategic minerals from the metallic nodules which are distributed across the deep ocean floors. The nodules can contain up to 50 per cent manganese and iron, and a 4 per cent mixture of copper, nickel and cobalt. These resources, which are especially prolific in the Pacific Ocean but in deep water of up to 6 000 metres and far offshore from any nation, pose problems of ownership. In the mid-1970s they were being regarded as the common heritage of mankind. An international sea-bed authority was proposed as a possible solution to the vexed question of exploitation, but these important issues of ownership, use and sharing of benefits have yet to be resolved.

So far as the precious metals are concerned, gold and silver are extensively used in making jewellery. The scarcity values of both metals encourages their hoarding as bullion and coins, and there is a financial function of gold bullion normally undertaken at international levels. Industrial use of silver is considerable in the preparation of photographic film, and there is a growing use of gold in the electronics industry where its excellent electrical conductivity is prized in the making of components.

World production of gold is dominated by two producers, South Africa and the USSR. Gold deposits are widely scattered in the USSR, but in South Africa are concentrated, along with other metal ores, in the Orange Free State and in the Transvaal around Johannesburg (Fig. 3.17). This mining region has become an important focus of economic activity in South Africa, especially in the urban complexes of Pretoria, Johannesburg and Vereeniging. Silver is produced largely as a by-product of lead, zinc and copper mining. Two LDCs, Mexico and Peru, lead world production followed by four MDCs, the USSR, Canada, the USA and Australia. These six countries account for nearly 70 per cent of the world output of silver.

Recoverable minerals

Following a classification suggested by J. Blunden, 1985, the *recoverable resources* can be divided into two broad groups; one group

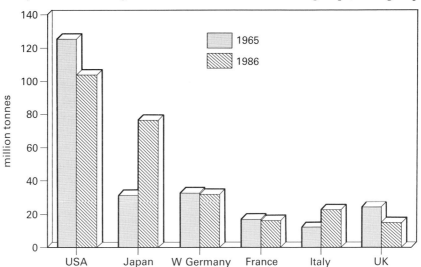

Figure 3.16 *Changes in steel consumption, 1965–1986*

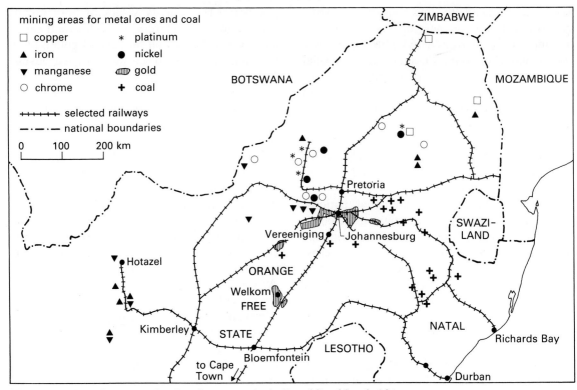

Figure 3.17 *Metallic, mineral and coal resources in the Republic of South Africa*

including common clays, sands, gravels and rocks is *widely dispersed*, but the second group of special clays and compounds like salt, potash and phosphate is *localised*.

The widely dispersed resources – sands, gravels and rocks – referred to collectively as *aggregates*, are important to the construction industries. Because they have low value by weight or volume they are uneconomic to transport over long distances, and are exploited as close to final markets as possible. Fortunately, aggregates can be extracted from surface working of geologically recent sedimentary deposits which occur in lowland areas where the majority of a country's population live and where building activity is concentrated.

Although it is an economic advantage that these resources are located in areas of demand, against this must be measured the effect that excavations have upon the landscape and the conflict that arises with other possible land uses such as housing. For a maritime nation like

Britain, one way of avoiding environmental clashes on land is to dredge the sands and gravels from offshore; about 12 per cent of the south-east England market is supplied in this way. A further advantage of using offshore sources is that the use of water transport allows materials to be brought to coastal markets at relatively low cost.

So far as the localised recoverable minerals are concerned, comment is restricted to five out of the large number occurring. Two of them, potash and phosphate, the bases of fertilisers, are produced in quantity by just a few countries, with the USSR being the only principal producer of both. Canada has immense reserves (5 000 million tonnes) of potash beneath the prairie provinces, actually found by accident during the course of drilling for oil. In world terms, Canada is by far the most important exporter of potash, sending large quantities to the USA. The USA has little of its own potash, but is a leading producer and substantial exporter of phosphate. However, since 1970, Morocco, with 50 per cent of the world's reserves, has emerged as the dominant world exporter of phosphate. As both these commodities are of relatively high value and subject to little weight loss on treatment, they can withstand the transport costs to distant markets.

Kaolin (china clay) production is concentrated in three nations, the USA, UK and USSR, which together account for 70 per cent of world production. China clay is used mainly in paper making and also in china ware. Britain produces high quality china clay, and exports 50 per cent of the total output. The coastal location of the large deposits at St. Austell in Cornwall is an advantage in helping to reduce the transport costs.

Sulphur is an indispensable element in chemical manufacturing and in the making of fertilisers. As native sulphur it is mined or pumped in solution from natural deposits such as those associated with the salt plugs in the Gulf south of the USA. Other leading producers of native sulphur are Poland, the USSR and Mexico. However, these sources are not very common and sulphur is also produced from sulphur compounds and by recovery methods at metal smelting works, power stations, oil refineries and at oil and gas fields. Recovery techniques, used to reduce effluent gases containing sulphur dioxide, have become so important that recovered sulphur accounts for half of the total world production. Future supplies are likely to come increasingly from recovery, given that environmental management objectives remain strong.

Common salt is a key compound used in the making of chemical feedstocks. Salt fields, beds of salt below the surface of the earth, are localised within countries but common to most, and hence the production of salt is widespread in world terms, with some maritime countries also producing salt by the natural evaporation of sea water. Where large salt deposits are near to other raw materials and to fuel supplies they have sometimes led to major industrial development as in the case of the Teesside chemical industry in the UK.

ASSIGNMENTS

5 a. For any one mineral in Table 3.2, construct compound columns to compare production in MDCs and LDCs.
  b. How is your selected mineral processed?
  c. Comment on the uses of your mineral.
6 Using Figure 3.8 and Table 3.2, contrast North America and South America in terms of mineral production.
7 a. Why is it that the activities of bauxite mining, alumina refining and aluminium smelting frequently take place at separate locations?
  b. Quote a specific example of each activity and comment on its growth since 1950.
8 a. Comment on two technological developments of the past 25 years that have affected mineral development.
  b. How have these developments affected resource availability?

MINERALS AND ECONOMIC DEVELOPMENT

The mineral economy of the MDCs

During the 19th century emergent industrial countries in Europe and America, especially Great Britain, Germany and the USA, experienced rapid economic growth which was founded in part on access to supplies of mineral ores and coal. Concentration of these resources in particular areas led to different rates of *regional economic growth*. However, major industrial regions emerged not solely on the basis of their ability to extract minerals from the ground, but also because of their capacity to convert them and imported raw materials into more valuable metals and into finished goods. In Britain, for example, the West Midlands was by the early 19th century a place of intense metallurgical activity. Its large iron output was forged and hammered into metal rods and bars to become the raw material input of chain and nail makers, and other metal fabricators. Large quantities of non-ferrous metals, copper, tin and zinc, were brought by canal or carted into the region and made into pots and pans and brassware. Markets for these goods abounded in the fast-growing towns and cities in the rest of the country and in other countries. From these sales, money flowed back to the region, becoming the capital to expand existing production and to develop new, higher-skill activities such as those in mechanical engineering. Similar examples are to be found within the Ruhr of West Germany and the Nord region of France.

This regional economic growth was associated with two components. One was the linkages between the various stages of metal making: from mining of ore, to ore processing, to metal refining and to metal fabrication. These are known as *forward linkages*. A region possessing all these stages of activity gains from the cumulative effect of production as well as sharing in the *value added* to the metal stage by stage. Value is added because the material brought in as a relatively low value primary good is sold as a high value finished good; for example, the transformation of a length of silver rod into a piece of fashion jewellery.

The second component is the spill-over effect to other activities which need to be set up to provide the goods and services demanded by the wage earners in the mining-related industries. This is the *multiplier effect*. In this case the exploitation of resources starts to attract investment from allied industries and supporting activities to the region, bringing about a broadly-based, well-integrated industrial structure that provides the foundations of future economic prosperity.

Minerals and regional economic development in the LDCs

In the light of the comments in the preceding paragraph, it might seem feasible for mineral-rich LDCs to base their present-day regional economic development on mineral exploitation and processing. The benefits of engaging in processing of ores would include additional employment, higher wages, more advanced skills, technical development and higher value exports. In the longer term, these activities might foster industrialisation and development of the kind experienced by the MDCs. However, it cannot be assumed that resource-based development of the kind experienced by the MDCs will automatically apply in a different era to the LDCs.

There is, however, evidence of economic development associated with mining amongst the established copper mining LDCs. In major producing countries such as Chile, Peru, Zaire and Zambia there is an integrated industry based on smelting and refining. Each of these countries smelts 90 per cent of the copper they mine. In Zambia the long phase of copper exploitation has resulted not only in metal processing at the mines, but also manufacturing activity and urban development focused on mining communities such as at Kitwe and Ndola (Fig. 3.18). There has not been much spread, however, into surrounding areas and the copper belt tends to remain a concentrated zone of development, highly dependent on this single resource, and standing in some isolation from the rest of the economy. There are considerable problems in building up other activity elsewhere in the country as the necessary infrastructure is lacking. Outlets for exports are made particularly difficult in Zambia's case as it is a land-locked state reliant on neighbours for access to ports which are at a distance from its borders. Zimbabwe and Bolivia face similar difficulties.

An increased share in processing has benefited bauxite producers such as Jamaica, Surinam and Guyana. Alumina works have been built in mining areas (Fig. 3.14) creating a degree of higher paid employment and higher value exports. Linkages with local activities remain limited, and there are no related industries capable of providing the necessary chemical input of alkalis needed to produce alumina from bauxite. The establishment of smelting works to make the aluminium metal is difficult because of the lack of cheap electrical power.

Energy resources of the right magnitude and cost are limited in the case of Caribbean producers, but the prospects for Brazil are more encouraging, given both the actual and potential HEP developments along with the large bauxite reserves.

Minerals and the national economies of LDCs

LDCs are significant but not dominant world mineral producers and their position in world terms has fallen slightly since 1970 as a result of the reduction of investment noted earlier. However, they supply about one-third of the minerals entering world trade, valued at some $9000 million in 1979.

Indeed, on a national scale a country should benefit financially from export earnings on the sale of minerals to foreign countries, from income from taxes on the mining companies and the workers and from royalties (production taxes) levied on the amount of mineral extracted. Practical benefits are possible gains in labour skills, the acquisition of new technologies and improvements to the national infrastructure.

Of the leading LDC mineral producers given in Table 3.2, five are heavily dependent upon mineral exports. As a proportion of total export earnings in the early 1980s, Chile and Peru obtained 60 per cent from minerals, mainly copper, and Indonesia earned 75 per cent from tin and nickel exports. Extreme dependence on the export of a single mineral characterises Zambia and Zaire, with 95 per cent and 75 per cent respectively of the earnings coming from copper. Thus the price fetched by minerals on world markets is an important issue affecting national income. Market prices of mineral commodities are subject to instability, as well as loss in value over a period of time. Attempts made by the United Nations to stabilise prices have not been successful (see the discussion in

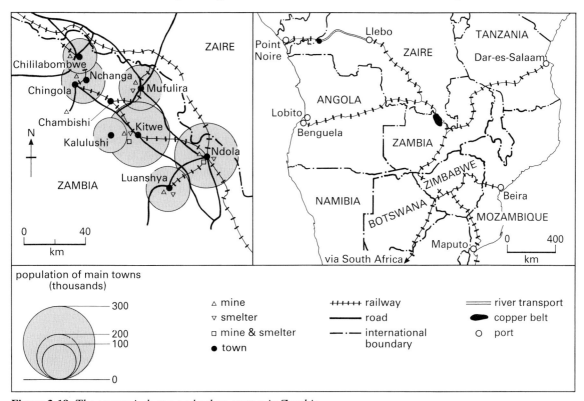

Figure 3.18 *The copper industry and urban centres in Zambia*

Chapter 8), and hence reliance on a single mineral export, or even a narrow range of mineral exports, is not always as advantageous as might be expected.

A key question for mineral-producing LDCs is how much of the money generated from foreign earnings is available as new capital to invest into additional mining capacity, mineral processing and associated manufacturing industry in order to promote new economic growth. All too often other demands have to be satisfied; in 1987, for example, Brazil, Chile, Mexico and Peru spent 30 per cent of their total export earnings on servicing and repaying debts.

Many difficulties arise because mineral production remains greatly dependent on the capital, technical expertise and skilled management provided by the TNCs which dominate world mining. The TNCs, having made their investments into mineral-producing countries, take out revenue when it begins to flow from successful mining operations. One estimate for Chile suggests that the American companies involved received $10 000 million over the period 1910–70, compared with an investment totalling $100 million. During the 1960s, around 40 per cent of the profits generated from LDC mining operations were sent back to the headquarter countries by TNCs.

In order, then, to secure greater control of their mineral assets, several of the LDCs nationalised the mining industries in their countries during the 1960s and the 1970s. This happened in the case of the three copper producing countries, Chile, Zambia and Zaire, and to sections of the bauxite/aluminium industry in Jamaica and Guyana. The newly formed state companies, however, have often found it difficult to operate these activities, partly because of a lack of sufficient numbers of skilled technicians and managers, but largely because of the complications of selling minerals into world markets which remain under the control of the importing countries or the TNCs. Breaking into metal production and fabrication is even more difficult. A solution to these difficulties has been tried in the form of partnership schemes, in which the mineral-owning country and one or more mining companies form a joint company to manage the mine projects in the country. This gives the host country some access to management skills and to markets. The political importance of such partnership schemes can be judged in the case of the copper industry, where about 60 per cent of production is now controlled by majority-held state companies.

ASSIGNMENTS

9 a. What two factors are suggested as contributing to the regional economic growth of MDCs?

b. What is meant by value added?

c. Describe the processes involved in adding value to primary metal inputs.

10 a. Name the main centres of the copper belt in Zambia.

b. Use your atlas to help comment on the extent to which these centres represent a concentration of urban population in Zambia.

c. Why is it difficult for economic activity to spread out from a single area of mineral development?

11 a. Name four LDCs which are heavily dependent on earnings from mineral exports.

b. Suggest two reasons why economic benefits are not easily gained from such mineral exports.

c. Comment on the ways in which the exploitation of minerals might help economic development.

4

Energy, the Economy and Renewable Energy Resources

ENERGY AND THE ECONOMY

The economic development of the industrial countries of the world has greatly depended on the use of machines. Machines have made it possible for people to work more productively. This growing use of machines has in turn resulted in increased energy consumption. Larger amounts of energy have also been needed to satisfy the heating, lighting and transport needs

of expanding industrial and domestic markets. In other words, economic growth, with rising industrial output, requires an increasing input of energy.

Energy and economic development

A close correlation exists between a country's level of economic development and the amount of energy it consumes (Fig. 4.1). The figure shows *energy consumption per capita* on the

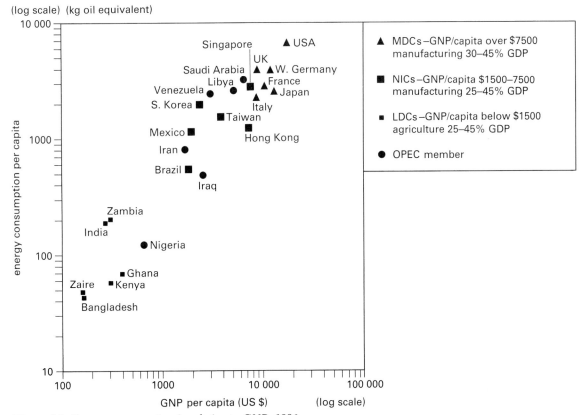

Figure 4.1 *Energy consumption in relation to GNP, 1986*

vertical scale plotted against *Gross National Product (GNP) per capita* on the horizontal scale. Note that the graph uses logarithmic scales on both axes. The unit *oil equivalent* is used as a convenient way of comparing different types of energy which have different heat outputs, for example, 1 tonne of oil is equivalent to about 1.5 tonnes of coal or 1 100 cu m of natural gas.

Notice how LDCs such as India and Kenya combine low GNP per capita with low energy consumption per capita and hence cluster towards the bottom left of the graph. There are exceptions amongst these LDCs, and Zambia's position on the graph shows that it consumes a relatively large amount of energy for its GNP/ capita. This is explained by the energy-intensive industries of copper smelting and refining in Zambia. The MDCs are at the upper right of the graph; their high GNPs are related to high energy inputs. Their industries and extensive transport systems demand energy. Also high up along the array of points lie some of the NICs, for example South Korea, Taiwan and Hong Kong. Countries in this group have greatly increased their manufacturing output since the early 1960s, leading to increased energy demand. Singapore's high energy use is because of its importance as a location for oil refining. Oil producing countries such as Saudi Arabia, Libya and Venezuela are also high in the list of oil consumers.

The graph also shows that the MDCs use about 20 times as much energy per capita as the LDCs. What is not shown is information about changes in *energy efficiency*, that is the additional energy associated with an increase in GNP. For many of the MDCs the ratio is now below 0.5, meaning that a 1 per cent annual growth in GNP is gained from an extra 0.5 per cent input of energy. Although, then, the MDCs remained major consumers of energy during the period 1970–85, there was a reduction in the amount of energy needed to produce each unit of goods or to run services. More effective energy use was achieved as a result of improvements to machinery; a decline in *energy intensive* industries such as iron and steel and ship-building; and the application of conservation measures.

In some LDCs, however, and particularly in the NICs, industrial development promoted a rise in energy intensity. These early stages of industrialisation are often based on heavy industries which are energy hungry and consequently there is a trend in these countries for energy inputs per unit of output to increase.

Energy flows in the economy

Hypothetical energy flows for a modern industrial economy are shown in Figure 4.2. Stage 1 is the production of *primary energy*: the mining of coal, the extraction of crude petroleum and natural gas, the harnessing of hydro- and nuclear power resources. Ignoring small contributions from lesser renewable energy resources, these four primary energies are taken as the inputs into Stage 2: the power producing industries. These industries provide the *secondary energy* to satisfy the heating, lighting and mechanical work requirements of consumers. Stages 3 and 4 are the transfers to and final sectors of use in markets. In the industrial markets fuels such as coke and fuel oil are delivered in bulk to large firms by rail or road transporters. The supply of gas is often arranged under long-term contracts, with deliveries made via pipelines. In the transport sector, airports are large points of demand for jet fuels, and bulk deliveries by pipeline are sometimes justified to these fixed locations. The domestic market is highly fragmented, with gas and electricity for heating and lighting supplied to each individual householder. Car owners make frequent purchases of petrol from filling stations. Thus a variety of transport methods is used to complete the transfer of secondary energy from the concentrated points of production at processing plants to the widespread markets of the end users.

There are sizeable losses in the system. As shown in Figure 4.2, some 30 per cent of the primary energy input is lost in conversion processes and in distribution. The largest losses are in the conversion of primary energy into electricity and in transmitting electrical power, yet

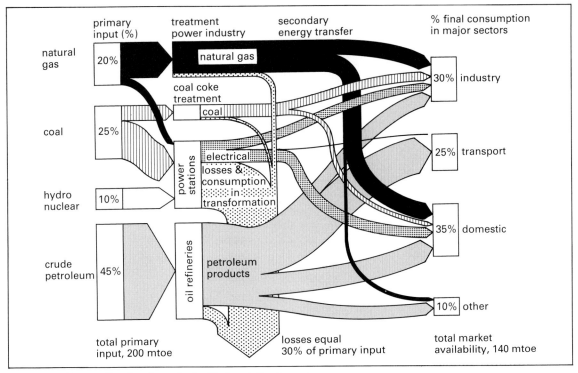

Figure 4.2 *Energy flow in a hypothetical industrialised country*

the compensating benefit is that electricity is clean, convenient and widely available.

The energy mix

A country's energy mix is the proportions of oil, gas, coal and other energy sources consumed as primary energy. Table 4.1 compares the mix for selected countries and summarises information for selected areas of the world. As the table shows, for most countries oil is the most important of the energy inputs followed by natural gas and coal, but there are exceptions. France has a large input of nuclear electricity and Canada of hydro-electricity, while the Netherlands' use of natural gas is larger than other countries.

The reasons for a particular mix in a country are complex, but are greatly influenced by availability and cost. For example, oil consumption in Europe expanded very fast in the 1960s. There were ample supplies available from the prolific oilfields of the Middle East and North

Africa, and these supplies could be brought cheaply to Europe using large tankers (Fig. 4.3). Oil was an efficient fuel to use compared with solid fuels because of its high calorific value and the ease with which it could be distributed to and controlled in homes and factories. Above all, oil was cheap. Oil, therefore, competed effectively in energy markets and gained market share, particularly at the expense of coal.

This era of low-priced oil ended abruptly in 1973 with war in the Middle East between Israel and the Arab countries. This gave OPEC (the Organisation of Petroleum Exporting Countries, formed in 1960) the opportunity to control oil prices. Although a geo-politically diverse group, OPEC's core of oil-producing countries in the Middle East and North Africa provided the political will to cut back production and force up the price of oil. The economic effects of this price rise were far-reaching, and were still being felt in the early 1980s in terms of employment structures and energy mixes.

	Oil	Natural gas	Coal	HEP	Nuclear	Total	Oil	Natural gas	Coal	HEP	Nuclear
	(million tonnes oil equivalent)						(per cent)				
Belg./Lux.	24	8	10	0	10	52	46	15	19	0	19
France	86	24	17	16	55	198	43	12	9	8	28
Italy	92	33	15	11	0	151	61	22	10	7	0
Netherland	34	30	8	0	1	73	47	41	11	0	1
W. Germany	115	43	73	4	32	267	43	16	27	1	12
UK	80	48	66	1	14	209	38	23	32	0	7
EC*	431	186	189	32	112	950	45	20	20	3	12
USA	789	460	480	67	145	1 941	41	24	25	3	7
Canada	75	46	35	76	20	252	30	18	14	30	8
Japan	222	39	76	19	43	399	56	10	19	5	11
USSR	439	549	310	56	43	1 397	31	39	22	4	3
L. America	228	79	23	93	2	425	54	19	5	22	0
M. East	135	54	3	3	0	195	69	28	2	2	0
S.E. Asia	141	21	49	10	21	242	58	9	20	4	9
WORLD	3 039	1 631	2 428	537	439	8 074	38	20	30	7	5

EC*   total of countries named. Percentages may not sum to 100 due to rounding error.

Table 4.1 *Primary energy consumption for selected countries, 1988*

Figure 4.3 *Oil tankers at Fawley refinery terminal, Southampton Water*

When OPEC cut oil production again in 1978, there was a short-term shortage of oil in the MDCs and oil prices again rose sharply. The high energy prices of 1979–83 triggered slower economic growth, a shift to less intensive energy applications and the adoption of energy conservation. Oil was no longer cheap, and growth in energy consumption was increasingly satisfied by other fuels as the graphs in Figure 4.4 show.

Fearing OPEC's control of oil supplies, many MDCs acted to diversify both the source areas of oil and the types of energy used. The UK was particularly fortunate in that natural gas had been discovered in the North Sea and consumption of this fuel rose dramatically after 1967 (as shown in Fig. 4.4). The UK also gained a measure of independence from imported oil as a result of oil discoveries. In France a great effort was made to increase nuclear energy, and by 1985 France was second only to the USA in the amount of nuclear power generated. Between 1970 and 1984 Japan greatly increased its use of both natural gas and nuclear energy.

The different energy strategies followed reflected national objectives linked to the need to supply sufficient quantities of energy at reasonable prices. In some cases, account had to be taken of the need to protect domestic energy industries, especially the coal industry, whilst in all cases security of supplies was essential. A set of strategies, based on the so-called 'Coconuke' policy (coal, conservation and nuclear power), were advocated in the mid-1970s. However, with public attitudes turning against the nuclear option this policy is no longer so appealing. Neither has there been much of a resurgence in the production and use of coal, at least in EC countries. In part this was due to the shift to natural gas and nuclear power. It was also related to the structure of the coal industry in several of the older industrial economies, as discussed more fully in Chapter 5. In many cases the more accessible coal seams have been worked out and, despite modernisation of coal mining and improved productivity, the delivered cost of coal from deep pits in the EC is high. It was countries like the USA, with access to surface deposits and hence lower production costs, and Japan, depending on imported coal, that increased coal use between 1975 and 1985, as shown in Figure 4.4.

Energy balances

Many countries depend on imported energy in order to satisfy their energy needs. As Table 4.2 shows, Japan, the USA and members of the European Community have negative energy

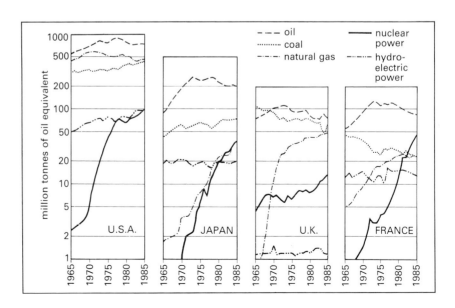

Figure 4.4 *Changes in primary energy consumption by type, 1965–85*

	Oil	Natural gas	Coal	HEP power	Nuclear	Total	Total demand	Energy balance (mtoe)	Oil balance
			Production (mtoe)						
Belg./Lux.	0	0	2	0	10	12	53	−41	−24
France	4	3	8	16	55	86	197	−111	−82
Italy	5	15	0	11	0	31	151	−120	−87
Netherlands	0	48	0	0	1	49	73	−24	−34
W. Germany	4	14	74	4	32	128	267	−139	−111
UK	114	40	63	1	14	232	208	24	34
EC*	127	120	147	32	112	538	949	−411	−304
USA	463	426	524	67	145	1 625	1 941	−317	−327
Canada	83	81	46	76	20	306	252	54	8
Japan	1	2	7	19	43	72	400	−328	−221
USSR	624	694	392	56	43	1 809	1 397	412	185
M. East	739	65	1	3	0	808	195	613	604
L. America	341	86	21	93	2	543	426	117	113
Africa	263	53	100	19	2	437	210	227	177

EC*   total of countries named
energy balance = total home production − total consumption
oil balance = home oil production − oil consumption

Table 4.2 *Primary energy production, consumption and balances for selected countries, 1988*

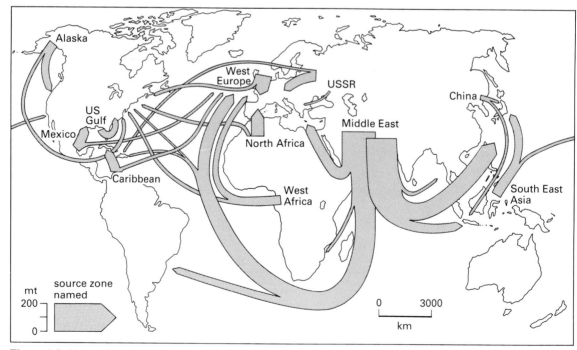

Figure 4.5 *Main oil movements by sea, 1988*

balances so far as the home supply of energy is concerned. The UK, with major resources of coal, oil and natural gas, is exceptional amongst EC members in that it has a positive energy balance. By making a great simplification according to *energy budgets*, judged very simply from home production minus demand, surplus and deficit zones of the world may be identified.

One major surplus zone is that of the Middle East petroleum producing countries, where home demand is small compared with production. There is also surplus production in the USSR and UK, which have such a range of energy resources that production levels exceed the substantial home demand. In contrast, and despite the scale of its energy production, the USA has an internal supply deficiency. Production of fossil fuels could reach higher levels in the USA, but, amongst other reasons, conservation objectives mean that there is a reliance on imports to add to supplies rather than pushing production closer to capacity limits. More clearly defined deficit zones are the major energy consumers like Japan and EC countries (excluding the UK) which are unable to satisfy their demand for energy from home production. There is also a number of LDCs where energy production is even less than the small amounts demanded.

Substantial transfers of energy are needed to satisfy the imbalances between spatially separated surplus and deficit zones. International trade in energy is dominated by oil, nearly 1 500 million tonnes entering into world trade in 1988 (Fig. 4.5). The Middle East, as the world's major supplier, stands out on this map, as do the principal oil movements to consumers in Europe and Japan.

ASSIGNMENTS

1 a. Explain the correlation between per capita GNP and energy consumption shown in Figure 4.1.
  b. Why are countries like the USA and Japan such large consumers of energy?
  c. What is meant by energy efficiency and why is it changing in the MDCs?

2 a. Draw compound columns to illustrate the percentage energy mixes of four EC countries.
  b. Describe the differences in their energy mixes and explain how they have arisen.
  c. For any two LDCs, find out about their energy mixes and attempt to explain them.

3 With reference to Figure 4.2:
  a. describe the main uses of coal in the economy;
  b. comment on how oil products are distributed to consumers;
  c. explain why electricity is produced, given that the losses of the primary energy inputs are so large.

4 Refer to Figure 4.4.
  a. How has total energy consumption in the UK changed over the period 1973–85?
  b. Compare these changes with those occurring in France.

5 Study Table 4.2.
  a. Comment on the energy production features of the European Community.
  b. Explain the major differences in production for any three countries.

6 For one MDC, suggest how climate, industrial structure and conservation practices might affect the intensity of energy use.

THE RENEWABLE ENERGY RESOURCES

Types of energy resource

Reference to Figure 1.6 shows the distinction to be made between the renewable (flow) types of energy and the non-renewable (finite) resources. Predictions of the lifetimes of these resources of energy are given by the curves in Figure 4.6. The sustained production of renewable resources like hydro, tidal and solar power is in contrast to the rising and falling output of finite resources. Look back to Chapter 1 for a discussion of the differences. Despite the attractive long-term production cycles of renewable resources, their contribution to present world

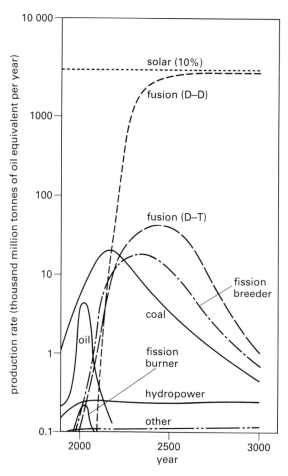

Figure 4.6 *Energy resource lifetimes*

energy needs is small. Even the most important of the developed renewable energy resources, hydro-electricity, provided only 7 per cent of the total primary energy consumed in the world in 1988. The range of renewable resources, though, is considerable and includes solar energy as radiation and as derived energy from the biomass, running water, wind and waves. Tides and nuclear fusion are other forms of renewable energy, as is geothermal energy, even though it is in the critical group, being depleted if over-exploited.

Solar energy – radiation

Incoming solar radiation is equivalent to 173 000 *terawatts* (a terawatt is a million, million watts).

This is 30 000 times greater than all the commercial energy the world uses in a year, but as a power source it is very inconveniently located at the top of the earth's atmosphere. Of this total, about 30 per cent returns to space by reflection and scatter, 47 per cent is absorbed in the atmosphere and 23 per cent in the water cycles.

Producing useful energy from the solar radiation available at the surface of the earth is something of a problem. This radiation is of low energy intensity, is intermittent and the amount varies according to latitudinal position on the earth's surface. To give some idea of the variation, over a year in the UK some 900 kWh/m^2 (kilowatt hour per square metre) strike the surface, but 2 300 kWh/m^2 at the tropics. In other words, the global distribution (Fig. 4.7) fails to match the pattern of market demand with its maxima located in the temperate climatic zones.

The cost of harnessing solar radiation to generate electricity is about twenty times greater than that of conventional methods. So far, development has been based on schemes serving local space heating and water heating needs, with only small inputs to electricity generation. Methods of tapping solar radiation are of two main kinds. The first are flat-plate collectors of the kind successfully adopted in Mediterranean and Middle East countries to heat water (Fig. 4.8). The second are the solar concentrators which use mirrors and focusing devices linked to thermal power plant. The Eurelios plant in Sicily is an example.

Techniques with wider application and suited to cool temperate regions include those based on the *passive solar design* of buildings and the *photo-voltaic cell*. Houses and offices can be designed to trap the solar energy falling on them and built with materials that act as heat stores and as insulators. The storage of heat is important as it overcomes the disadvantage of heat variation associated with solar energy. New houses at Milton Keynes, England, constructed to conform with these principles of heat conservation, have proved to be very energy efficient. Photo-voltaic cells produce an

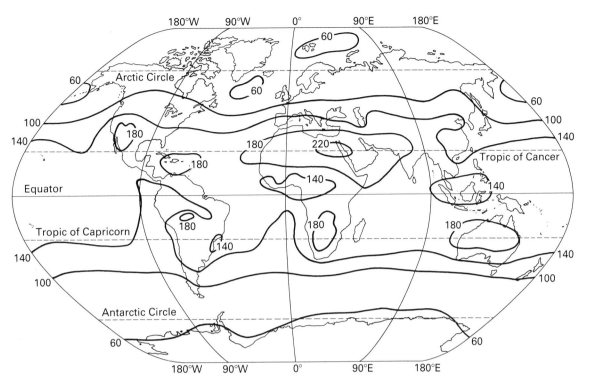

Figure 4.7 *Distribution of mean solar radiation at ground level*

electric current when activated by incident light; heat is not needed. They have a potentially wide geographical application and, despite their high cost, are being introduced on a small scale.

Energy from biomass sources

Plants fix carbon and store energy from the sun as carbohydrates. Fossil fuels are the accumulated organic product of the sun's past energy. Energy from the biomass, however, can be continuously derived by using natural vegetation, by growing *energy crops* or by using *biomass conversion processes*. In many rural areas of the LDCs natural woodland supplies as much as 80 per cent of the energy used. As these are critical resources subject to depletion if over-exploited, a solution is to conserve resources by combining sustained yield principles in the management of natural forests with the planting of new timber resources in other areas.

Figure 4.8 *Flat-plate solar collectors at Lod, Israel*

The allocation of land to energy crops is a problem in many countries because of land scarcity. There is a conflict of interests when the land is also needed to provide staple food crops. Even in a country the size of Brazil there is criticism of the policy of growing sugar cane as the raw material for industrial alcohol, despite the fact that the alcohol produced is a valuable substitute for imported petroleum products. Of the new cars sold in Brazil, 25 per cent have alcohol-adapted engines. In the USA, 'gasohol', a mixture of gasoline and alcohol made from maize and small grain crops, has been sold since 1980. About 3 per cent of the USA's primary energy was coming from biomass sources, including wood and crop waste, in the early 1980s. Because of the high cost of, and dependence on imported petroleum, EC countries have invested in biomass research. One of the research groups has suggested that up to 14 per cent of the fossil fuel part of the energy requirement of the EC could come from biomass sources without restrictions being imposed on food output.

An alternative to energy crops, and hence a more appropriate strategy in LDC economies, is to use conversion processes to make *biogas*. This is commonly done on a small scale in south-east Asia, where human and animal wastes are fermented in the absence of air to produce methane. The process is similar to that used at UK sewage works where methane is generated to supply some of the energy needs of the works. In an agricultural economy, though, a major disadvantage is the removal of valuable sources of soil nutrients from areas where animal manure is collected, although in compensation small amounts of nitrogen rich residues are available from the biogas process.

Hydropower

The water wheel has a long history of use as a means of providing mechanical energy, especially for the purpose of grinding corn. Watermills contributed to the industrial advance of Britain in the 18th and 19th centuries, being used to pump water from mines, power furnace bellows, hammers and grinding wheels in the metal trades and to drive machinery in textile factories. Even after the widespread adoption of the steam engine, the use of waterwheels persisted. As late as 1840 some 25 per cent of the total power capacity at textile mills in Britain was from waterwheels.

However, even with the more efficient over-shoot wheels there are severe limitations on the amount of power that can be produced, the restriction being that the head of water cannot be much more than the diameter of the wheel. A large watermill would be rated at 10 Kw capacity. Much more power can be derived from a water-driven turbine to produce electricity. This technology dates from the late 1800s and was pioneered in the USA. By applying water under pressure at the turbine, at least 60

Region	Potential (technically usable)	Operating and under construction	Utilisation (percentage)
	(million kilowatt)		
North America	360	164	46
Europe	160	107	67
USSR	250	52	21
China	217	12	6
Asia	610	62	10
Africa	358	23	6
Latin America	432	75	17
WORLD	2 430	502	21

Table 4.3 *World hydropower, 1980*

utilisation = percentage of potential that is operating or under construction per cent efficient energy conversion is achieved. Consequently, during the 20th century hydro-electric power has become the principal form of water power.

Hydro-electric power installations tap the vast amount of energy that flows in the hydro-logical cycle. Of this only a tiny proportion, about 2 400 million kW, is regarded as techni-cally usable because of fluctuating flows in rivers or the difficulties of constructing dams. The power capacity operating and under construc-tion in 1980 was 502 million kW, distributed amongst continents as shown in Table 4.3.

The last three continents quoted – Asia, Africa and Latin America, which include many of the LDCs – account for nearly 60 per cent of the total world potential. Much of the hydropower in these areas remains to be uti-lised. Utilisation is about 20 per cent in Latin America (Fig. 4.9) but only 6 per cent in the continent of Africa. Virtually none of the 180 million kW of hydropower in the Congo Basin, Zaire, has been harnessed, and only 0.3 per cent out of a possible 130 million kW in Indonesia.

Hydro-electricity is attractive as a renewable form of energy, but it is costly to develop on a large scale because of the amount of engineering work required. At costs of $1 000 per kW in-stalled, an investment of $1 200 million would be needed for a 1 200 MW (megawatt) plant. LDCs have limited capital to pay for the con-struction of a large-scale hydro-electric power plant. The best physical sites are often in remote locations, so that, apart from the costs of dam construction and engineering work, the trans-mission of electricity to markets is costly.

Despite such problems, the growth in the amount of hydropower installed in some LDCs has been considerable, especially in Latin America where an additional 160 000 million kWh were produced between 1975 and 1985. For a rapidly industrialising state like Brazil, with a physical geography endowed with vast water power potential, it has made sense to build hydro-electric power plants. Much of this development has focused on supplying power to the important economic area of south-east

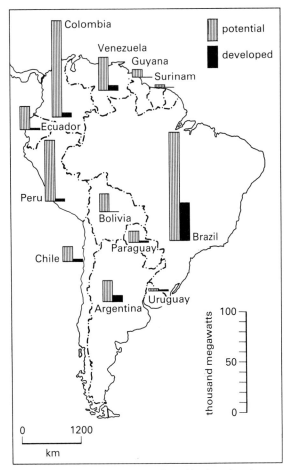

Figure 4.9 *Potential and developed hydro-electric power in Latin America, 1986*

Brazil between Rio de Janeiro, Sao Paulo and Belo Horizonte. During the 1970s, very large plants were under construction on the Parana River. Those at Jupia and Ilha Soltreira will have a total final installed capacity of 4 600 MW and that at Itaiupu, a joint development with Paraguay, a capacity of 13 000 MW (Fig. 4.10).

In tropical Africa several major schemes can be cited as evidence of the progress made to date. The market situations make interesting contrasts. Four of the largest schemes are: Cabora Bassa, Kafue, Kariba and Volta, with capacities ranging from 700 MW to 1200 MW. Much of the power from Cabora Bassa, Mozambique, is intended for markets in the Republic of South Africa, while the Kariba and

Figure 4.10 *The Itaipu Dam on the Parana River between Paraguay and Brazil*

Kafue projects have significantly added to energy supplies for industries, especially mining, in part of Central Africa. The first phase of the Volta scheme in Ghana was completed in 1966 at a cost of US $200 million. The power station at Akosombo provides 99 per cent of Ghana's electrical power. Behind the dam was created one of the world's largest man-made lakes. Losses of other uses of the land have some compensation in the development of fresh water fisheries, but the principal associated economic development, and the market for 66 per cent of the power produced, is the aluminium works at Tema.

It might be more appropriate for many LDCs to develop mini hydro-electricity schemes, rather than go for projects on the grand scale. Many such opportunities exist in India where low-head hydropower units could be built at existing irrigation canals, and there is considerable scope for similar units in south-east Asia. These small schemes have the merit of fitting into the rural economy without forcing radical social and environmental change. They are not very expensive to construct and they save on transmission costs.

In the MDCs, many of the best sites for water power development have already been used. Nearly 50 per cent of the potential has been harnessed in the USA and over 65 per cent in Europe (Table 4.3). Hydro-electric power has been systematically developed over many years in the USA, but even so only 4 per cent of the total primary power input is from this source. Most potential for this source of power in the USA is in the Pacific zone. In Canada the massive potential at Churchill Falls, Labrador, and at James Bay, Quebec, has been tapped with plant of 5 000 MW capacity installed at each of these recent developments. The objective of many of the older schemes was simply to supply electrical power to domestic and/or industrial users, as from those plants along the Appalachian Fall Line, at Niagara

Falls and those of the Canadian Shield along the St. Lawrence. In other places multiple objectives aim to combine water supply, flood control and irrigation as well as the production of electrical power. These include the high-dam schemes of the Rockies along the Colorado, Colombia and Snake rivers, and the schemes with regional economic objectives such as those of the Tennessee Valley Authority (TVA). Flood control and irrigation, along with power production, also characterise several of the massive projects engineered by the Soviet Union, which include the major series of dams along the Dnepr, Volga and Yenisi rivers. In Australia the complex Snowy Mountain scheme not only provides power but also transfers water across the divide to feed tributaries of the Murray and Murrumbidgee Rivers. These rivers in turn extend irrigation to the dry zones of the Murray-Darling basin.

In 1989 about 6.5% of world energy came from hydro-electric power. As a contribution to future world energy needs, and despite the desirable properties of continuous and pollution-free supply, hydro-electricity is estimated to remain small, as shown by Figure 4.6. This is because of the technical and economic limitations which will act to restrict the amount of capacity installed; not all the potential can be tapped.

Energy from wind and waves

Of the 370 TW of power associated with wind and waves, 20 TW is considered to be technically extractable as wind power. *Wind turbine* technology is now well advanced, and given the adoption of development programmes, several of the MDCs, including the USA and the UK, could be providing up to 20 per cent of their electricity needs from wind power by the end of this century. The economics of wind-generated power are, however, complicated by the discontinuous nature of the output. This limitation can be overcome if the output is linked to a national grid, otherwise stand-by facilities are needed to secure a continuous supply to customers. There are also environmental considera-

tions. Single large wind turbines would have major landscape impact as each unit would be the height of a transmission pylon with rotors up to 100 m in diameter. Alternatively, *wind parks* could be developed, that is groups of small machines concentrated at exposed sites as shown in Figure 4.11. In the UK, wind parks are under evaluation at Langdon Common, Durham, Capel Cynon, Dyfed; Cold Northolt, Cornwall. Wind generators could play a particularly useful role in serving remote rural markets in MDCs and scattered village communities in LDCs. Small-scale decentralised supply of this kind would fit the market pattern in many of the LDCs rather better than individual large HEP plant.

Despite a considerable research effort, the technical problems of harnessing wave power on a commercial basis are not yet fully mastered. The UK has examined the use of rocking vanes, pistons to create air pressure, oscillating water columns and hydraulic pumps, but the research effort was greatly scaled down in 1985. A great deal of wave power is available potentially to the maritime nations; for the UK,

Figure 4.11 *Wind park: groups of small wind turbines, California, USA*

a total of 100 000 MW is estimated. Even if technical problems were overcome, the main disadvantages are the very high capital costs of constructing such an energy system and the costs of transmitting the electricity to the national grid if it were to supply large national markets. The positive aspects are that the power is more or less continuously available, non-polluting and suited to serving scattered demand in remote coastal areas.

Tidal power

Direct use of tidal currents is possible and tide mills have a very long history of use dating back to Roman times. The power output from tidal currents is small even if modern turbines submerged in tidal channels are used. More power can be gained from barrage schemes in which water impounded behind the barrage at high tide is let out to drive low-head turbines on the falling tide, or which make use of both flow and ebb tides through the barrage.

Generally, on a world scale, coasts with a combination of high tidal ranges and funnel-shaped estuaries provide the most advantageous conditions for tidal power development. The White Sea (USSR), Kimberley (western Australia), the Bay of Fundy (Canada), and bays along the north-east coast of the USA all have suitable physical conditions. One major commercial scheme in operation is that at La Rance near St. Malo, France, with a capacity of 240 MW. A pilot scheme on the Bay of Fundy

is being monitored for the ecological effects of the barrage.

In world terms then, there has been little development of tidal power. This is because many of the sites with high potential are remote and the cost of transmitting power to distant markets would be uneconomic. Furthermore, the capital costs of construction are high relative to those for tapping other energy sources. It is estimated that from the world's tidal basins regarded as suitable for power developments, the amount of power technically available might be only 15 000 MW. This explains the modest contribution of tidal power to the world energy forecasts as given in Figure 4.6.

In Britain, the Severn, Mersey and Humber estuaries, the Wash and Morecombe Bay all have considerable potential. In the 1981 study of the Severn, an Inner Barrage scheme (Fig. 4.12) with a capacity of 7 200 MW was identified as being the most cost effective. Even so it would be a high capital cost venture at an estimated £5 600 million in 1981, and would have many environmental consequences. Hydrological changes upstream would affect sedimentation, possibly alter mudflats and threaten wildfowl sanctuaries. Although tidal power schemes are free from pollution hazards, there are other significant environmental issues to be faced.

Nuclear energy; fusion

As the line labelled Fusion D-D in Figure 4.6

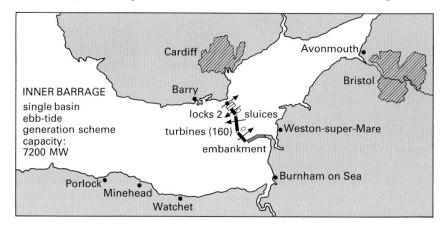

Figure 4.12 *The Inner Barrage Scheme, Severn Estuary*

implies, nuclear fusion is a route to a renewable energy resource. In this type of reaction, light nuclei are fused together and when this happens energy is emitted; this is the kind of reaction which is taking place in the sun. This is a process which is very difficult to copy and, despite interest in 1989 in a *cold fusion* process based on electrolysis, research is likely to concentrate on methods which use a plasma of gas heated to extremely high temperature in order to energise hydrogen nuclei sufficiently for them to fuse. This is done in a doughnut-shaped vessel, or *torus*, in which the gas is kept away from the walls of the vessel by means of a magnetic field. One of the isotopes used is deuterium and is reasonably abundant, but the other, tritium, is not. This explains why the curve for Fusion D-T, although involving a large quantity of energy, still has the characteristic shape of a non-renewable resource. If the reaction is based on deuterium nuclei, how-

ever, then the situation alters dramatically. The resources of deuterium from sea water are super-abundant, but immensely difficult technical problems will have to be overcome before this energy source is unlocked from the sea stocks.

Geothermal energy

Heat sources exist beneath the earth's crust in the form of hot dry rocks, and as steam and hot water from aquifers and springs. Strictly speaking they are only renewable resources if the heat extracted is less than the heat accumulating in the source rocks. Areas of the world with geothermal energy potential are shown in Figure 4.13, indicating a relationship with plate margins and areas of mountain building. The exploitation of hot dry rocks, such as granite, involves drilling through the surface rocks in order to reach the hot rocks below. The rock at

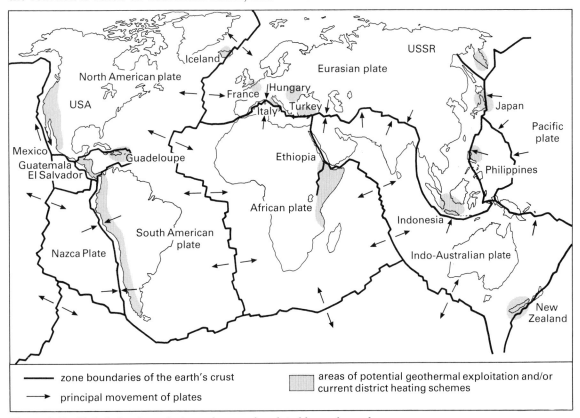

Figure 4.13 *Global plate boundaries and areas of exploitable geothermal energy*

the base of the hole is shattered by letting off explosives so that water pumped down the hole can circulate through the broken rock and absorb the heat. A second borehole is used to draw up the hot water or steam to the surface. Experimental work in New Mexico, USA, indicates that a thermal power unit of up to 50 MW capacity is feasible at the research site. The Camborne School of Mines, UK, is involved in a £11 million Hot Rocks project which entails drilling 2 km down into granite rocks. Results are encouraging, but the project is not commercially viable because development costs are high.

Steam and hot water can be obtained by tapping aquifers located in geothermal fields. These are the natural reservoirs which accumulate steam and hot water, some giving rise to the natural phenomenon of *geysers*. There are installations in several countries where geothermal steam is sufficient to generate electricity. Generating capacity is greatest in the USA at 1 300 MW, followed by the Philippines and Italy, each with around 500 MW, and Mexico, Japan and New Zealand with 200 MW each.

Prospects for renewable energy

As shown by Figure 4.6, apart from the potential contributions from solar and nuclear fusion, those from other renewable resources are comparatively small when measured at a world scale. Nevertheless, for a number of countries and individual regions renewable energy has significant potential, although there are many technical problems to be resolved before efficient use of some of the renewable energy sources is possible. Finally, there are difficulties arising from the geographical separation of several of the best source zones, for example of solar energy, tidal and hydro-power, from markets. In the medium term, therefore, and at least into the first quarter of the next century, reliance on fossil fuels, that is oil, natural gas and coal, seems inevitable.

ASSIGNMENTS

---

7 a. Draw up a list of factors which are likely to affect attempts to develop large-scale production of solar energy.

  b. Examine the prospects and problems involved for LDCs in attempting to make more use of energy derived from the biomass.

8 a. Using data from Table 2.4, draw column graphs to compare fuelwood use in African countries.

  b. Find out about the fuelwood crisis in the Third World and comment on the proposals for dealing with the crisis.

9 a. Draw up a list of the main physical features likely to favour the development of a country's potential hydropower.

  b. Examine the difficulties involved in developing the hydropower potential of any one LDC.

10 Why is the commercial application of alternative energy resources such as solar, waves and wind, so difficult?

5

Non-Renewable Energy Resources and the Power Industries

PETROLEUM RESOURCES

Petroleum resources are the hydrocarbons naturally occurring as gases, liquids or solids. Initially in this chapter attention is focused on *natural gas* and *crude oil* as the important hydrocarbons used as energy sources. Natural gas consists mainly of methane. Natural gas is not only an excellent fuel for heating purposes, but is also a valuable feedstock for the petrochemical industry. It occurs both in gasfields and in oilfields as a mix with oil, when it is referred to as *associated gas*. Many of the oilfields of the North Sea have large quantities of associated gas.

Crude oil consists of a very large number of different hydrocarbons and hence is a complex material. Generally speaking, light crudes are more valuable and have higher heating values than heavy crudes. Sulphur compounds are serious contaminants in some crude oils, as they are with natural gas, and extra costs arise in refining these oils in order to remove these pollutants. Petroleum products made by refining crude oil include the light fuels such as petrol and jet fuels used in engines, and heavier ones such as fuel oil used in furnaces.

Petroleum exploration relies on sophisticated ground and aerial surveying techniques. Computer analysis of artificially created seismic wave patterns through underground rocks has improved the identification of possible oil bearing structures, hence guiding the positioning of exploration wells known as *wild cat* wells. In some parts of the world, prolific oilfields are found in dome-shaped underground *oil traps* in which high pressure gas above the oil forces oil to the surface when the drill penetrates the flank of the dome.

World petroleum reserves

The world's known oil and natural gas reserves are geographically concentrated: just five countries account for 60 per cent of all the proved oil reserves, while the USSR and Iran together possess 50 per cent of the natural gas resources (Fig. 5.1; Table 5.1). These data on petroleum

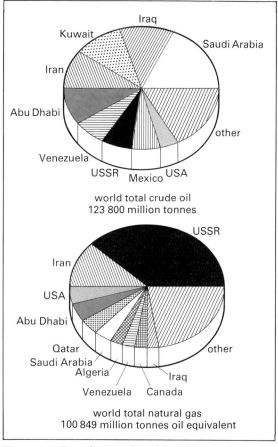

Figure 5.1 *Distribution of world crude oil and natural gas reserves, 1988*

resources are for proved reserves. This is the quantity of petroleum, as either oil or gas, which, at current prices, is indicated by geological and engineering information to be recoverable from known reservoirs by using existing technology.

World proved crude oil reserves of 124 000 million tonnes in 1988 are enough to last for 40 years at present rates of production. This lifetime of oil is the reserve amount divided by the production rate, referred to as the *R/P ratio*. The ratio for natural gas based on reserves of 100 000 million tonnes of oil equivalent (mtoe) is 58. This higher value for natural gas is because it is being consumed at a slower rate than oil.

Table 5.1 shows that a country's production of crude oil does not necessarily correspond to the reserves it possesses. High rates of oil production in the USA, USSR and the UK lead to low R/P ratios. These high levels of production are related partly to the needs of the large home markets and partly to political and economic interests in maintaining a powerful oil industry. In these countries, therefore, known oil reservoirs are fast being depleted and in order to find more oil a continuing programme of exploration is necessary. In contrast, Middle

East producers have high R/P ratios. This is not only because of their large reserves, but also because production is well below oilfield capacity.

Estimates of the world's ultimate resources of crude oil vary. These estimates are based on the probability of finding oil in suitable geological formations in new areas. Extra oil will also come from the application of improved technology at existing oil and gas fields. The world's total oil resource has been put at around 275 000 million tonnes by a number of experts, but one analyst, Professor P. R. Odell, Director for International Energy Studies at Erasmus University in the Netherlands considers three times this amount more likely. For natural gas, the average estimated quantity is some 230 000 mtoe.

Whatever the ultimate amounts of either oil or gas might be, the present geographical realities are clear: for the political economy of world oil, the most significant fact is that OPEC (as defined in Chapter 4 and Fig. 5.2), has 75 per cent of the proved reserves. Dislocation from this region, as shown by the invasion of Kuwait by Iraq in August 1990, can result in a rapid increase in oil prices.

	Reserves			Production		R/P
Countries by rank	**Million tonnes**	**Cumulative per cent**	**Countries by rank**	**Million tonnes**	**Cumulative per cent**	**ratio**
Saudi Arabia*	23 100	19	USSR	624	21	13
Iraq*	13 400	30	USA	463	36	10
Kuwait*	12 700	40	Saudi Arabia	257	45	90
Iran*	12 700	50	Mexico	141	50	54
Abu Dhabi*	12 100	60	China	136	55	23
Venezuela*	8 300	66	Iraq	128	59	105
USSR	8 000	72	UK	114	63	5
Mexico	7 500	78	Iran	113	67	112
USA	4 400	82	Venezuela	96	70	87
China	3 100	85	Canada	83	73	14
Libya*	2 900	87	Nigeria	68	75	32
Nigeria*	2 200	89	Kuwait	67	77	190
OPEC	91 800	74	OPEC	1 031	34	89
WORLD	123 800	100	WORLD	3 031	100	41

Table 5.1 *Proved crude oil reserves and production, 1988, for leading countries*

Reserves given for countries with more than 2000 million tonnes
Production for countries producing more than 65 million tonnes
R/P ratio: Reserves/Production   *   member of OPEC

OPEC and the world petroleum economy

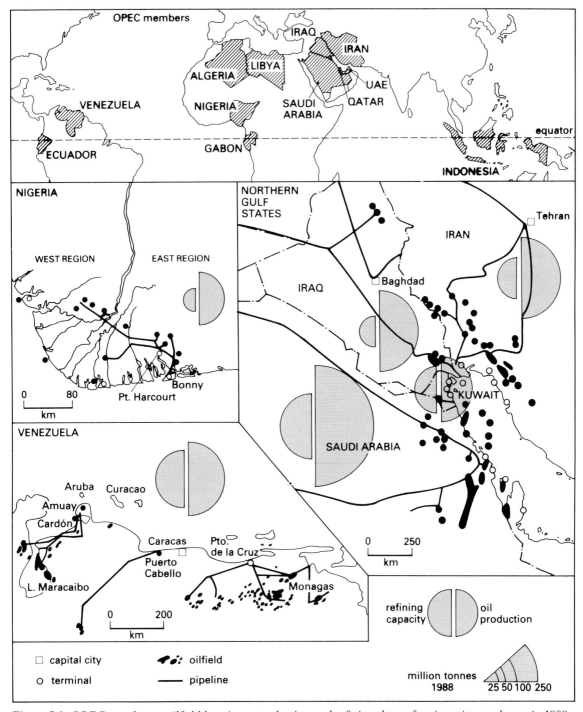

Figure 5.2 *OPEC members – oilfield locations, production and refining shown for six major producers in 1988*

Prolific oilfields with low production costs have enabled several OPEC members (Fig. 5.2) to gain a major role in world oil production. Of the total of 1 030 million tonnes produced by OPEC in 1988, 70 per cent was from the Middle East, the location of several of the world's *super-giant oilfields*, that is fields with reserves exceeding 1 000 million tonnes. Fast development of the Middle East oilfields by American and European oil companies in the 1960s was stimulated by rapid growth in demand in Japan and Europe. The Middle East oilfields located at the head of the Persian Gulf are well placed to take advantage of sea transport, although long hauls to markets in Japan and Europe are involved as shown in Figure 4.5. The sea routes to Europe are either via the Suez Canal or the Cape of Good Hope. The scaling-up in size of oil tankers after 1960 helped to ease costs on the long Cape route. The use of this route was increased at times of conflict between Middle East countries. During the Arab–Israeli war of 1967 and the Iran–Iraq war of the mid-1980s, for example, oil movements through the Suez Canal and via transcontinental pipelines to the Mediterranean coast in Lebanon and Syria were disrupted.

In contrast to oil production, natural gas production in the Middle East is small (Table 5.2). Natural gas is a commodity which has a large volume to value ratio. It is not cost effective to send it to Europe by pipeline. To export it, the gas is first liquified at very low temperature and then sent out as *liquified natural gas* (LNG) in special refrigerated tankers similar to that illustrated in Figure 5.3. The use of large versions of these tankers is helping to reduce the cost of transport and hence total costs, leading to new export opportunities, especially in Japan. Algeria, which has exceptionally large gas reserves, has the advantage of proximity to Europe and has invested in production facilities to give it the highest natural gas production of any of the Middle East or African producers (Table 5.2).

Apart from the Middle East, substantial contributions to OPEC oil production come from Venezuela, Indonesia and Nigeria. Most of Venezuela's output is from the Maracaibo fields (Fig. 5.2). Large reserves of heavy oils occur in the Orinoco Basin, the full development of which will need the stimulus of high oil prices. Indonesia has an increasing production from offshore fields, and with small needs of her own, is an important exporter, especially to Japan.

Countries by rank	Reserves			Countries by rank	Production			R/P ratio
	mtoe	Cumulative per cent			mtoe	Cumulative per cent		
USSR	38 265	38		USSR	694	40		55
Iran*	12 602	50		USA	426	65		11
USA	4 770	55		Canada	81	70		30
Abu Dhabi*	4 681	60		Netherlands	48	73		33
Qatar*	3 997	64		UK	40	75		13
Saudi Arabia*	3 719	68		Algeria	39	78		68
Algeria*	2 658	70		Indonesia	31	80		68
Venezuela*	2 602	73		Mexico	28	82		68
Canada	2 426	75		Norway	27	84		81
Iraq*	2 423	78		Saudi Arabia	23	85		162
OPEC	39 630	39		OPEC	162	9		245
WORLD	100 849	100		WORLD	1 736	100		58

Table 5.2 *Proved natural gas reserves and production, 1988, for leading countries*

Reserves given for countries with more than 2400 million tonnes
Production for countries producing more than 20 million tonnes
R/P ratio: reserves/production
* member of OPEC

Figure 5.3 *The Northwest Sanderling LNG carrier Western Australia*

As noted in Chapter 4, OPEC forced up oil prices in the 1970s. Although for a time oil demand in the MDCs remained high, eventually the market responded and oil consumption fell. Faced with declining demand, OPEC tried to stabilise the situation by cutting back production, and in 1988 was producing 460 million tonnes less oil than in 1978. Equally, many oil-importing countries have tried to reduce their dependence on OPEC by seeking alternative sources. Outside the OPEC areas the major oil companies have found new reserves and still control 20 per cent of world reserves, Shell alone accounting for 1 200 million tonnes.

Petroleum developments in non-OPEC areas

	1973	1978	1983	1988	Change 1973–1988 per cent
		million tonnes			
Saudi Arabia*	365	410	256	257	−30
Kuwait*	138	97	45	67	−52
Iran*	293	262	122	113	−61
Iraq*	99	126	54	128	29
Nigeria*	100	94	61	68	−32
Venezuela*	179	115	97	96	−46
Mexico	27	66	147	141	424
Norway	2	17	32	56	+
UK	–	53	115	114	+
OPEC	1 619	1 495	903	1031	−36
WORLD	2 844	3 093	2 766	3031	7

* member of OPEC
– less than 1 million tonnes
+ very large increase

Table 5.3 *Changes in crude oil production since 1973 for selected countries*

Throughout the 1960s, the transnational oil companies, dominated by Exxon, Royal Dutch Shell, BP, Chevron, Gulf, Mobil and Texaco, held close control of world oil, especially pricing policy. However, as the political and economic power of OPEC strengthened in the early 1970s, the role of the oil companies as oil producers in OPEC countries diminished and eventually decision-making over prices and levels of taxation and production passed to OPEC.

The reduced oil production by OPEC is in sharp contrast with increases in countries such as Mexico, the UK and Norway (Table 5.3 and Fig. 5.4). These changes represent an important relocation of oil investment resulting from a shift of exploration and development into non-OPEC areas in the period after 1975. In Mexico, for example, following major discoveries in the

Figure 5.4 *Changes in oil production since 1973, OPEC and non-OPEC comparisons*

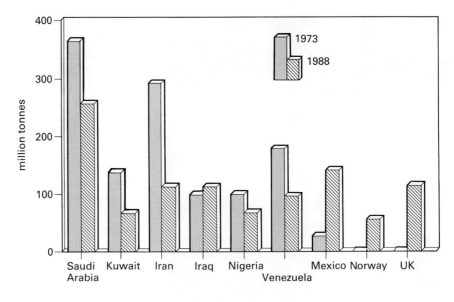

Figure 5.5 *The Mexican oil industry*

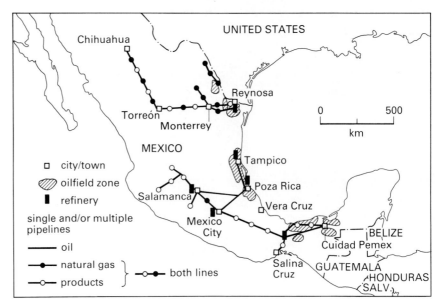

southern states of Chiapas and Tabasco and in adjoining offshore areas in the Gulf of Mexico (Fig. 5.5), the national oil company, Pemex, built up new capacity, increased production and sold large quantities of oil to the USA.

The fast rise in oil production in the UK is shown in Table 5.3. Several factors combined to stimulate oil developments in the UK. These included high oil prices, an interest in reducing dependence on OPEC sources, improvements

in offshore exploration techniques and the introduction of legislation for allocating licences. The UK oilfields discovered up to the end of 1988 have 570 million tonnes of reserves left. A further 1 230 million tonnes might ultimately be recovered. As shown in Figure 5.6, the offshore oilfields lie towards the central areas of the North Sea, with those in the northern sector about 400 km from land. Whether or not it is economic to build a pipeline to link oilfields to onshore terminals depends on the field's size, its distance from shore and its relative position in the North Sea. About 75 per cent of the 109 million tonnes of oil produced in 1988 was delivered by pipelines to terminals at Sullom Voe, Flotta, Cruden Bay and Nigg Bay. Another pipeline delivers oil to Teesside from the Ekofisk field in Norwegian waters. Of the crude oil produced in the UK in 1988, one-third was refined at UK refineries and 70 million

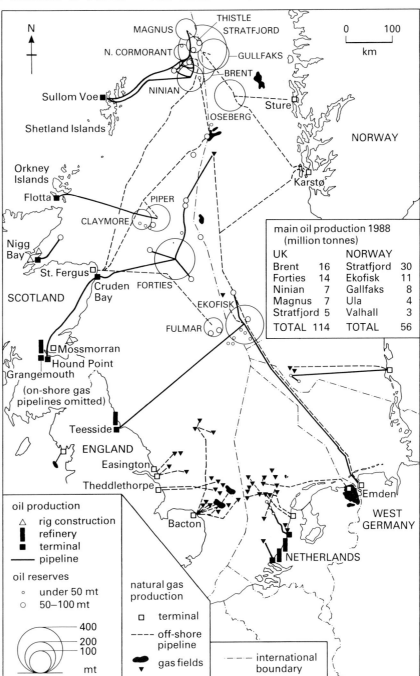

main oil production 1988 (million tonnes)			
UK		**NORWAY**	
Brent	16	Stratfjord	30
Forties	14	Ekofisk	11
Ninian	7	Gallfaks	8
Magnus	7	Ula	4
Stratfjord	5	Valhall	3
TOTAL	114	TOTAL	56

oil production
△ rig construction
▌ refinery
■ terminal
— pipeline

oil reserves
∘ under 50 mt
○ 50–100 mt

400
200
100

mt

natural gas production
▢ terminal
- - - off-shore pipeline
◆ gas fields
–·– international boundary

Figure 5.6 *North Sea oil and gas. (Largest oilfields shown by name and size of reserves.)*

Figure 5.7 *The landscape consequences of oil-related development at Sullom Voe, Shetland Islands*

tonnes exported. Small contributions to total oil production are made from onshore fields. The largest of these is Wytch Farm, Dorset, with reserves of 38 million tonnes. Numerous small oilfields exist in Nottinghamshire and Lincolnshire.

As shown in Figure 5.6, the development of the UK's oil resources has produced a new petroleum economy made up of oilfields, pipe-line networks, onshore terminals, service bases and downstream facilities at refineries. The regional onshore effect has been mostly felt in

Scotland. In some areas, the environmental consequences of the oil industry have been far reaching. The Sullom Voe terminal (Fig. 5.7) on the western shores of the Shetlands occupies 400 ha and is equipped with storage tanks, a power station, liquid petroleum gas plant and effluent treatment works. These facilities are all in an area which was formerly a remote crofting community.

As well as oil, the UK is rich in natural gas, with proved reserves of 590 mtoe. The southern gas fields (Fig. 5.6) are linked by short pipelines to terminals at Easington, Theddlethorpe and Bacton. Gas from the Frigg complex of gasfields in the northern part of the North Sea is piped to the large terminal at St. Fergus. Natural gas associated with the northern group of oilfields is fed by pipeline to Mossmorran in central Scotland for treatment.

The economic significance of the UK continental shelf petroleum resources is considerable. Oil and gas sales earnt £9 000 million in 1988, whilst a further £3 000 million was collected by the Government in royalties and taxes. Industry has benefited from oil company spending on exploration, rig construction, pipelines and

terminals to the tune of £50 000 million between 1965 and 1984. A labour force totalling 30 000 is employed in the offshore activities.

The United States, formerly the world's greatest oil producer, has not been self-sufficient in oil production since 1948 and now relies on imports for 40 per cent of its crude oil needs. Exploration effort to find new oil has increased. This effort involves drilling to find extensions to existing oilfields and exploration in the outer continental shelf areas and in the hostile environments of the Arctic. Despite oil finds such as those at Prudhoe Bay, Alaska, with 1.5 million tonnes in place, oil production at 463 million tonnes in 1988 was short of the 790 million tonnes demanded. The leading oil producing states are Alaska, Texas, Louisiana and California. Texas and Louisiana dominate natural gas production, accounting for 70 per cent of the total.

Large amounts of oil and gas are supplied by pipelines and tankers to the important markets of the North East and Midwest, USA, where local production of petroleum is small (Fig. 5.8). The Alaskan oilfields are not well placed to serve such distant markets. Oil is sent from

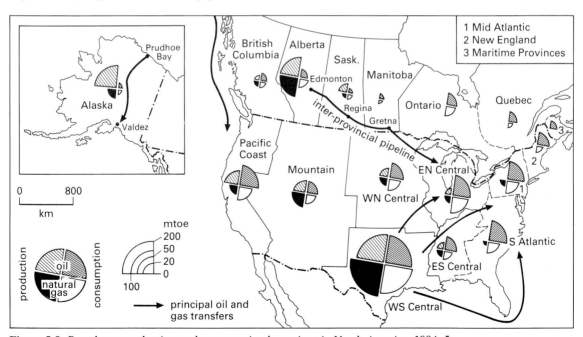

Figure 5.8 *Petroleum production and consumption by regions in North America, 1984–5*

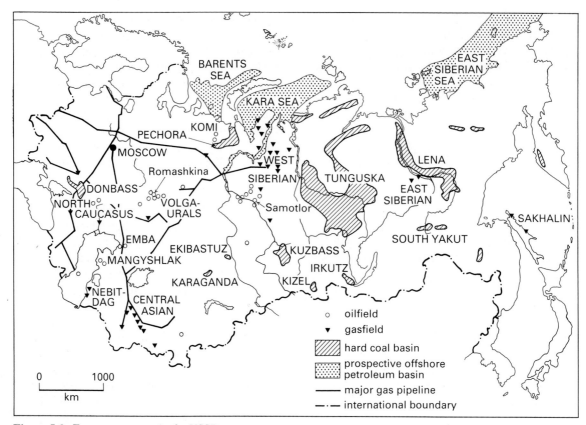

Figure 5.9 *Energy resources in the USSR*

these fields by pipeline across Alaska to the ice-free port of Valdez, whence tankers distribute it to markets along the Pacific coast, and via the Panama Canal to Canadian and USA markets. As Figure 5.8 shows, Canadian oil and gas production is highly concentrated in Alberta, which accounts for over 80 per cent of the total hydrocarbon production of Canada, whereas demand is greatest in Eastern Canada. Oil and gas are pumped through pipelines to Canadian and USA markets.

In 1975 the Soviet Union outstripped the USA to become the world's largest oil producer. Eighty per cent of the USSR production comes from extensive oilfields in the Volga/Urals and west Siberia areas, with exceptionally large contributions from two super-giant oilfields, Romashkino and Samotlor, which together are estimated to contain 30 per cent of Soviet oil reserves. West Siberia and Soviet Central

Asia (Fig. 5.9), are major developments since 1960, while the original oil-producing areas of Caucasus and Baku are now relatively insignificant. Future expansion is likely to focus on west Siberia and even further east in central and east Siberia. The centre of gravity of Soviet oil production is thus tending to be pushed further away from the principal home and European markets. Oil and gas are transferred westwards by transcontinental pipelines. The USSR satisfies the major proportion of the petroleum needs of its neighbouring *Comecon* members (countries allied to the USSR to develop trade and resources) and also sells oil and gas to Western Europe. Additional gas supplies can be drawn from Iran which has a pipeline link to the Soviet network. On the other side of the continent, the relative proximity of the Japanese market is a spur to development of the east Siberian oilfields.

Environmental issues

Exploration and development of petroleum resources lead to environmental change. The building of the infrastructure means the removal of vegetation and the grading of land for roads and buildings. Although production wells can be reasonably inconspicuous, storage and processing facilities are more intrusive as shown in the scene at Wytch Farm, Dorset (Fig. 5.10). Furthermore, as the scale of production increases, so does the potential for environ-

mental impact. For example, at the Wytch Farm oilfield, the operating company, BP, is anxious to extend drilling to Poole Harbour and Studland Bay areas by building an artificial island offshore. Installations like oil refineries have major consequences. There was considerable controversy at the time of building the Fawley refinery in the New Forest area. In some environments the need for special engineering techniques leads to obvious features as in the case of the raised pipeline taking oil

Figure 5.10 *Oilfield development at Wytch Farm, Dorset*

Figure 5.11 *The trans-Alaska oil pipeline. The insulated pipeline is raised above ground level to avoid damage to the permafrost zone*

across Alaska (Fig. 5.11). In offshore areas the abandonment of disused production platforms causes problems. Plans to deal with this in the North Sea include the toppling of the upper structures of the rigs and the monitoring of plugged seabed wells.

Some oil spillage at sea is inevitable with off-shore oil production and supply. In general, exploration and production cause 5 per cent of oil spills, tanker operations and accidents 50 and 30 per cent respectively, and coastal refineries 15 per cent. Reported spills from UK North Sea oil production averaged 1 750 tonnes a year between 1985 and 1988. Oil was also dumped at the rate of 20 000 tonnes a year between 1985 and 1988 from waste mud expelled by drilling rigs and water extracted along with oil from production wells. These amounts compare with an average oil production of 117 million tonnes per annum over the same period. On occasions, uncontrolled oil flows occur as a result of the *blow out* of a well. One blow out off shore from Mexico lasted for ten months and spilled out a quarter of a million tonnes of oil. Tanker accidents are the cause of con-centrated spills affecting coastal localities. The grounding of the Exxon Valdez tanker in March 1989, for example, produced an oil slick of 35 000 tonnes which drifted onto the envi-ronmentally sensitive coastline of Prince William Sound, Alaska. Remedial action involving the use of chemicals to break up the oil can have unfortunate further adverse effects on marine organisms. Preventative action would be better.

Tankers which have double hulls could be built as a safety measure, although this would increase the cost of construction, and hence of oil transport.

ASSIGNMENTS

---

1 a. Using data from Table 5.1, draw pairs of column graphs to compare oil reserves and production for four members of OPEC.

  b. Comment on the factors which have affected the R/P ratios of these countries.

  c. What problems are involved in exporting natural gas from Middle East producers?

2 a. From Table 5.3 identify the OPEC members with the largest falls in oil production and suggest reasons for these falls.

  b. For the UK, comment on the location pattern of oil production (Fig. 5.6).

  c. Suggest why oil pipelines from the North Sea oilfields are built mainly to the UK and not to Norway.

  d. What are the main kinds of onshore installa-tions in Scotland?

  e. What has been the environmental impact of these installations?

3 With the aid of Figure 5.8:

  a. comment on the main petroleum producing regions in the USA;

  b. compare the Pacific Coast and the East North Central regions in terms of petroleum supply and demand;

  c. what are the problems in delivering Alaskan oil to the East Coast of the USA?

4 a. How much larger is the USSR's oil production than the USA's?

b. With the aid of your atlas, comment on the environmental problems involved in the exploitation of the west Siberian gasfields.

c. Where are the main markets for this gas and how are they supplied?

5 a. With the aid of Tables 5.1 and 5.4, comment on the differences in the world distribution of reserves of crude oil and coal.

b. What are the economic consequences of this distribution?

COAL RESOURCES

World coal reserves

The world's coal resources are some five times greater than those of oil and have a markedly different distribution. About 35 per cent of the total reserves are in the USA and the EC, whilst the USSR and China account for a further 30 per cent. The proved reserves are very large indeed, at some 580 000 million tonnes of hard coal (*anthracite* and *bituminous coal*) and nearly 450 000 million tonnes of brown coal (*sub-bituminous coal* and *lignite*). These reserves would last for more than 200 years at present rates of production (Table 5.4).

The use of coal

As a proportion of the total primary energy used in the MDCs, coal has become less important since the early 1960s. Even in the period after 1970 when oil prices were rising rapidly, coal consumption in the EC countries in particular was in decline, as shown in Table 5.5. By 1988 coal contributed only 20 per cent to the EC's total energy consumption. Nonetheless, the total amount of coal used in the EC is still substantial at around 200 mtoe. Power stations are the principal markets, accounting for 60 per cent of consumption. Although in Japan and the USSR there was an absolute increase in the amount of coal used in the period between 1970 and 1988, again there was a fall in its percentage contribution to total energy consumption. As Table 5.5 shows, there have been substantial increases of coal consumption in China and the USA, and these two countries, along with the USSR, are the leading world consumers of coal. The market in the USA is principally for

Countries by rank	Reserves			Countries by rank	Production			R/P Ratio
	Hard coal	Other coal	Total		Hard coal	Other coal	Total	
	thousand million tonnes				million tonnes			
USA	131	131	262	China	885	75	960	175
USSR	108	136	243	USA	607	263	869	301
China	155	14	168	USSR	610	175	785	310
Australia	29	45	74	E. Germany.		317	317	63
W. Germany	24	35	59	Poland	191	70	261	161
South Africa	58		58	India	180	9	189	74
Poland	28	14	42	W. Germany	79	108	187	316
E. Germany	0	20	20	Australia	134	42	176	420
India	12	2	14	Czechoslovakia	26	101	127	na
UK	9	1	10	UK	104		104	87
WORLD	579	443	1 023	WORLD	3 240	1 460	4 700	218

Table 5.4 *Coal reserves and production for selected countries, 1988*

hard coal: anthracite and bituminous coal
other coal: sub-bituminous and lignite

Country/ Region	Coal/ Consumption* 1970	1988	Percentage change
	million tonnes oil equivalent		1970–1988
UK	92	66	−29
W. Germany	90	73	−18
EC**	149	124	−16
Japan	60	76	27
USA	330	480	46
USSR	294	310	6
China	252	581	131
WORLD	1 635	2 428	48

* bituminous and sub-bituminous coal

** EC (the original six)

Table 5.5 *Coal consumption, 1970 and 1988*

coal-burn in power stations, but there is a wider pattern of demand in China and in the USSR because of the greater use of coal by industry and railways. Countries with extensive lignite deposits, for example West Germany, East Germany, Poland and the USSR, use these resources to fuel power stations located at the lignite fields. The costs of mining using open-cast methods are low at these near-surface deposits, but their low calorific values mean that large quantities are burnt with a correspondingly large output of smoke and carbon dioxide.

Finally, an increasing use of coal is notable amongst several of the LDCs, particularly Brazil, South Korea and Taiwan. The increased use of coal in these economies is in part from home production, but largely from imported coal. In each case, coal imports doubled in the period 1980–87. Coal, as one of the energy resources, plays a role in aiding industrialisation and programmes of electrification.

The major producers and consumers of coal

Although the number of mines in operation in the United States decreased by over 1500 between 1965 and 1985, coal production actually increased by nearly 250 million tonnes from 480 million tonnes to 635 million tonnes. Much of this extra output came from new low-cost mining based on strip-mining methods in Kentucky, Montana and Wyoming (Fig. 5.12), which off-set a decrease in production in several states where the Appalachian coalfield is worked.

The application of giant excavating equipment (Fig. 5.13) at the extensive coal deposits

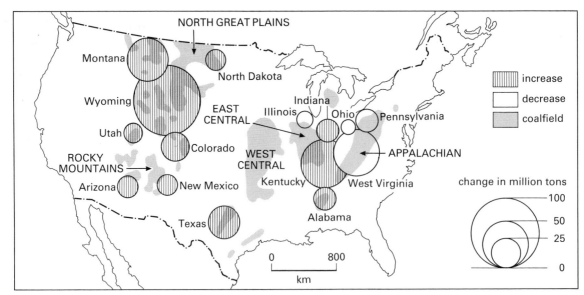

Figure 5.12 *Changes in coal output by states, USA, 1965–83*

Figure 5.13 *Large-scale coal mining operations in western USA*

of the Mountain States such as Wyoming and Montana effects major economies of scale, giving low production costs. Further, as these coals have a low sulphur content, they help keep down the costs of controlling atmospheric pollution when burnt at power stations. There are two disadvantages arising from the development of these coalfields. Firstly, there is the environmental issue of mining in areas formerly without much industrialisation. Secondly, the separation of these coalfields from the markets and ports in the east of the USA has transport cost implications, although this disadvantage is offset by the low production costs. Most of the haulage is by rail, but some movement is by river and, experimentally, by slurry pipeline.

In contrast to the United States, where coal mining has spread to new areas, there is in-creasing regional concentration of coal production in the EC. In the UK the older coalfields in Scotland, South Wales, Northumberland and Durham have long been in decline, largely on account of high costs associated with difficult geology and the depletion of the more easily-worked seams. Investment in the industry, following the 1974 Plan for Coal, has favoured development at the eastern margin of the Derby, Nottingham and Yorkshire coalfields, but even here output has declined as shown in Figure 5.14. The UK industry faces major problems over markets. In the home market, there is dependence on the demand from electricity generating stations and to this extent the coal industry is vulnerable to the decisions taken by the companies that produce electricity. External markets in the EC are competed for

Figure 5.14 *Changes in hard coal production at European Community coalfields, 1961–81*

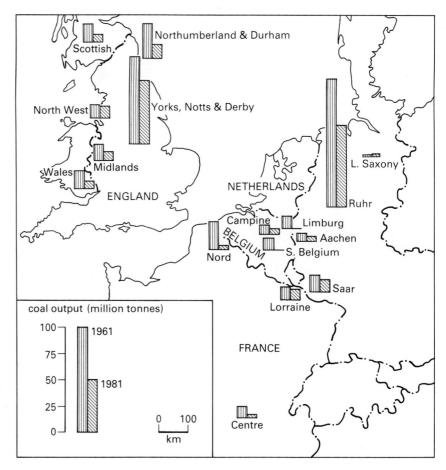

by other countries, with Poland, the USA, Australia and South Africa able to deliver coal more cheaply to Europe than can Britain.

West Germany is the other major EC coal producer, with large amounts produced from lignite and brown coal as well as hard coal. Hard coal output (79 million tonnes in 1988) is mainly from the Ruhr coalfield, where active mines are now concentrated in the central sector as shown in Figure 5.15, the southern sector being worked out and the northern sector too deep for economic mining at today's coal prices. Germany also takes large amounts of lignite from the extensive deposits at Ville. Elsewhere in the Community the picture is one of decline, to the extent that in some cases production has virtually ceased.

The major heavy industrial regions of the USSR – the Donbass and Kuzbass – are both producers and consumers of much of the coal produced in the Soviet Union. Some 90 per cent of the USSR's vast coal resources are in Soviet Asia and a long way from the markets of the west. Production has increased relatively faster east of the Urals compared with the west. The Donbass is disadvantaged by high cost mining of deep thin seams compared with the more easily worked Kuznetz and Karaganda coalfields (Fig. 5.9). Low cost strip-mining at the Ekibastuz coal basin to the south-east of the Urals led to a rapid build-up of production there in the 1970s. The main problem of coal supplies in the Soviet economy is transport, due to the great distances between the newer large coalfields and markets.

Much new investment in the coal industry has gone to Australia, where BP, the British oil company, is one of the most important investors

Figure 5.15 *The Ruhr coalfield in 1983*

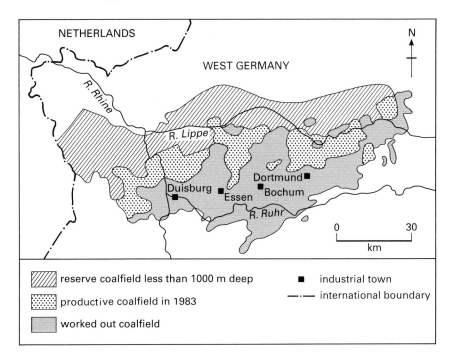

in Australian coal. New South Wales and Queensland possess the bulk of Australia's coal reserves. The coal basins near Sydney and Newcastle (Fig. 3.12), have had a long period of development and serve markets in the power, iron and steel industries of the region. The vast Bowen Basin resources in Queensland were extensively developed after 1960 following the signing of contracts to supply Japan. Investment here included the building of rail links and high-capacity coal handling berths at ports such as Hay Point and Gladstone.

The hard coal reserves of the Republic of South Africa are amongst the largest in world terms, and twice the amount in Australia (Table 5.4). The pit head price of South African coal is amongst the lowest in the world. Since the oil crises of the 1970s South Africa has built up its capacity as a coal exporter. New terminal facilities at Richards Bay, which serve the coalfields in northern Natal (Fig. 3.17), have a capacity of 44 million tonnes a year. Coal is a significant source of energy in South Africa itself given the lack of oil resources. About 50 per cent of the coal produced is used at thermal power stations.

Relatively low cost mining also characterises Polish production which is concentrated at the vast mining operations at Gliwice-Katowice in southern Poland. Political and economic factors, especially the need for foreign earnings, have encouraged the development of a major coal exporting industry.

Environmental issues

Important spatial changes in world coal production have occurred since 1960. Mines have closed in many old established regions, in the UK, the Ruhr (West Germany), the Nord Coalfield (France), the coalfields of Belgium and the Netherlands, and Pennsylvania (USA). This has caused economic distress in these regions and a legacy of environmental degradation. When mines are closed down, there is a need to deal with the resulting dereliction left behind in the form of abandoned buildings and equipment, waste tips and waterlogging from subsidence (flashes). In Abercarn, South Wales, for example, landscaping of derelict land on the old

101

Figure 5.16 *Coalfield reclamation at Abercarn, South Wales*

coalfield has created recreational open space (Fig. 5.16) and sites for industry.

Environmental conflicts are also associated with the development of new mines, as in the western USA. In England the National Coal Board is acting to limit the impact of the new mines at the Selby coalfield, leaving pillars of coal as supports in order to limit subsidence. However, it will be impossible to hide the new infrastructure of railways, screening and handling plant and houses.

The burning of coal at power stations causes atmospheric pollution through the release of gases such as sulphur dioxide and carbon dioxide. In Europe there is concern about sulphur dioxide (acid rain) pollution in particular. Preventive measures can add up to 10 per cent to costs, but effective methods are available especially for the removal of sulphur dioxide. Concern over carbon dioxide and its association with atmospheric warming, though, could act to limit the use of coal at power stations.

ASSIGNMENTS

---

6 a. Using data from Table 4.1, Chapter 4, for the EC and UK, compare the pattern of coal consumption with other fossil fuels.

b. Why has coal demand fallen since 1965 in the EC?

c. What are the problems in supplying the coal needs of the EC?

7 a. With the aid of Figure 5.12 and your atlas, comment on the regional shifts in coal mining in the USA.

b. What are the cost benefits and limitations of these shifts?

Figure 5.17 *Pernis oil refinery at Rotterdam*

8 a. Examine the adverse environmental issues associated with coal mining development.
  b. How can reclamation of former coal mining areas be achieved?
  c. Comment on the social and economic benefits of such reclamation.

THE POWER-PRODUCING INDUSTRIES

As discussed in Chapter 4, people and industries use energy in a secondary rather than a primary form. Oil refineries and electricity generating stations are needed to convert primary energy inputs into fuels that are convenient for consumers.

The location of petroleum refining

Crude oil is not itself a usable end product. As mentioned earlier, it is refined to make the gasolines, jet fuels, diesel and fuel oils and lubricants that are needed. These products are made by distilling crude oil, followed by chemical treatment and blending at refineries. Refineries are capital intensive industrial plant with production units and storage tanks separated out over a large area, and hence they have demanding space requirements (Fig. 5.17). Oil refineries are built at one of three types of location: *resource, intermediate* or *market*. A large part of the world refining capacity is market-orientated. Table 5.6 shows the relatively greater importance of refining in the European Community and in Japan as opposed to a resource zone such as the Middle East. However, refining capacity in the EC market area has been cut back since 1978 whilst new capacity has been built in the Middle East. There are more complex patterns of both resource-located and market-located refineries in the USA and USSR.

A combination of economic and political factors affect the choice of refinery location. Part of the economic explanation is illustrated in the model of hypothetical transport costs (Fig. 5.18). Here an oilfield and market are shown separated from each other by sea. The total transport cost at a place is made up of the cost of transporting crude oil from R plus the

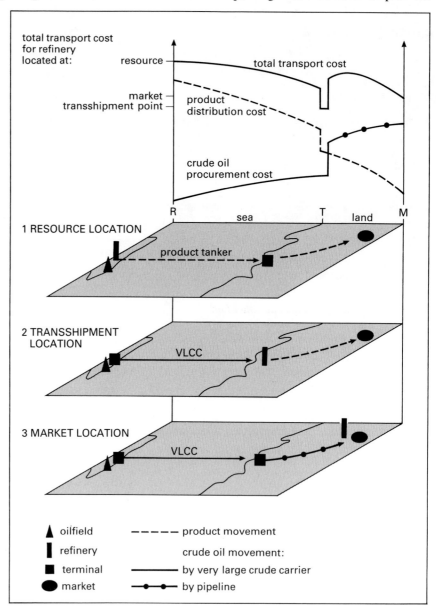

Figure 5.18
Hypothetical transport costs affecting oil refinery location

	Refining capacity 1978 1988 million tonnes		Change 1978–88 per cent
USA	865	793	−8
USSR	498	611	23
Japan	263	215	−18
France	172	90	−47
Italy	209	117	−44
Netherlands	90	69	−23
UK	125	90	−28
W. Germany	154	82	−47
Euro 7	802	483	−40
S. Arabia	32	68	117
Kuwait	29	37	30
Iran	52	26	−50
MIDDLE EAST	168	216	28
Venezuela	72	60	−17
Mexico	49	89	81
WORLD	3 887	3 701	−5

Euro 7   original six, plus UK

Table 5.6 *Changes in petroleum refining in selected countries, 1978–88*

cost of distributing products to M. If a refinery is located at the oilfield, i.e. the resource location R in map 1, total transport costs are high because of the cost of sending mixed cargoes of products to market in relatively small tankers. It is cheaper to locate the refinery at the coast near the market, the *transshipment* point T, map 2. Crude oil can be shipped at low cost in very large crude carriers (VLCCs) and suffers little waste on processing. Further savings are gained at the transshipment point by the reduction in handling costs. The short haul of products by rail or road to market adds to costs, but not to the extent of wiping out the cost advantages at T. It is assumed that a location at the market, point M on map 3, would nearly match the cost at T because of the efficient delivery of crude oil to the refinery through a large capacity pipeline.

A situation of coastal and inland refineries, a combination of maps 2 and 3 (Fig. 5.18), is a rough approximation to that in the European Community. Figure 5.19 shows the oil refinery locations at a time of peak capacity in 1980. Investment in the industry was influenced not only by transport cost considerations, but also by the growth in market opportunities after 1950. The region was also favoured for security reasons given the very large capital investment involved. Much of the initial capital was provided as dollar aid by the USA, aimed at the economic recovery of Western Europe after the Second World War. Investment in oil refining was also closely linked to the development of a petro-chemical industry. Because a refinery needs space and access to deep water, estuarine sites, with open flat land near to deep water, provide favourable site conditions. Such sites also correspond to *least-transport cost locations*. Refineries at Rotterdam, Marseilles/Fos, the outer Thames and Milford Haven are at this type of site, the locations reflecting the ideal one of map 2 (Fig. 5.18). Coastal refineries of the kind suggested by map 2, but with much closer contact with markets, correspond to the situation in Japan. Large refineries at major port complexes as in southern Honshu are located close to industrial and population concentrations.

The pattern of refining in the USA is more complex. A proportion of the USA's refining capacity is at oilfields. In oil-producing states like Texas, Oklahoma and California, refineries serve local markets, and some also send products by pipeline or tanker to more distant markets in the Midwest and north-east USA. Refineries have also been built in these market areas and are supplied either by imported oil or home-produced oil delivered through pipelines.

Despite the attraction of markets as locations for refineries, capacity has also been built at or near oilfields in countries such as Saudi Arabia, Kuwait and Venezuela (Table 5.6). In some cases these reflect decisions made in the early days of the petroleum industry, when there was a high degree of waste during processing, when

Figure 5.19 *Oil refining locations in selected EC countries, 1980*

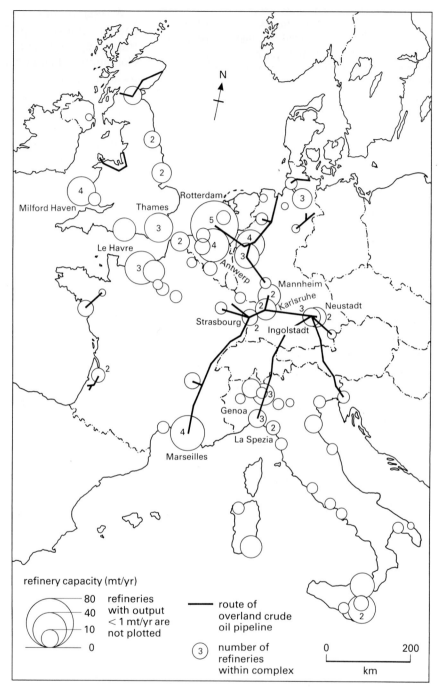

markets were less concentrated and transport economics were not so advantageous to bulk crude oil movement. Since the mid-1970s, OPEC members have developed oil refining and petro-chemical manufacturing as a way of diversifying their oil industries and of reducing their dependence on crude oil exports.

Those LDCs without oil resources have few economic incentives to build refineries. One reason is that, in order to gain scale economies in refining, markets must be large enough to justify a refinery of 5 million tonnes per year capacity. Such a *threshold capacity* is a problem for many LDCs where markets are limited. Another reason is the lack of capital for investing in such an industry.

Location of coal-fired power stations

Many large thermal power station plants were built in the MDCs during the period from 1950 to 1970 in order to satisfy rapid increases in demand for electricity. Where markets coincided with ample primary energy resources, the choice of type of plant was essentially straightforward. In the USA, for example, natural gas is used as the main energy source in power stations in southern states such as Texas and Louisiana, but coal in the north-east, in Pennsylvania and West Virginia.

Where supplies of fuel and markets are spatially separated, decisions have to made about power station location. In the early days of the industry, it was not economic to transmit electricity over long distances; towns were often supplied with electricity which was generated locally at comparatively small power stations which used coal brought in from coalfields some distance away. High-voltage transmission now allows electricity to be distributed over distances of up to 1 600 km at economic cost. In the UK, the adoption of a high-voltage national grid system in the 1960s made it cheaper to transmit electricity to markets from power stations near coal resources than to transport the equivalent amount of coal to power stations located in market areas. There are additional benefits in using a national grid for distributing electricity. The grid network as a whole acts as an integrated power system. Generating stations are interconnected so that together they contribute to a national market. The largest and most efficient power stations can be used to supply the average daily demand, called the *base load*, while older, more costly plants can be switched on to cope with *peak demand*. This procedure, known as *merit-order-loading*, means that the newest, high-capital cost plants are utilised as continuously as possible.

The location of large coal-fired power stations in the UK (Fig. 5.20) reflects the economies of using a national grid. There is regional concentration of power stations along the River Trent at the margin of the Yorkshire, Nottinghamshire and Derbyshire coalfields. The riverside sites allow water to be abstracted for cooling purposes as well as providing for the disposal of spent water. Rail links between power stations and coal mines are short and circulating *merry-go-round* trains help to reduce the delivered costs of coal. Automated 1 000 tonne unit-trains are loaded on the move at collieries and dispatched to power stations where they are unloaded through bottom-opening doors. The surplus power produced in the region is sent through the grid to other markets, especially to those in the south-east of England.

Nuclear power stations

Where there are large regional markets which have no local fossil fuels, an alternative to importing electrical power is to construct nuclear power stations which use uranium as a fuel. This is feasible because of the low weight ratio of uranium input to energy output. One tonne of natural uranium is roughly equivalent to 10 000 tonnes of coal in terms of the electrical power that can be produced, depending on the type of reactor. At a national scale one argument is that it is a sound strategy to use nuclear energy in order to conserve and to reduce dependence on fossil fuels. Advocates of nuclear power have also argued for it on the grounds of its lower costs compared with thermal power stations fired with fossil fuels. This is a debatable point. Figures published in 1981 by the International Energy Agency indicated that power produced at nuclear plant could be as much as 25 per cent cheaper than from oil-fired plant and marginally cheaper than from coal-field plant located in the EC and Japan. However, a clear-cut economic case for nuclear power failed to be made at the 1988 Sizewell Enquiry in the UK. The cost of dismantling old nuclear power

Figure 5.20 *Major fossil fuel power plants and nuclear power plants in England and Wales and part of the EC, 1989*

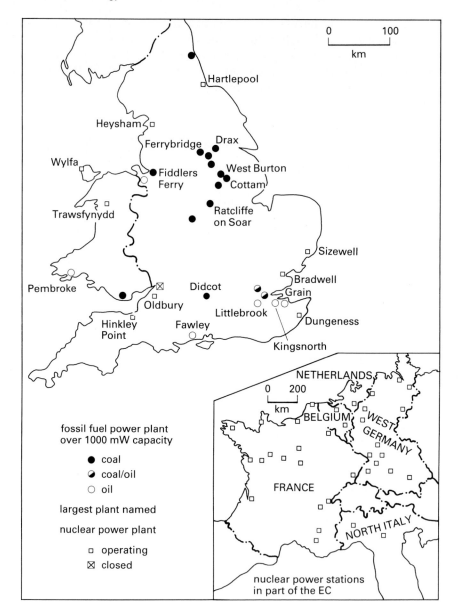

stations should also be considered. The cost of decommissioning eight of Britain's first nuclear power stations built in the 1950s has been put at between £5 000 million and £20 000 million. Finally, a case for nuclear energy can be based on its freedom from carbon dioxide production. Against any possible cost and other benefits, however, are deeply-held public concerns about the disposal of radioactive waste and the safety of nuclear reactors.

In a nuclear reactor, energy is released by the controlled breakdown, or fission, of uranium. This control is achieved by using a moderator such as carbon to slow down neutrons and by control rods made of cadmium or boron to absorb neutrons. The rods are lowered into the reactor pile to slow the chain reaction down, or raised in order to speed it up. On the breakdown of the uranium atoms energy is released which can be extracted as heat to raise steam.

Figure 5.21 *The Sizewell nuclear power station, 1989*

Country	Installed nuclear capacity (million kilowatt)	Contribution by main type of nuclear reactor to total nuclear (per cent)	Contribution of nuclear to total installed generating capacity (per cent)
USA	78	PWR (66)	11
France	38	PWR (95)	43
USSR	28	PWR (41)	9
Japan	24	PWR (46)	14
Germany FR	16	PWR (56)	17
UK	10	GCR/AGR (97)	15

Table 5.7 *Leading countries producing electricity from nuclear power plant, 1985*

PWR   pressure water reactor
GCR/AGR   gas cooled and advanced gas cooled reactor

The reactor fulfils the same task as a coal-fired boiler in a conventional power station. A coolant is used to take the heat from the reactor and transfer it via a heat-exchanger to the generating plant. Water is used as the coolant in *pressure water reactors* (PWR) and carbon dioxide in *gas cooled reactors* (GCR). Most nuclear power stations world-wide are of the PWR type, with only the UK relying extensively on gas cooled and advanced gas cooled reactors (AGR) (Table 5.7).

About 15 per cent of the electricity produced in the UK comes from nuclear power stations, the locations of which are shown in Figure 5.20. The sites chosen are coastal, relatively distant from large population centres but near important regional markets. Although there has been a slowing down in the programme, Government estimates suggest that by the end of the century the equivalent of 95 million tonnes out of a total of 186 million tonnes used at all thermal stations will come from nuclear fuels. Future nuclear power stations in Britain are likely to be of the PWR design of the type under construction at Sizewell in East Anglia (Fig. 5.21).

Of Western European countries France has followed an active policy of nuclear development based largely on pressure water reactors. The French nuclear programme has been argued for on the grounds of cost effectiveness, balance of payments savings, security of energy supplies and the importance of a nuclear engineering industry to the national economy. So much electricity generating capacity has been built in France that there is a surplus for export, including some to the UK through a

109

submarine cable. However, in other countries in Europe and in the USA, public concern about safety, environmental pollution, and increasingly, about the disposal of radioactive waste, has caused a slowing down in the rate of development of nuclear power. Opposition has strengthened following the reactor disasters at Three Mile Island, Pennsylvania, USA, in 1979 and at Chernobyl in the USSR in 1986. The fire in the nuclear pile at Chernobyl caused the spread of a radioactive dust affecting several north-west European countries as noted in Chapter 1. No utility company has ordered a nuclear power plant in the USA following the Three Mile Island failure.

Uranium is a finite resource, but abundant. The known reserves of uranium in non-Communist countries, mostly in the USA, Canada, Australia and South Africa, are of the order of 5 million tonnes, which is enough to last 125 years at present rates of consumption. This consumption is related to the small part of the natural uranium consumed as fuel in the present types of *burner reactors*. The energy resources available from uranium would be vastly extended by using *fast breeder* reactors because they use a much larger part of the uranium fuel and also produce another fissionable material, plutonium. Fast breeder reactors are in an early stage of development and are very costly to build, but they are significant because they have the potential to open up large energy supplies as indicated by Figure 4.6. Amongst western countries, France is leading in fast breeder reactor technology with its Superphénix plant near Lyon.

WORLD ENERGY PROSPECTS

Pessimistic views about world energy supplies were commonly expressed in the late 1960s and early 1970s. Since then, a slowing down in the rate of increase in demand and improvements in supplies suggest that these views were too alarmist, although there is a continuing need for husbanding resources on a global scale.

Energy demand

World demand for energy rose by 30 per cent in the five years from 1968 until 1973, but only by 13 per cent between 1982 and 1987. A slow-down in economic growth partly explains the change, but it is also due to improved energy efficiencies and to energy conservation. Improvements in industrial technology mean that a lower ratio of energy consumption per unit of GNP is required now compared with that in the 1960s. This ratio was about 0.3 kg of energy for each dollar of GNP in Japan and the European Community in 1985 and 0.5 kg in the USA. Advances in engine efficiency in the transport sector are especially important, because, as shown in Figure 4.2, this is a large oil user. Improvements in heat treatment in industry have also led to greater energy efficiency.

Conservation is an attractive route to reduced demand for energy resources. It has the merit of helping environmentally by reducing both heat output and gas pollution. Improved design and insulation are capable of saving 50 per cent of the costs of space heating of buildings. Energy conservation in industry is possible by recycling used materials. The use of scrap in steel making is estimated to save 30 per cent of the energy required to produce steel from iron ore, while savings of 78 per cent have been quoted if recycled glass is used in glass manufacture instead of raw materials.

In the energy industry itself there are two conservation methods which could be applied more extensively. One is the reduction of gas flaring (the burning-off of waste gas) at oilfields. The second is to use spent hot water from power stations. The water is suitable as a low-grade heat source for district heating, that is in the central heating of offices and homes near to power stations.

Energy supply

On the supply side, changes have already occurred in response to the 1970s energy price increase. These triggered several important changes including a search for new oil sources, the use of substitutes for oil and the increased use of nuclear power. The search for oil has brought in new, but costly, resources, often in harsh environments like the Arctic and deeper offshore zones of the North Sea. Hitherto under-explored areas in Latin America, Africa and south-east Asia have yielded more oil, and changes in political attitudes have led to the release of new areas for exploration in the South China seas. Hence a wider range of supplies is emerging.

Oil supplies could also be extended by using non-conventional resources. Very large quantities of oil occur as oil shales and tar sands, possibly as much as the present known reserve of oil itself. The distribution of these resources favours the DMEs, large quantities being located in the USA, Canada and Australia. The cost of extracting the oil from these deposits is far too high to be economic at present oil price levels, but these resources remain a possibility should there be future energy scarcity.

Optimistic views about the future role of coal at a global scale were expressed in the early 1980s, with the World Coal Study suggesting that coal consumption by the end of the century might be some 2.5 times the present level. To supply such a vastly expanded world market, big increases in investment in mining capacity, shipping and ports would be necessary. The scale of the physical impact of port development can be gained from Figure 5.22 which

Figure 5.22 *Terminal for coal shipments at Newport News, Virginia, USA. Coal from the West Virginia, Virginia and Kentucky coalfields is exported.*

indicates the scale of the coal exporting facilities at Newport News, Virginia, USA. In Europe, existing deep-water ports such as Rotterdam, Le Havre, Dunkirk and Fos could be developed as transshipment ports. However, as noted earlier, pollution worries are likely to limit this degree of expansion.

Energy prospects in less developed countries

The poorest countries in the world are characterised, along with other low consumption data, by their limited use of energy (Fig. 4.1). For these small needs these countries rely heavily on oil imports, often to the extent of 55 per cent of the commercial energy used. The cost of these imports has risen greatly since 1970 compared with the value of primary goods exported by the LDCs. In many Third World countries there is a problem of *rural energy impoverishment*, that is village communities have poor access to an energy infrastructure. They are without dependable supplies of electricity and may have difficulty affording other fuels such as kerosene and diesel oils. Resolving such energy needs through large-scale schemes is difficult on account of the capital costs involved and the dispersed nature of internal markets. Instead, solutions based on local schemes, at low cost and of low social and environmental impact, seem best. A 'small is beautiful' approach along the lines already noted in Chapter 4 is more appropriate to future energy provision in many LDCs than grand schemes.

ASSIGNMENTS

---

9 a. Why is a transshipment location for an oil refinery a cost effective one?

  b. With the aid of Figures 5.18 and 5.19, comment on and explain the distribution of oil refineries in the UK.

  c. How have the problems of supplying oil products to interior markets of the EC been resolved?

10 a. Study Table 5.6 and comment on the changes in oil refinery capacity.

  b. Suggest why some Middle East oil producers have expanded their oil refining industries since 1978.

11 a. What is meant by a base-load power station?

  b. Comment on the reasons for locating power stations at coalfields rather than in market areas.

  c. How do the locations of nuclear power plant differ from those of coal-fired plant in Britain?

  d. Comment on two reasons for building nuclear power stations and on two reasons against doing so.

12 a. Why did the rate of increase of energy demand slow down in the 1980s?

  b. What kinds of infrastructure development would be needed to serve a major expansion of coal use in the 21st century?

  c. What is the case for limiting the use of coal?

6

Manufacturing Activities

The prime driving force in the economy is demand for goods and services. Manufacturing firms respond to this demand by making the articles that people want and they also stimulate demand by offering new products. There is fierce competition in the market place with firms vying with each other to attract customers by offering value in terms of the price, quality and design of products.

In the manufacturing process itself, raw materials are converted into semi-finished or final usable products. This is the role performed by *secondary industries* which transform the natural and semi-processed materials of the *primary industries*. Industrialists decide on the methods of production and on the location of manufacturing plant (Fig. 6.1), and thus are important decision-makers in the economic system.

FACTORS AFFECTING MANUFACTURING

A factory is needed in order to assemble the production and material inputs necessary to make goods. As suggested in Figure 6.1, manufacturing involves decisions about the procurement of the production inputs of land, raw materials, labour and capital. Decisions have to be made about where to locate the factory in relation to the sources of the various inputs and to market opportunities for end products. The skill of the industrialist, or *entrepreneurship*, in decision-making is often regarded as the fourth factor of production. In order to operate an efficient business, the industrialist has to take account of the factors affecting costs and revenue.

Land cost

As noted in Chapter 2, it is expensive to buy the land on which factories and other facilities are to be built. Because the value of land varies from place to place, it exerts a locational influence on industrial activity. Land within urban areas is particularly costly and many firms seek cheaper sites elsewhere, thus contributing to industrial and employment decline in the older urban areas.

For industries engaged in large-scale processing, such as the steel and chemical industries, a lot of space is taken up by plant and consequently availability of cheap land is a factor in the selection of a site. If sites are sought in rural areas then environmental issues arise, with restrictive conditions perhaps being imposed to limit the landscape impact of the industry. For those industries needing only a small amount of space the environmental issue can have a different effect. These firms might seek a location at a place because of its landscape quality. The trend is for light industries which are not tied to specific site needs, that is *footloose industries*, to locate in areas perceived to be environmentally attractive (Fig. 6.2).

Energy resources

In the early days of industrial development, factories were built at water power sites and on coalfields because fixed energy resources exerted a powerful influence on location. The high costs of moving coal, together with the large quantities needed by industries, led in the 19th century to a concentration of European and American industry on coalfields, for example, the cotton industry in Lancashire, steel making and engineering in the Ruhr (West Germany) and Pittsburgh (USA). In contrast, in the 20th century, the widespread availability of electricity, the relative ease with which fossil fuels are transported and the more efficient use of energy have combined to reduce the need for industry to be near sources of energy, except in special cases like the smelting of aluminium.

Raw materials

Industries which use large amounts of raw materials, and especially those affected by a high *weight loss* in manufacture, are pulled towards resources. Locations with ease of access to resources, such as at ports and estuaries which offer transshipment economies of the kind discussed in the last chapter, are efficient locations for industries such as oil refining, iron- and steel-making and heavy chemical production. Generally, however, raw materials have less influence on the location of industry in the 1990s than they had even 50 years ago. Changes in processing methods and in the bulk transport of raw materials mean that transport costs are likely to be a smaller proportion of total production costs than in the past.

This is especially so for light industries making semi-manufactured products. As the cost of inputs is small, contact with outlets for components is more important than access to materials. These industries are located near to larger assembly firms which are their markets.

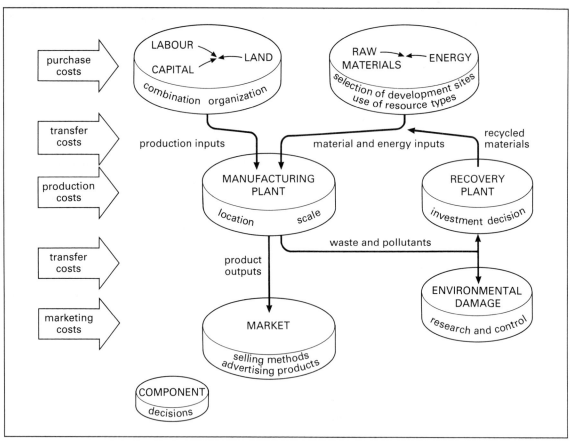

Figure 6.1 *The manufacturing production process*

Figure 6.2 *Light industry located on the outskirts of Lowestoft, Suffolk*

There is what is known as *linkage* between the various firms carrying out separate stages of manufacturing. Car component firms in relation to car assembly plant are an example. This results in a clustering of firms, as has been the case amongst light engineering, clothing and furniture manufacturers, and, more recently, electronics as discussed later in the chapter.

Labour

The effect of labour costs on location is limited by the extent to which the labour force is mobile. Within a country, high wages in one place should in theory attract workers, especially the younger members of the workforce. Hence as more labour moves in, wage rates should fall and labour costs even out from one region to another. In practice, *labour immobility* and sometimes *unionisation* act against an evening-out of costs. Other characteristics of the workforce are often just as important as its cost, particularly the skill of the workforce and its adaptability to new production methods.

The degree to which labour has an influence on location depends upon the type of industry. *Labour-intensive* manufacturing is more likely to be attracted to low-cost labour areas than is capital-intensive industry. Large firms, in particular, are able to seek out such low-cost regions on a world scale and have done so in south-east Asia, where the combination of labour availability, its relative low cost and lack of trade unionisation has attracted investment.

Capital

Capital as money for financing developments is not locationally fixed, although there can be advantages for firms if they locate in areas where banks have expertise in lending to industrial clients. Capital becomes fixed when it is invested in the form of buildings, equipment, power plant, roads and railways. As a result, it is often easier for a firm that wants to expand production to stay where it is and add to existing facilities rather than move. This is the idea of *industrial inertia*, i.e. the tendency for firms to continue at an original site. Staying put is an attractive option because local services can still be used and contacts with local firms and markets maintained. Indeed, as capital itself is *depreciated*, that is written off, by a firm over a period of time, it is access to facilities and links to other firms that are often the more important factors of inertia.

The market

Figure 6.1 suggests a single market as a simplifying idea. In reality, even a single market has demand varying within it. This kind of variation was suggested by A. Lösch in his analysis of markets. He likened the structure of a market to a cone, with demand falling as distance from the supplier increases and the costs of transport push up prices to consumers, making it more expensive for them to purchase goods. Thus demand is greater in the central area and diminishes towards the periphery as shown in Figure 6.3. Large regional or metropolitan markets are likely to be made up of several interlocking cones of demand.

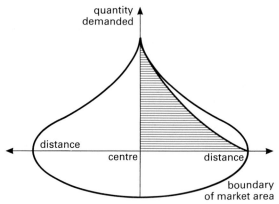

Figure 6.3 *Demand for goods or services in relation to a central supplier (after Lösch)*

Demand also varies spatially because of the differences in the purchasing power of people. This is the idea of *economic potential* which is measured in terms of the each area's total personal income and its national accessibility. In Britain, a zone of high economic potential stretching from London and the South East to the West Midlands is shown in Figure 6.4. Regions like this, where purchasing power is concentrated, are attractive to firms considering new locations. Large companies, though, are likely to view market opportunities beyond such regional scales. Markets are seen by large companies to be international in scope, which partly explains the move towards multiplant production.

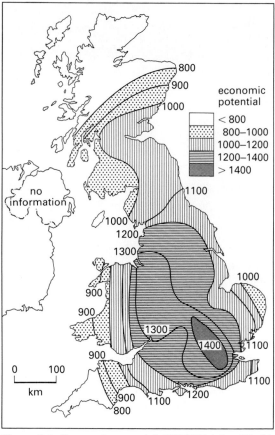

Figure 6.4 *Economic potential, UK 1960 (after Clark)*

RESOLVING THE PULLS OF LOCATION FACTORS

Few raw materials are available everywhere. Unless raw materials and markets coincide, there is a range of possible locations for a manufacturing plant, with a pull backwards to materials in one direction and forwards to the market in the other. The question of industrial location is: where along the economic space from raw material to market should the manufacturing plant be located?

The cost minimising solution

A partial solution to this problem, based on minimising costs, was presented by A. Weber in 1909. His analysis of industrial location was

116

strongly influenced by the heavy burden which transport costs imposed on total costs. Weber took raw materials and market to be at fixed locations. *Transport costs* were calculated as a simple function of the weight of materials times the distance they were moved. *Land costs, manufacturing costs* and the *price of products* were assumed to be the same everywhere. In this model, price cannot be controlled by any individual firm, which means that revenue is the same for all manufacturers no matter where they are. Any industrialist who wants to maximise profits will locate where the cost of production is least, that is at the place with the lowest total transport cost.

Figure 6.5 shows least-cost sites under different conditions. The circles on the diagrams are *isotims*, which are lines of equal transport cost showing how costs increase the further a factory is from a source of raw material, S, or from a market, M. Assume in Figure 6.5(a) that the transport rate is £1/tonne/km and that 10 tonnes of product are made from a *pure raw material*. As defined by Weber, a pure material is one which loses no weight on manufacture. In this case there is no single site which has the lowest total transport costs. It makes no differ-

ence if the plant is at S, from where it would cost £200 to send ten tonnes of product to the market 20 km away, or at M, where it would cost £200 to bring in ten tonnes of raw material from S. At intermediate locations along a straight line between S and M, the two transport costs involved always add up to £200, but locations away from this line involve higher costs. This is proved for any place by adding together the two transport costs to produce a new line of total transport cost called an *isodapane*. The isodapane for £300 is drawn on the diagram.

In Figure 6.5(b), the raw material is assumed to be impure, or *gross* as Weber described it, so that it loses weight on processing. This means that the low-cost location is pulled towards the raw material. Weber used a *material index* to indicate this pulling effect. The index is a simple ratio of the weight of the raw material input to product output. A value of more than one indicates a pull to raw material and a value of less than one to market. The example in Figure 6.5(b) assumes weight loss of 50 per cent on processing so that twice as much of the resource is needed to make one tonne of product. If 10 tonnes of end product are still made and the transport rate remains £1/t/km, the respective

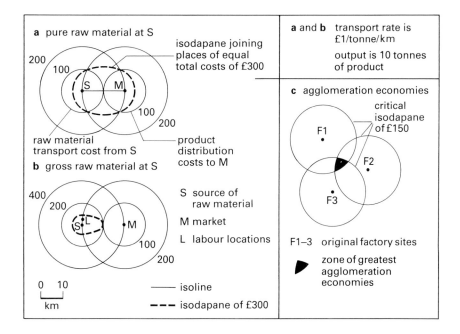

Figure 6.5 *Solutions to least-cost siting of industry using isodapanes*

isotims around S become £200 and £400. Raw material has the greater pull on location, and the least cost site is at S, it being cheaper to send 10 tonnes of finished product from S to market than to bring 20 tonnes of raw material to a plant located at the market. At no site other than S is the total transport cost as low as £200, and hence this is the only location which will allow an industrialist to maximise profits given that revenues are everywhere the same.

More complicated situations can be analysed using isotims, for example allowing the complication of more than one source of raw material. Weber's own analysis included two sources and a market represented by the points of a triangle, which then allowed various pulling effects to be examined. This variation is examined later on.

Diversion from the least-cost transport site

Weber also drew attention to ways in which industry might be diverted from the *least-cost transport site*. If some places offer low labour costs or if firms gain agglomeration economies by locating there, then the lower production costs could offset the handicap of additional transport costs compared with the least-cost site. In Figure 6.5(b), for example, if the labour element is £4.5 per tonne at L but £10 a tonne at S, then it would be cheaper to locate at L. This is because total costs at L are £250 + £45 and at S are £200 + £100. Weber went on to argue that the effect of labour depends upon its cost relative to the costs of procurement and distribution; this ratio per tonne of product he referred to as the *labour coefficient*. Generally, the early stages of processing, i.e. metal refining, have low coefficients and the later stages of manufacture, making cars and domestic goods, have high ones.

The separate idea of *agglomeration economy* is shown by Figure 6.5(c). Here, each factory, F_{1-3}, is at a site of least cost, relative to its sources of raw materials and its market. It would be worthwhile for these factories to cluster together if the resulting savings in production costs were greater than the additional transport costs incurred by not locating at the

least-cost site. Figure 6.5(c) assumes that agglomeration saves £150 per tonne of output. Around each original factory is drawn an isodapane of additional transport cost of £150. These isodapanes are critical in this example because only in the shaded zone where the three circles intersect are the agglomeration economies enough to offset higher transport costs.

Agglomeration, or concentration of industry at certain places, is a characteristic of industrial location. Agglomeration economies arise for several reasons but mainly because of the way firms can gain from links with other firms, as already mentioned for example by buying components or semi-finished materials. Agglomeration also gives rise to *external economies*, that is the opportunity for a firm to use the wide range of infrastructural and other services of the locality which are provided for all firms.

Limitations of least-cost solutions

Several researchers have refined Weber's work in attempts to overcome the transport and market simplifications. As mentioned earlier, transport costs do not rise simply with distance, but at a rate which slows down as distance increases, that is they are *tapered*. This means that places distant from supply points are not so disadvantaged. (See Chapter 8 for a more detailed discussion of transport topics.) The effect of transport costs on the location of oil refining was discussed in the previous chapter. The illustration used there, Figure 5.18, showed that under certain conditions the lowest transport cost site was the transshipment point.

In a study of the Mexican steel industry, R. A. Kennelley showed that by applying Weber's model based on the distances that materials and product were moved, a least-cost site for a steel plant was predicted to be about 160 km west of Monterrey as shown in Figure 6.6. By improving the model simply by adjusting transport costs to take account of freight rates, the least-cost site was indicated to be at Monterrey, coincident, in fact, with the actual location of Mexico's steel plant with the lowest costs. Thus the general principles underlying

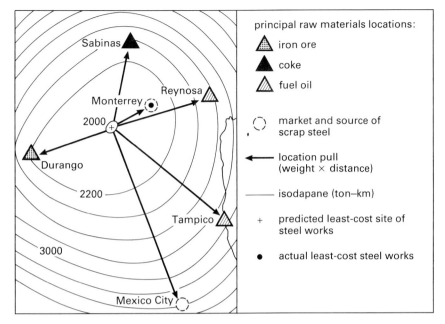

Figure 6.6 *Predicted and actual least-cost steelworks in Mexico*

the Weberian approach to industrial location were shown to apply in this particular study.

However, transport costs are not so critical now as they were when Weber analysed industrial location. Also the practice of processing raw materials before they are sent out from resource areas means that there is less wastage on final processing. Energy inputs are small now compared to the situation in the 19th century when metal processing industries concentrated on coalfields. Then, some 10 tonnes of coal were needed to make a tonne of iron metal, but today just a little more than half a tonne is sufficient. For this reason, iron ore supply costs are more significant to the modern iron and steel industry.

There is still an interest in keeping transport costs down in the case of heavy industries like iron- and steel-making in which the volume of inputs is high. Integrated steel works in many MDCs are located at coastal sites in order to receive imported iron ore and to take advantage of bulk transport economies at transshipment points. The distribution of large steel works served by iron ore handling terminals with deep water access is shown in Figure 6.7 for the EC. Other examples are at Sparrow's Point, USA, and at port complexes such as Fukuyama,

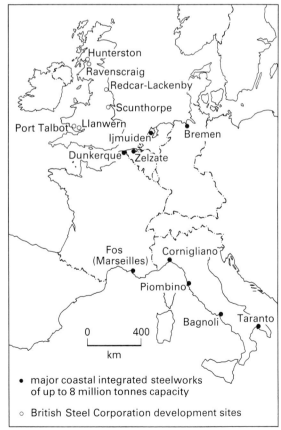

Figure 6.7 *EC coastal steelworks*

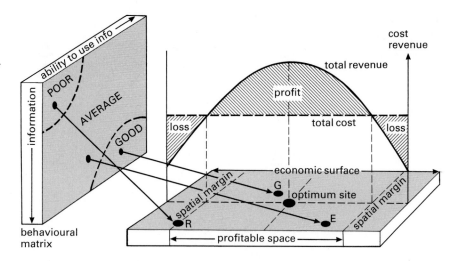

Figure 6.8 *Space-revenue and space-cost curves (after D. M. Smith) with indication of behavioural effect on location choice*

Kawasaki, Kitakyushu and Wakayama in Japan, and at Inchon and Ulsan in South Korea.

The least-cost explanation is less satisfactory when analysing the location of light industry. For these industries, with small input needs, transport cost minimisation is unimportant and other influences, such as the physical environment, are of greater significance.

Seeking profitable industrial locations

The least-cost approach is one-sided in its argument in that revenue is not allowed a locational effect. Industry can survive without occupying the least-cost site provided that a reasonable profit is made. A model which focuses on the balance between cost and revenue, and introduces the idea of the margins to profitability is that of D. M. Smith (1971). In an adapted form of this model (Fig. 6.8) variations in revenue across economic space are shown, with total production costs held constant. The best, or *optimum*, site is at the one place which has the highest revenue and is most profitable, but an industrial plant could be located right up to the spatial margins of profitability and still stay in business, even though in such a position it is more vulnerable if prices fall or costs rise.

By considering economic space as the surface over which an industrialist has some freedom of action, behavioural influences on location choice can be introduced. This approach allows the industrialist to be viewed as someone who is not necessarily motivated to extract maximum profits, nor perfectly informed about sites, nor always able to use information wisely. The consequences of such decision making are shown in Figure 6.8 by filtering decisions through a *behavioural matrix*. This shows how there can be different outcomes depending on how well a firm can collect and use information. Generally speaking, a large firm can afford to collect and make detailed analysis of a wide range of data. By doing so, a good site, G, is selected near to the optimum site. Companies that are unable to investigate so thoroughly, or to use information effectively, might end up at a riskier position at the economic margin, R. Finally, some industrialists might decide to make less profit but gain more lifestyle satisfaction, known as *psychic income*, by deliberately choosing to locate in a pleasant environment, perhaps at E, even though this is some way from the economic optimum. Thus the locations shown, chosen for whatever reason, entail different profit levels and different risk elements if economic conditions change.

The idea of spatial variation both in production costs and in revenue is introduced in Figure 6.9. Look first at the imaginary situations for 1885, when energy needs were very demanding and coalfields gave low production costs (Fig. 6.9(a)). Sites with different

Figure 6.9 *Hypothetical change in regional prosperity*

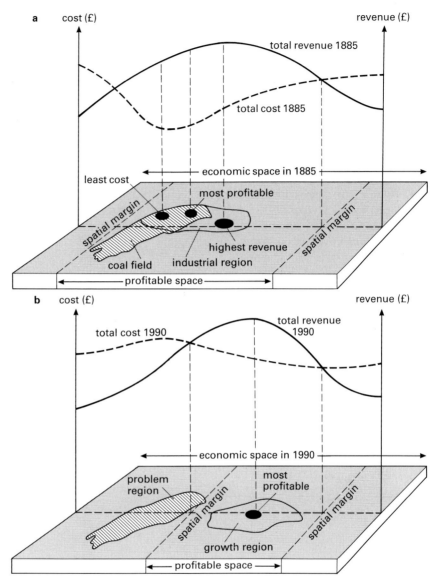

conditions are projected from the graph onto a possible economic surface. For convenience of discussion, specific sites are picked out on this surface instead of lines of equal profitability or revenue. Note that the most profitable site shown is one with the greatest profit midway between the least-cost and highest revenue locations. The general circumstances in the figure are akin to those at UK coalfields like Durham, Lanarkshire or Staffordshire during the late 19th century.

Figure 6.9 can also be used to suggest changes over time. The situation for 1990 (Fig. 6.9(b)), is one in which the pattern of production costs have risen so that the coalfield is no longer profitable for industry, especially as revenue has also dropped in this area. The old heavy industries are facing economic difficulties. Several such resource-based industrial regions in Europe have become *problem regions*. Figure 6.9(b) assumes that industry has moved away from the high-cost coalfield and into the *growth region* where the balance of costs and revenue produce a profit.

REGIONAL ECONOMIC DEVELOPMENT

Industrial evolution

The changes shown by Figure 6.9 suggest that the coalfield region has passed through a sequence of industrial evolution, from initial growth to final stagnation or decline. Over a period of time, some regions prosper while others decline. These changing regional fortunes are related to the *core-periphery concepts* developed by G. Myrdal (1957). Myrdal argued that polarisation of economic growth results from *cumulative causation*. As shown in Figure 6.10, the process is one of circuits of development resulting from the location of new industry in the region. One expansion path is through local employment and population. This increases the pool of skilled labour which is then attractive to new industry. A second pathway is based on new capital and enterprises which foster expansion of service industries. A third

effect is that of increased wealth of the community which provides money through taxation which is used to improve the infrastructure. These positive feedbacks are enhanced by the development of local firms and service industries which in turn serve new industry and local markets.

As a result, the core region becomes characterised by fast economic growth focused on urban-industrial concentrations. Although peripheral regions stand to gain from the purchases made from them, that is from beneficial *spread effects*, according to Myrdal negative influences are often more powerful. These are the *backwash effects* which drain resources, people and talent away from peripheral regions, while the core prospers and regional inequalities persist.

Government intervention

Governments often act to help resource-based and agricultural peripheral regions which are

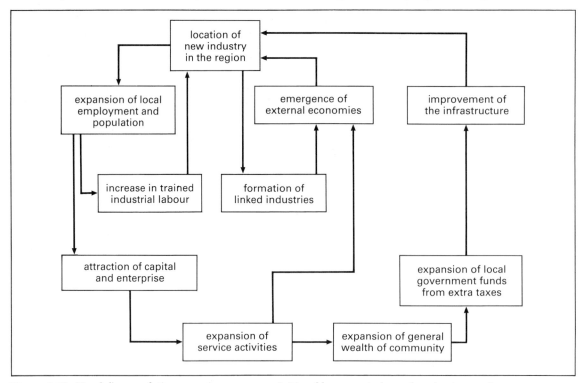

Figure 6.10 *Myrdal's cumulative causation processes, initiated by a new industry locating in a region*

Figure 6.11 *European Community regional aid, 1975–84, and selected peripheral regions*

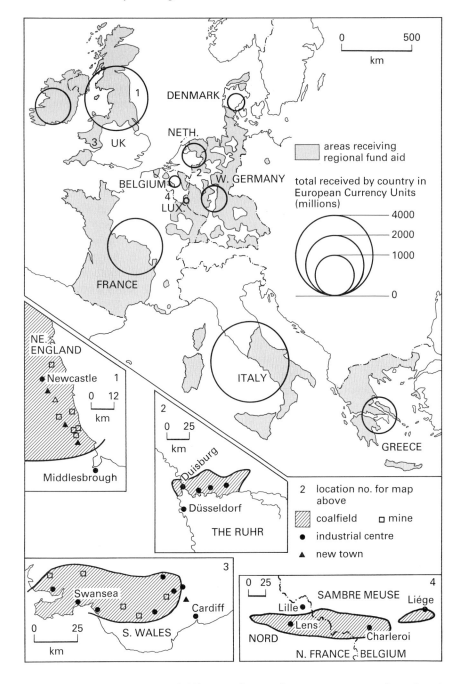

lagging behind the rest of the economy. Assistance is also given to the older industrial regions which are facing decline. Through their intervention policies governments exert a considerable influence on industrial location. Many regions in the European Community (Fig. 6.11), receive assistance as part of regional policies aimed at reducing inequalities. In France, for example, part of the action taken was through the *metropoles d'equilibre* policy. The idea was to set up growth poles at eight major cities, including Bordeaux, Lille, Lyons and Strasbourg, is an attempt to draw economic growth away from the Paris region. Regional aid in the European Community is now being directed more to selected backward areas, with help going to small businesses, tourism and rural job creation. Aspects of this new direction are to be seen in the Integrated Mediterranean Programme directed at southern France, southern Italy and Greece.

Assistance to problem regions in the UK through subsidies, tax benefits and the building of new factories was strongly focused on Special Development Areas in the mid-1960s, with lower levels of provision in Development Areas and Intermediate Areas. During the 1980s the assisted areas were more narrowly defined and greater attention was paid to cities with serious social and economic difficulties. Enterprise Zones were established to help regenerate selected urban areas blighted by derelict land. Twenty-five such zones, housing over 700 re-located firms, had been established by 1985 at a cost of £130 million. One zone which has witnessed dramatic commercial regeneration is that of the Isle of Dogs, London (Fig. 6.12), where the disused Millwall and India Dock areas provided a large amount of space for redevelopment close to the City of

London. Further action to tackle derelic-tion problems in urban areas was taken in the 1980s by setting up eleven Urban Development Corporations. Their task is to deal with the redevelopment of the 15 000 ha of waste land in parts of the metropolitan districts and selected large cities.

ASSIGNMENTS

1 Trace Figure 6.5a.
  a. On your tracing draw the £500 isodapane.
  b. Find the least-cost site if product distribution costs were twice those of raw material movement.
  c. Suggest why product distribution is likely to be more expensive than raw material movement.
2 Make a copy of Figure 6.8.
  a. Draw a new straight line to show higher total costs.
  b. Suggest causes for such increased costs.
  c. How is the firm at R affected by this change?
  d. How might this firm act to overcome the new conditions?
3 Study Figure 6.9.
  a. Compare the pattern of total costs in 1885 with those in 1985.
  b. Suggest reasons for the increased costs on the coalfield.
  c. What action might a government take to assist such a problem region?
4 a. Describe the site features of the industrial area shown in Figure 6.2.
  b. Suggest the nature of the production inputs likely to be used by light industry in this locality.
5 Identify and comment on the fourth expansion path (Fig. 6.10).

Figure 6.12 *Industrial/commercial buildings at the Enterprise Business Park, Isle of Dogs, London*

CHANGES IN MANUFACTURING ACTIVITY

Far-reaching changes affecting the organisation and location of manufacturing industry in the market economies have been gathering pace since the mid-1960s. Industrial restructuring is affecting several of the MDCs. Two main pro-cesses are involved in this restructuring. One is the concentration of activity into large firms, the other is de-industrialisation. In a number of LDCs, however, industrialisation forces are at work, especially in the NICs. Finally, in many of the former CPEs, industrial production is being affected by a need to make more consumer goods in order to satisfy growing demand for household and electrical equipment and by the re-organisation of production along market economy principles.

Large companies and manufacturing

Manufacturing has become increasingly concentrated into large companies since the early 1960s. Nearly 90 per cent of all industrial assets in the USA is held by just 1 per cent of manufacturing firms, with 25 per cent of production accounted for by the top 100 companies. The world's top ten manufacturing companies are shown in Table 6.1. They are large organisations on several counts, but especially in terms of their world-wide sales and by the number of people employed. The sales and assets of several of these companies exceed the total value of output as measured by GNP in many non-oil LDCs apart from NICs.

The companies shown in the table specialise in making motor vehicles, chemicals and electrical goods. Specialisation helps a company gain economies of scale. Indeed the large amount of capital needed to build factories equipped with high-technology production facilities demands the resources of a very large company or of the state. Many companies have become large because of their success in producing well-designed or innovative products, for example, International Business Machines (IBM) as an innovator of computers. This sort of success propels the growth of a firm as the money earned can be reinvested in additional production capacity and in research and development.

Firms also become large by buying up or merging with other companies. If they take over companies in the same line of business the process is referred to as *horizontal expansion*. Some companies deliberately diversify their activities by merging with or by buying dissimilar companies. If the range of activity is extended by taking on resource development, it is known as *backward integration*, but if it shifts towards marketing, then the process is *forward integration*. An oil refining company moving into petro-chemical manufacture would be forward integration.

Improvements in transport and communications are significant factors in enabling these large companies to function efficiently. Telecommunications allow management to keep informed of the actions of the various departments and to pass decisions quickly down the line. Equally, on the production side, inter-plant transfers of materials and components can be

Table 6.1 *The world's ten largest manufacturing companies, ranked according to sales in 1987*

Company	HQ/Country	Activity	Sales $ (thousand million)	Employees (thousand)
General Motors	USA	Motor vehicles	102	813
Ford	USA	Motor vehicles	72	350
IBM	USA	Computers	54	389
Toyota Motor	Japan	Motor vehicles	42	84
IRI	Italy	Metals	41	422
General Electric	USA	Electronics	39	302
Daimler Benz	W. Germany	Motor vehicles	38	326
AT&T	USA	Electronics	34	303
Du Pont	USA	Chemicals	31	140
Volkswagen	W.Germany	Motor vehicles	30	260

Excluded are natural resource related companies
Other large employers (thous): Siemens (359) W. Germany, electronics
Philips (337) Netherlands, electronics

moved quickly and cheaply and be very precisely controlled as in *just-in-time* deliveries to assembly lines. However, to achieve speedy information flow and accurate decision-making, companies have to be organised in a highly structured way.

The organisational structure of large firms has been described as being like a three-tiered cake (Fig. 6.13). The base is large and made up of numerous basic work processes, or manufacturing units, which are separated out over an extended economic space, giving rise to what is known as the *multi-plant* firm. The middle layer is the office structure dealing with day-to-day administration. The top layer is the high-order management level, located at the headquarters (HQ), and responsible for the strategic planning of the firm.

As these different functions are carried out at separate locations there is a *spatial division of labour*. To a large extent, headquarter offices concentrate at *information-rich* cities. London has about 65 per cent of the HQs of the 500 leading UK companies and New York 30 per cent of those in the USA. For American companies operating in the EC there is a clear concentration of headquarter functions in capital cities as shown in Figure 6.14. For most large companies, routine office functions are located in main towns from which the manufacturing plant, which is spread across several regions or even countries, are administered. This organisation of activity means that strategic decisions, for example about opening a new factory or possibly closing an old one, are made by a high-level management at a distance from the area where the consequences of the decisions will be played out.

Large companies are often active in more than one country. These are *transnational companies* (TNCs). They are companies which make direct foreign investment by spending capital outside the parent country. The TNCs employ an estimated 45 million people to account for nearly 25 per cent of world manufacturers.

De-industrialisation

In several DMEs the proportion of the working population employed in manufacturing industry has declined since the mid-1960s, a change referred to as *de-industrialisation*. After 1966, growth in manufacturing employment slowed down and then between 1973 and 1983 went into decline, with the decline in the UK running at 3 per cent per annum. This particular period coincided with world recession, and all countries, apart from Japan, listed in Table 6.2 registered a drop in the percentage employed in

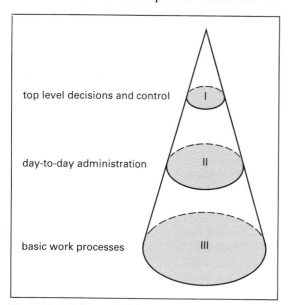

Figure 6.13 *The vertical division of control within a transnational corporation (TNC)*

Country	Value added $bn 1986	Manufacturing Percentage of total employment 1966	Manufacturing Percentage of total employment 1983	Number employed (thousand) 1980
USA	836	28	20	19 210
Japan	574	24	25	10 252
W. Germany	295	53	33	7 141
France	161	29	24	5 002
Italy	140	26	25	3 333
UK	118	35	25	6 462
Canada	60	24	18	1 853

Table 6.2 *Manufacturing output and employment change for selected DMEs $bn = $ thousand million*

Figure
6.14 *Geographical distribution of the European regional headquarters of United States TNCs*

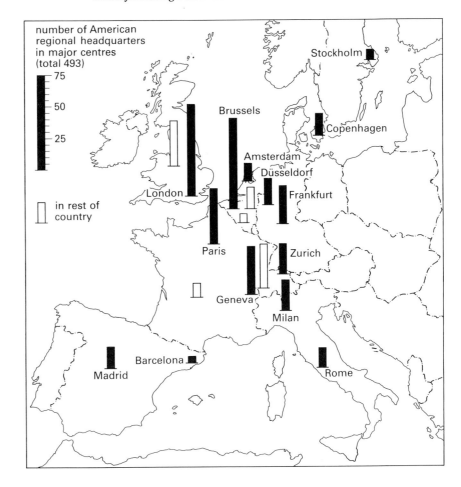

number of American regional headquarters in major centres (total 493)

manufacturing activities. Despite these changes, however, all these countries remain important manufacturing nations, with millions of people employed in these industries and with large amounts of value being added to original raw material inputs by the manufacturing process.

A simple explanation for de-industrialisation is to be found in the sector, or maturity, theory (Chapter 1 and Fig. 1.16.) This is the idea of the progression of the economy to a mature phase in which service activities (commerce and trade, business and personal services, banking and insurance) expand in response to the demands of an increasingly affluent population. Consequently, the proportions employed in other sectors, especially manufacturing, decline.

De-industrialisation, in the sense that fewer people are employed in manufacturing, is also

due to technological progress. Improved methods of production lead to higher output with fewer workers being needed as jobs are taken over by machines. The use of robots for welding and paint-spraying in car manufacturing is an example. A further cause of de-industrialisation in some of the older industrial countries is competition from Japan and the NICs. Well-designed products of high quality have led to deep penetration of USA and European markets by Japanese companies and hence to a smaller market share by home companies. The consequences for three traditional industries, iron and steel, shipbuilding and textiles, are recorded in Table 6.3, while Figure 6.15 shows the changes for steel production. Despite increased productivity in the USA and the EC, especially in the UK, steel output in

Figure 6.15 *Changes in steel production, 1970–85*

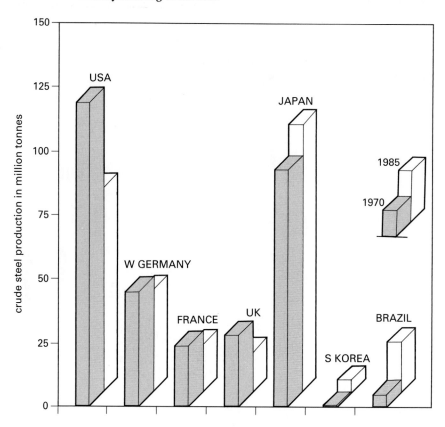

	Crude Steel Production			Merchant Ships Launched			Cotton Yarn Production		
	1970	1985	1970–85	1970	1985	1970–85	1970	1983	1970–83
	(thousand tonnes)		(change percent)	(thousand tonnes)		(change percent)	(thousand tonnes)		(change percent)
USA	119 000	80 000	−33	345	173	−50	1 525	1 064	−30
W. Germany	45 000	40 000	−11	1 717	599	−65	239	168	−30
France	24 000	19 000	−21	975	183	−81	237	149	−37
UK	28 000	16 000	−43	1 260	152	−88	184	97	−47
Japan	93 000	105 000	13	10 648	9 500	−11	507	438	−14
S. Korea	–	5 000	+	–	2 784	+	91	478	425
Brazil	5 000	20 000	300	102	406	300	118	535	353
WORLD	594 000	690 000	16	24 384	19 710	−19	10 447	11 624	11

– negligible
+ very large

Table 6.3 *Changes in manufacturing output for selected industries and countries, 1970–85*

these countries has declined in contrast to the increases in Japan and some NICs.

Does de-industrialisation matter? It certainly hits hard in some regions because manufacturing decline is related to the structure of industry. Regions most affected by unemployment and recession are those where steel-making, ship-building and textile industries, together with coal mining, have predominated in the past. It may matter less to the national economy if there are gains in productivity and if actual loss of output is made good by service activities. Banking, insurance, shipping and other services like tourism can all earn foreign income for the economy. Britain's economy has shifted from one founded largely on manufactured goods to one reliant on non-manufactures, mainly the export of oil and services. Service activities contributed £5000 million to Britain's earnings in 1985. What may be less desirable is loss of labour skill and innovation in manufacturing, with the possibility of progressive decline in production capability so that new goods are supplied increasingly from imports rather than from home firms.

Industrialisation in LDCs

Some LDCs have enclaves of industry built up by past colonial powers, quite often in relation to the exploitation of minerals. Comment on some of these mineral-rich countries, such as Nigeria, Zambia, Malaysia and Chile, was made in Chapter 3. Generally, industrialisation is viewed by many LDCs as a means of promoting economic and social change, a view encouraged by economic models such as Rostow and the recent success of the NICs.

An initial step is for the LDCs to establish industries to produce at least some of the many goods required. Economic development of this kind would save on the costly importation of goods and is a process which is known as *import substitution*. A problem with this kind of industrialisation is that capital equipment has to be bought in order to set up manufacturing plant. The further step of bringing about an *export-based economy* is an even more difficult process. Competing on world markets where other countries have expertise and provide sophisticated products is a problem for any country at an early stage of industrial development.

Even in a country like India with a varied resource base and long-established industries in iron and steel, textiles and chemicals, exports remain small. India's total manufacturing output in 1986 was considerable, and at nearly $40 000 million *value added*, made India the twelfth most important world manufacturing nation. However, manufacturing value is low when measured by per capita output. The total value of manufactured goods exported was about $580 per worker compared with $8 200 per industrial worker in South Korea.

Some other LDCs, the NICs (Table 6.4), and especially the 'four tigers of Asia' are characterised by fast rates of increase in industrial production. If you have a portable cassette

Country	GDP per capita	Labour force in manufacturing	Annual average change in industrial production		Exports of goods		Balance of trade in goods
					total value	per capita value	
	U.S.$	thousand	per cent	per cent	$thousand million	U.S.$	$thousand million
	1985	1985	1970–80	1980–85	1985	1985	1985
Brazil*	1 549	7 524	8.8	−0.2	24	177	10
Mexico*	2 260	2 575	7.0	1.3	22	283	8
Hong Kong	6 273	933	10.2	na	30	5 544	−1
Singapore	6 832	294	11.6	1.3	23	8 917	−3
S. Korea	2 091	3 500	18.8	10.4	30	735	−1
Taiwan	3 095	2 098	13.5	5.9	31	1 606	11

* Labour force in 1980. Industrial labour force for Brazil
na: not available.

Table 6.4 *Newly industrialising countries*

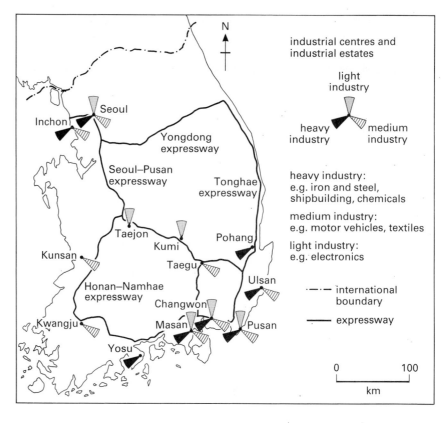

Figure 6.16 *Industrial centres in the Republic of Korea (South Korea)*

player it is likely it was made in one of the four tigers, Hong Kong, Singapore, South Korea or Taiwan. Their fast economic growth has been founded on the export of manufactured goods. Initially, a narrow range of goods, mainly textiles and clothing, spearheaded the development, but in the 1970s output was diversified. South Korea is a good example of this development path. Its strong export-based economy developed from an original emphasis on heavy goods such as steel, ships and petrochemicals, and then expanded into cars and electronics, with locations at port complexes and other centres as shown in Figure 6.16.

Countries like Brazil and Mexico have their own large internal markets. Their industrialisation strategy, especially Brazil's, contrasts with the export-based style of the Asian NICs, as it was founded on import substitution in order to supply home markets from local industries thereby reducing the level of imports. New domestic industries were protected in the early

stages by tariff barriers designed to keep out competing goods. Industrialisation was also helped by investments made by foreign companies who built plant to manufacture the types of consumer goods which could not be produced initially by Brazilian firms. Strong phases of growth between 1968 and 1974, coincided with major investment by the TNCs, especially from the USA. These TNCs account for some 15 per cent of total capital investment which tends to be in more modern and technically advanced plant. There are benefits from these foreign investments in the form of new technology, the creation of a demand for components and the possibility of a surplus output for export. Against this, profits earned by the TNCs are drawn out of the Brazilian economy.

Industry in centrally planned economies

During early periods of planning in the USSR following the revolution, emphasis was placed on heavy industrial development in order to make producer goods, i.e. the tools and machines needed by industry itself. Coal and raw materials were essential inputs for the iron and steel industry. The steel works at Donbass and newer works at the Ural Mountains and Kazakhstan reflect the locational pulls to resources. However, along with the greater availability of alternative energy such as oil and natural gas, has come a diversification of production into petrochemicals and non-ferrous metallurgy. Location factors have also changed with growing market demand for more consumer goods. Two opposing influences thus affected the spatial development of Soviet industry in the post-1960 period. One was the growth of labour-intensive industry in the older industrial centres to the west of the Urals and the other the growth of resource-based activity in more remote areas in Siberia, the north-west and Kazakhstan. However, even though proportionately more investment went to these eastern locations, the greatest amount of production remains in the older established regions further west.

ASSIGNMENTS

---

6 a. From Table 6.1 work out the sales per employee for each of the motor vehicle companies.

b. Comment on and attempt to explain the differences between the companies in terms of productivity as measured by sales per employee.

c. What are the advantages of large-scale industry?

d. What are the spatial consequences of such industrial organisations?

7 a. With reference to Table 6.2, work out the value added per employee for each country.

b. Draw a set of bar graphs to compare the countries on the measure calculated for (a).

c. Suggest reasons for differences in productivity between the countries presented in (b).

d. What is meant by de-industrialisation?

e. Why is de-industrialisation such a significant process in the DMEs?

8 a. Examine the ways in which LDCs might industrialise their economies.

b. What are the benefits and disadvantages of industrialisation in a Less Developed Country?

9 Use the data in Table 6.4 to comment on the economies of the Asian countries.

SPATIAL CHANGES IN MANUFACTURING ACTIVITY

The components of change discussed above for the market economies are closely interrelated and have significant spatial consequences. On a world scale, there is increasing internationalisation of production and the emergence of important new manufacturing nations. This global dimension is strongly affected by the location decisions made by TNCs. On a regional scale, manufacturing is in decline in many of the old industrial areas. In compensation, new high-technology industries are promoting economic growth, especially in those regions perceived as environmentally attractive.

The global pattern of industry

The largest of the TNCs have spread activities so widely around the world that they have created a global system of manufacturing. A good example of this is the automobile industry. The production and marketing of cars is dominated in world terms by the countries shown in Figure 6.17. In terms of ownership, this pattern is complicated by the control of production by a small number of internationally-operated motor companies, each of which is organised as a *multi-plant* operation spread across several countries. There is often a complex flow of materials and partly finished products between plants. Parts are sometimes sent as *completely knocked down* (CKD) kits for assembly elsewhere. Figure 6.18 shows the complexities of

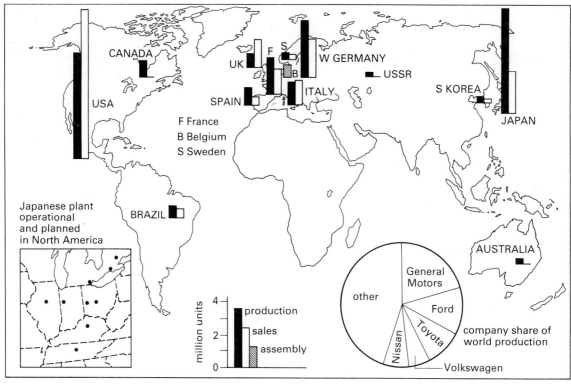

Figure 6.17 *Major world production and sales of passenger cars, 1986*

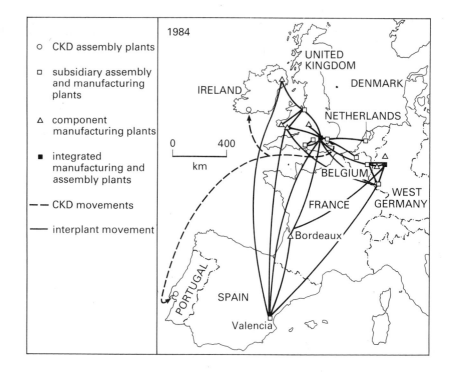

Figure 6.18 *The location of Ford Motor Company operations in western Europe, 1984*

the Ford Motor Company's operations in the EC. The world's largest motor company, General Motors, has manufacturing plant, research and development (R & D) establishments and marketing facilities in some twenty countries.

The growth of Japanese car production (Fig. 6.19) in the past ten years or so has resulted not

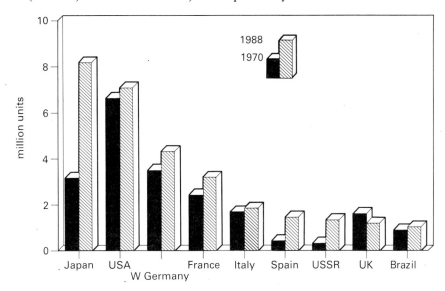

Figure 6.19 *Major car producers in 1970 and 1988*

Figure 6.20 *Nissan car plant in Sunderland, UK*

Figure 6.21
Manufacturing employment change by state, USA, 1977–85

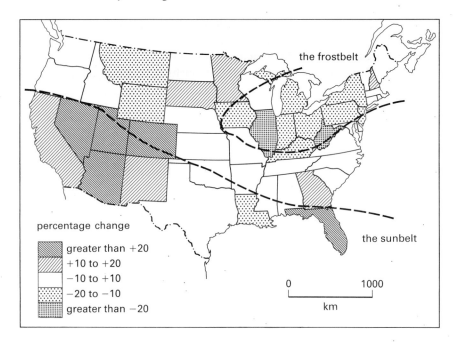

percentage change

greater than +20
+10 to +20
−10 to +10
−20 to −10
greater than −20

0   1000

km

the frostbelt

the sunbelt

only in an increasing volume of vehicle exports from Japan, but also in the building of manufacturing plant in North America and Europe by major Japanese companies such as Toyota, Honda and Nissan. Nissan has built a major assembly plant in Sunderland in north-east England (Fig. 6.20) and Toyota has one near Derby.

The global system of manufacturing involves the transfer of capital between countries. These transfers are no longer dominated so strongly by USA and European companies as they were in the 1960s. Cross transfers of capital occur, with Japanese and other Asian countries becoming increasingly important. These investment flows have tangible results. At one time, American, European and Japanese investment led to a considerable expansion of sub-assembly manufacture in east Asian countries, but now plants are being built by Asian firms in the USA and Europe. See Chapter 8 for further discussion of these changes.

Regional changes in the older market economies

Since the mid-1960s, industry has been moving

from older industrial regions while new industries have tended to favour regions peripheral to the old industrial cores. The old industrial regions with cramped sites, high land costs and congested transport systems compare unfavourably with many parts of the periphery with their open and environmentally attractive space, such as in the 'sunbelt' localities of the west and south in the USA. The map of changes in manufacturing employment in the USA in Figure 6.21 shows the old 'manufacturing belt' to have a shrinking workforce in comparison with growth in the south-west and some southern states. As usual, care is needed when analysing this picture. High positive changes are often because of the initial low manufacturing base, so that a small increase in output shows as a large percentage change. Changes also relate to the time period analysed. Had the earlier period 1967–80 been selected, then Texas would have stood out as a fast-growing manufacturing state. What has happened since the early 1970s is that a drop in employment in oil-related industries like petrochemicals has offset growth in 'high tech' ones. The trend, however, is for manufacturing growth to favour the sunbelt rather than the old core, the frost belt. It will, though, take some time for the sunbelt to catch up. The value of per capita output in Ohio was around $6 000 in 1985 compared with Florida's $2 000.

Movement from the older industrial regions and from congested urban locations also occurs in European countries. Regions most affected by manufacturing decline and associated unemployment and recession are those where coal mining, steel-making, shipbuilding and textile industries have predominated in the past. Regions experiencing growth, on the other hand, are those attracting new light industries and service industries. In France the Mediterranean area is increasingly favoured for new light industry. Places in southern Germany, the upper Rhine and in south Bavaria, especially in the vicinity of Munich, have experienced fast rates of economic growth and manufacturing expansion. The rapid expansion of some regional economies is associated with *high-technology* (sunrise) industries. High-technology industry includes a wide range of manufacturing, most commonly electronics, but also aerospace and pharmaceutical industries, and the making of scientific and optical equipment.

Exceptionally fast growth of the electronics industry characterised the Santa Clara Valley, California in the late 1960s. At one time, nearly 50 000 jobs a year were being created. The agglomeration of so many industries here is explained by their need to have close contact with research institutions such as Stanford University, and also with the larger electronics and aerospace companies of the locality. Although the industry has spread to the nearby states of Arizona, New Mexico and Texas, where there are less congested conditions, but California still accounts for some 30 per cent of the USA's output of electronic equipment and employs 400 000 people in the industry.

Much of Britain's electronics industry has spread along the M4 in the vicinity of Heathrow and in south Berkshire. Here there is opportunity for firms to have contact with government research establishments. Attempts have also been made to provide conditions favourable to high-tech industry at science parks which are

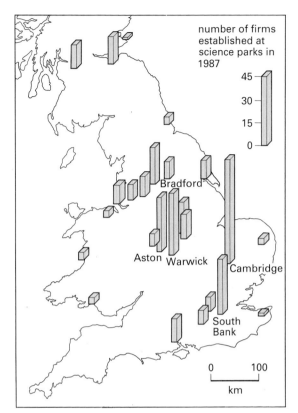

Figure 6.22 *Science parks in the UK, 1987*

located at university sites, the idea being to encourage technology transfer between academic and commercial worlds. About £90 million has been invested, creating 7 600 jobs at 26 science parks (Figs. 6.22 and 6.23). This puts the UK second to the USA in the number of parks developed and well ahead of other European countries. At the largest of these parks in Cambridge, there are 68 companies.

Much research and development in the high-technology industries is taking place in Japan. As in the UK and USA, the Japanese electronics industry is highly concentrated, most of it in the south Kanto region at Tokyo (Fig. 6.24), where there is some 60 per cent of Japan's computer and space equipment industry as well as a concentration of electronic component manufacturers. Several of the major appliance companies, Hitachi, Sony, and JVC, act as markets and as organisers of production for smaller companies clustered near them. In this

Figure 6.23 *The science park at Cambridge – spacious layout and good access to roads characterise the park*

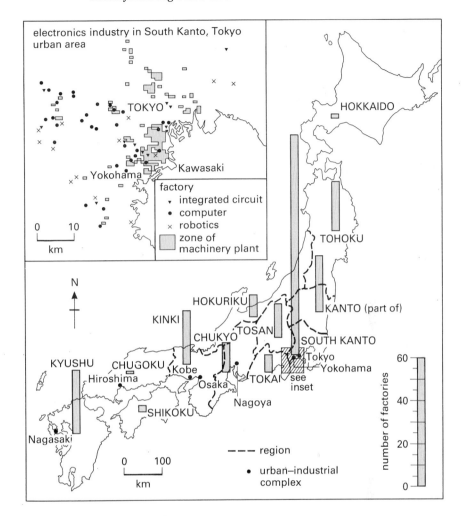

Figure 6.24 *Electronics industry distribution in Japan by regions, and the South Kanto area, 1982*

Industrial movement from urban areas

Taking place within the broader regional patterns are important smaller-scale changes. These involve the closing down of premises in central urban areas (Fig. 6.25) and a shift of firms from central locations to suburban or rural locations. So far as Britain is concerned, the larger the urban area, the greater is the manufacturing employment decline. A key explanation for the shift of industry from urban areas is that of *space constraints* in central areas. This makes it difficult to build new premises and road links to accommodate modern industry's machinery and transport needs. It is much easier to build single-storey factories at *greenfield* sites in the country. Generally, communication improvements have enabled greater separation of producer and consumer. As the Cambridge Econometrics Group put it 'What we are witnessing is an unravelling of the 19th and early 20th century industry concentrations, which were the result of the inflexibility of transport and power systems.'

area there is a highly concentrated manufacturing system making up an industrial-technological complex. It is this successful type of new industrial region that competes so fiercely against similar technically advanced regions in the USA and in Europe.

Figure 6.25 *Industrial decline in an urban area*

ASSIGNMENTS

---

10 Using Tables 6.2, 6.3 and 6.4, exemplify the main changes in the industrial poles of the world since 1960 which have been outlined in this chapter.

11 a. What is import substitution industrialisation?
  b. Why do LDCs attempt it?
  c. What are the difficulties of developing the economy on the basis of import substitution?
  d. Comment on the alternatives to import substitution.

12 a. What is meant by a multi-plant industrial company?
  b. With the aid of Figure 6.18, describe the pattern of the Ford Motor Company's operations in Europe in 1984.
  c. Give reasons for the location pattern in 1984.

7

Service Activities

SERVICE ACTIVITIES AND THE ECONOMY

The many different kinds of service transactions between consumers and suppliers take place in the goods and services market described in Chapter 1 and shown in Figure 1.1. To buy goods, private consumers use the services of shopkeepers and other retailers. They obtain other services from a wide variety of sources; banks and insurance offices, education and government institutions, garages and repair shops, theatres and sports centres. Firms in the production sector and those in the service sector itself need support from finance, transport and communication services. All these varied service activities are sometimes placed in one large category, the *tertiary sector*. However, as a country's economy develops, so its service activities become wider-ranging and more complex, and hence it is useful to separate out a set of higher-level services from the rest of the tertiary group and place them in the *quaternary sector*.

The quaternary sector includes financial, educational, research and administration functions. These are closely involved with the collection and processing of information and with decision-making. This information-handling, rather than goods-handling, distinguishes quaternary activities. The tertiary sector is left with routine personal and business services on the one hand, and distribution services (wholesale and retail activities, plus transport and communications) on the other. Transport and communications are used by all sections of the economy, including other service activities, and

because they have such universal importance they are discussed separately in the following chapter.

Types of service occupation

One way of classifying service occupations is shown in Figure 7.1, which is based on data for the UK. As can be seen from the figure,

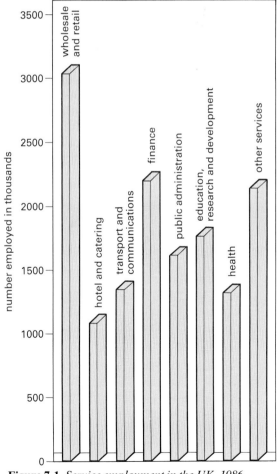

Figure 7.1 *Service employment in the UK, 1986*

wholesale and retail trades account for a large part of all service employment, 20 per cent in 1986. *Wholesalers* are firms that deal in and store large consignments of goods, often re-packaging them into smaller lots before dispatch to retailers. *Retailers* are responsible for the direct sale to the final personal customer. Although employment in these two services increased in Britain during the twenty-five years after 1960, it has remained fairly static since 1985. This is largely because of the scaling up of the size of outlets so that more goods are sold per retail unit and per employee.

In contrast, the *finance sector* has expanded by nearly 30 per cent during the period 1980 to 1986. The banking, insurance and property sub-branches of this sector have all increased, but the most striking growth has been in *business services*, which have increased by 44 per cent. These are professional groups, like accountancy and other financial and manage-ment consultancy businesses.

Many people in the UK are employed in *education*, a total of 1.75 million including re-search and development. Other state dominated services are health and public administration, the latter including defence and national and local government services. Employment in *hotel and catering services* has become more impor-tant along with the growth of tourism and recreation. Demands on all these activities have increased as greater prosperity has given some people more disposable income to spend on non-essentials. Tourism is a very significant in-ternational operation, with many visitors coming to the UK. The final category in Figure 7.1 – *other services* – is made up of a mixed collection of services, including recreational, cultural and personal services.

It is important to note that Figure 7.1 is based on people employed directly in the service sector. There are many workers in the primary and secondary industries who carry out service tasks. These are the office staff who deal with sales and purchases, wages and personnel services. Generally speaking, the proportion of office and management staff in industry, the so called *white collar* workers, has increased whilst that of production (*blue collar*) workers has fallen.

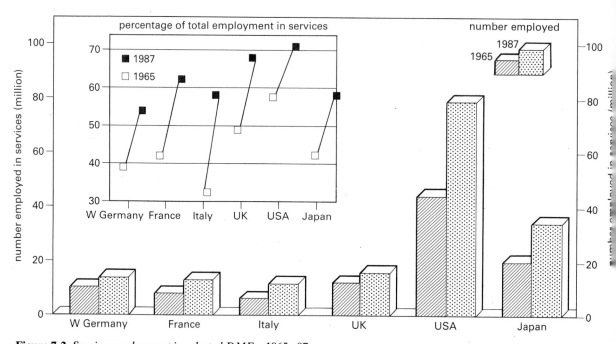

Figure 7.2 *Service employment in selected DMEs, 1965–87*

Table 7.1 *Service employment in LDCs and DMEs*

Average percentage	Year	Low income LDCs	Upper middle income LDCs	Developed market economies
Service employment	1960	14	31	44
	1981	15	42	56
GDP from services	1960	27	49	54
	1981	29	51	61

The growth of service employment

Over a period of twenty years since the mid-1960s, employment in service industries has increased in all the DMEs (Fig. 7.2). There are several reasons for this. These advanced societies use a great deal of equipment that requires servicing and repair. As noted above, people have more leisure time to spend on non-productive activities like recreation. Wealthy nations make extensive provision of social, health and educational services so that the state is a major employer of service workers, with many people working in government departments. Industrial and commercial firms demand more sophisticated support from a wide range of financial and business consultants, and from equipment maintenance companies.

As shown by Figure 7.2, the total number employed in service industries rose by between 3 million and 5 million in the four EC countries shown and by 33 million in the USA. In all these countries employment in service activity as a proportion of total employment has increased. These percentage changes (Fig. 7.2) reflect the shift to *post-industrial society*. This is a characteristic shift as advanced economies mature, and employment moves out of agriculture and industry and into services as suggested by the sector model of development (Chapter 1 and Fig. 1.16). By the late 1980s, several of the DMEs had over 60 per cent of their workforce employed in services, although West Germany, Italy and Japan were lower at around 55 to 57 per cent.

Amongst the LDCs there is a contrast between low-income countries and others, as shown by Table 7.1. There was only a weak shift towards the service sector by the low-income countries. The relatively low employment in services reflects the level of development of these countries. Poorer countries make less provision than richer ones for social services, whilst the large employment in primary activity inevitably means a lower percentage in other sectors.

Growth in services was clearly greater in the case of upper-middle income countries, a group which includes the NICs. Along with manufacturing growth in these countries, there has been increased demand for administration and for transport and communications in order to support rapidly growing export activities. The service sector's growth is also linked to urbanisation, simply because urban dwellers create new demands for transport and local government services.

ASSIGNMENTS

---

1 a. Describe the composition of service employment in the UK as shown in Figure 7.1.

 b. Give reasons for the growth in importance of financial services and of transport and communications.

 c. Suggest why employment in retailing has not grown as fast as that in other services.

2 a. Explain why, amongst the advanced market economies, West Germany and Japan have a relatively low percentage of service employment.

 b. Comment on the scale and nature of the service industries in the LDCs.

3 a. In what ways does the quaternary sector differ from the tertiary sector?

b. What is meant by the term 'post-industrial society'?

c. Why is the USA regarded as having progressed further towards a post-industrial society than other countries?

THE SPATIAL ORGANISATION OF SERVICE ACTIVITIES

As services are provided for and by people, it is not surprising to find that there is a relationship between the population size of a place and the number of services offered there, as suggested in Figure 7.3. Two concepts, *threshold size* and *range of a good*, help explain this relationship. These concepts were developed from W. Christaller's work on central place theory which he carried out in the 1920s.

Central places are settlements that provide goods and services for the people living there and in the surrounding area over which the place has an influence. Outlets for services, shops, banks and so on, are clustered at central places, and are provided irregularly as distance from these places increases. Any business sup-

plying goods or services, whether a shop selling groceries or a broker selling insurance, needs a minimum number of customers, the *threshold population*, in order to generate sufficient revenue to stay in business. These customers include local people and others attracted from areas further away. The total area from which customers are drawn to the centre is its *market area*. Generally speaking, because transport costs reduce the amount people can spend, more goods and services are sold near to the centre and less further away, as shown in the Lösch model (Fig. 6.3).

How much people are willing to pay to travel to a particular centre, and hence the distance they travel, depends upon the type of goods or services being purchased. Cheap goods like groceries, purchased frequently, have a small range as it is not worthwhile for customers to travel long distances to buy them, unless they are bought in bulk or at the same time as other goods. Before the advent of supermarkets and hypermarkets, it was therefore a convenience for people to have these shopping facilities, selling what are known as *low order* or *convenience goods*, in the neighbourhood. For people without cars it still is.

On the other hand, a business selling expensive, or *high order goods*, such as items of furniture which are bought infrequently, needs an extensive market area in order to tap a sufficient number of people. When setting out to buy these expensive items, people like to compare styles, prices and quality. Thus a clustering of stores in a large centre is a benefit to both the customers and the retailers. If these stores are located near each other in one large centre, each will tap a large threshold population and people will be willing to travel a long distance to the centre in order to compare the goods on offer from store to store. However, as discussed later in the chapter, there are changes to this concentration in town centres because transport improvements are giving people ease of access to stores located outside or at the edge of the town.

Comparison shopping also applies to fashion goods. When buying new clothes a consumer

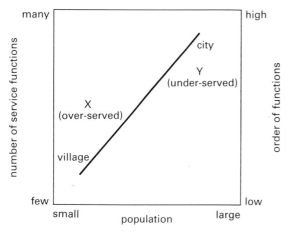

Figure 7.3 *Hypothetical relationship between population size and services*

may wish to compare what Marks and Spencer has to offer with that at C & A, British Home Stores, Top Man and Next. Only in a large centre will several major stores be present. Indeed, large firms require high threshold populations of around 100 000 for stores in central locations. Furthermore, in large towns and cities, specialist services are available, for example, at major hospitals, at investment banks and at government departments.

There is, then, a hierarchy of central places, with the largest places offering not only the highest order of goods, but also all the lower orders. Moving down through the scale of towns by size, services gradually reduce in number and sophistication (Fig. 7.3), until, at village level, only convenience shopping and personal services are left, if there is any retail activity at all apart from the ubiquitous public house.

The location of service activity within central places

Wholesale and retail activities These distributive trades deal with the exchange of goods between producers and consumers. As noted earlier, wholesalers serve retailers by storing, packaging and delivering goods in bulk. The separation of the two activities, however, is no longer clear-cut for the simple reason that many of the large retailing companies operate their own warehousing and transport services. Such integration has become more common along with growth of the multiple retailers like J. S. Sainsbury, Tesco and Marks and Spencer, and with the development of *retail warehousing*. In the past wholesale warehouses were often located near central markets, i.e. in the transitional zones of cities. Favoured locations are now likely to be in suburban areas or on industrial estates out-of-town. The famous London wholesale markets for fruit and vegetables and for fish have been moved from their central locations at Covent Garden and Billingsgate and the vacated sites redeveloped for other commercial functions, as shown in the case of Covent Garden in Figure 7.4.

Figure 7.4 *New commercial uses of the former fruit and vegetable market at Covent Garden, London*

Although the *central business districts* (CBDs – the central area in which retail, office and civic functions are concentrated) of towns and cities no longer have such a dominating hold on retail activities, there is still a strong retail presence in these central areas. Explanation of this concentration can be based on the principle of *bid rent* (Fig. 7.5). Retailers depend on occupying locations which are highly accessible

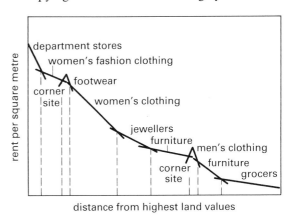

Figure 7.5 *Hypothetical rent gradient in one direction from the point of highest land values within a major unplanned shopping centre*

to potential customers. They are prepared to pay high costs in rates and rents to occupy the city centre where mass transport is focused. The firms controlling department stores and multiple stores seek out prime, very expensive, sites at the intersections of principal shopping streets where they share large pedestrian flows and gain from agglomeration at the centre. These stores vie with each other by setting out attractive window displays to invite comparison shopping.

Smaller retailers, selling a limited range of goods, clothes, jewellery or shoes, also need to attract customers, but they find it costly to occupy sites on the High Street where rates are high. Solutions are found either by setting up shop in side streets, or by minimising the frontage used along the High Street, or by occupying space on upper floors of buildings. Although upper-floor locations are often suitable for functions such as insurance and financial services, they are not so desirable to retailers who depend on shoppers seeing their goods in the window. Even a narrow foothold on the High Street can be preferable because of the flow of potential customers there. A short shop front, though, creates a problem because of the loss of window display. Ingenious solutions are devised, with jewellery and shoe shops often making window bays part of the shop entrance. Owners of fashion boutiques in enclosed shopping precincts sometimes use removable partitions along the shop front so that when the shop is opened there are no barriers to customers. Stylish clothes are displayed and popular music played loudly to lure unwary shoppers off the street and into the store.

Thus the central shopping area is not totally dominated by a few mega-stores, but retains a mix of shops of different sizes in different locations, offering a broad spectrum of shopping opportunity to potential customers. Land use in the CBD as a whole is made up of more than retail use, of course. Other users pay to occupy central locations, and there is jockeying for position in relation to how much firms are prepared to bid for accessibility. In large cities this is reflected in the emergence of specialist

quarters with distinctive zones in retail, wholesale, office, entertainment and civic functions.

Office functions and office locations Offices function by receiving, processing, transmitting and acting on information. At headquarter offices the information is used to guide decision-making, and, as noted in Chapter 6, these high-level office functions are located in large, information-rich centres. With several firms in the same locality, there is face-to-face business contact which helps speed decisions and can lead to innovative projects. Firms gain from agglomeration economies by using the established infrastructure of services. Some cities, often capital cities, have international functions, especially in finance, and may be chosen by major firms for headquarter locations because this gives access to important financial services, as well as to government departments. Despite decentralisation of offices, London and Paris retain dominating roles as cities for headquarter offices, as do New York and Los Angeles in the USA (Table 7.2).

For HQ offices, prestigious locations in the CBD are sought. In the City of London, financial services cluster in a zone within 1 000 metres of the Bank of England. In capital cities, government departments are located near each other, often in impressive office blocks, as for example along Whitehall, London, and on Capitol Hill, Washington DC.

Spatial concentration in the city centre, where public transport systems converge and ensure access to a large workforce, is a characteristic of office location. Exceptionally high workforce/visitor densities are associated with sky-

City	Number of firms with HQs in city	Number in financial sector
New York	72	47
Los Angeles	26	15
Dallas	17	5
Chicago	16	6
San Francisco	13	5

Table 7.2 *The five leading cities for headquarter office location in the USA, 1987*

144

Figure 7.6 *New York City office skyscrapers with Empire State building and World Trade Centre*

scrapers. The World Trade Centre, New York (Fig. 7.6) is estimated to have a daily flow of 50 000 workers and 80 000 visitors.

Services operated by the state

In any country, the state, both at central and local levels, is a major employer of office workers. Interestingly, the LDCs spend proportionately more of their national budget on their civil service than do the DMEs. Spending in most LDCs is heavily committed to central government administration in the capital city, but in the DMEs spending is spread more broadly on people-related services such as education and health.

Information was given in Table 1.1 about some of the differences between nations in the provision of these important services. In most DMEs, for example, there are around 20 to 25 pupils per teacher, but in the LDCs commonly over 200, and in some African countries as many as 400. Health provision is strikingly different, in terms of hospital provision, with one hospital bed per 1500 persons in the LDCs, but only 80 persons in the DMEs.

The DMEs are relatively well provided for in welfare services, but even so there is often an imbalance of provision from one region of a country to another. Educational success rates in England and Wales show higher performances for counties near London and in Wales than elsewhere. There are considerable regional differences in health services in Britain, as indicated by variations in hospital waiting lists, with relatively long waiting lists in the northern part of the Midlands.

ASSIGNMENTS

4 For a shopping centre you visit:
  a. record how major stores and minor stores differ in the way goods are displayed;
  b. comment on differences in location of these two types of store;
  c. compare your results with those selected in Figure 7.5;

d. comment on how some of the minor retailers minimise their space needs in the High Street location.

5 a. Write a short account to explain why wholesale trades have moved out from central city locations, as in the case of London.

   b. How are the vacated sites being used?

6 a. With reference to Figure 7.3, suggest reasons for town X and city Y being over- and under-provided with services.

   b. For a central area known to you, contrast the location of supermarkets and banks.

7 a. Why is it that some retailers are prepared to pay high bid rents in order to occupy the central areas of towns?

   b. Why in cities is there often a sorting out into distinctive zones of functions in the CBD?

DECENTRALISATION OF SERVICE ACTIVITIES

Although there is still a considerable concentration of services in the central areas of towns and cities, there is an increasing amount of *out-of-town* shop development. There are several reasons for this. People have moved out to suburbs and the country areas around large towns, and the service industries have followed them out there. Access to places has changed so that many people prefer to use their car instead of public transport. There is serious congestion on urban roads in central areas where routes converge. Parking is difficult as well as costly in the centre of towns and cities. In contrast, out of town there is greater freedom of movement by road.

In other words, accessibility has changed from being public-transport-based and radial, to being car-based and orbital. Significant new locations for the distribution services are out of town at intersections of main roads or at links to motorways as suggested in Figure 7.7.

Changes in retail location

In the USA, many out-of-town shopping centres have been built since the 1950s. So extensive has this process been that, in many cities, the CBD accounts for only about 10 per cent of total city retail sales. By 1980, some 22 000 out-of-town regional centres located in or near the fast-growing suburban areas of North American cities accounted for 42 per cent of all retail sales.

The largest centres have floor space of around 100 000 m^2 and parking for over 5 000 cars (Table 7.3). These large enclosed shopping

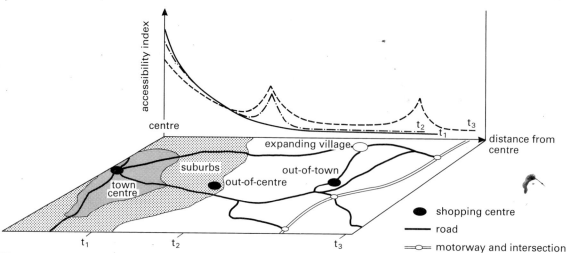

Figure 7.7 *Model of changing accessibility in three time periods and location of shopping centres*

Table 7.3 *Characteristics of new regional shopping centres*	Floorspace (1000 m² approx)	Shop units (number)	Car space (number)
Out-of-town centres, North America			
Yorkdale, Toronto	116	100	6 500
Tyson's Corner, Washington	90	105	6 000
Cross Country, New York	70	60	6 500
In-town centres UK			
Victoria Centre Nottingham	60	88	1 670
Arndale Centre Manchester	90	200	–
Out-of-town centre UK			
Metro Centre, Gateshead	120	na	9 000

malls include two or three *anchor stores*, that is nationally renowned retailers who will attract customers from distant areas, together with a large number of smaller units. One type of arrangement is shown in the example of York-dale, Toronto (Fig. 7.8).

A similar trend is much more recent in Britain, but in 1985 nearly 60 per cent of all proposed shopping developments were for out-of-town locations, half of these being at sites close to the M25 around London. Until 1986, however, a true equivalent to the American out-of-town regional shopping centre did not exist in the UK. Instead, there were a number of in-town enclosed shopping centres, several of which had floor areas, if not car space and site

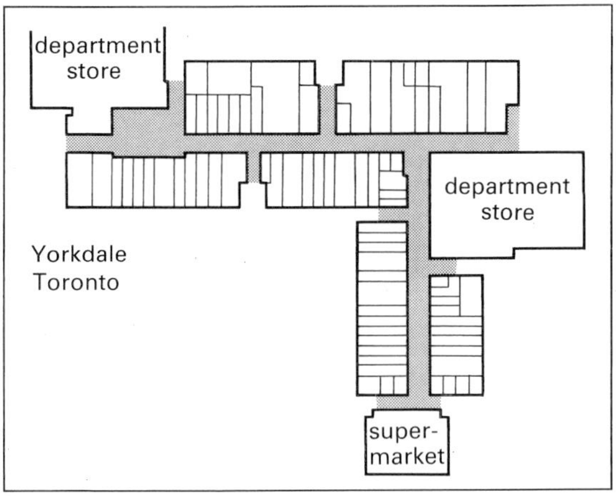

Figure 7.8 *The Yorkdale shopping centre, Toronto, Canada*

area, on the same scale as American centres (Table 7.3). The first UK out-of-town regional shopping centre was opened in 1986 at Metro Centre near Newcastle-upon-Tyne. This is the largest purpose-built shopping centre in Europe, with over 120 000 m² of retail floor space, plus leisure areas and space for 9 000 cars. The design (Fig. 7.9) has features in common with American shopping malls. There are several anchor stores, in the form of department stores and chain stores, plus numerous smaller units. Metro Centre aims to make shopping a family leisure activity, and the site has a funfair, children's village and ten-screen cinema.

Other responses to changes in car ownership, accessibility and population distribution in the UK are to be seen in the development of superstores, retail warehouses and hyper-markets. These trends represent a major scaling-up in the size of retail outlets and are associated with the concentration of ownership into a relatively small number of major firms. The retail geography of the UK is greatly affected by the presence of companies such as J. S. Sainsbury and Tesco, which between them control 30 per cent of grocery sales, and by Marks and Spencer with 16 per cent of the clothing market.

Superstores sell convenience goods aimed at the one-stop, car-based, once-a-week shopper. They are usually at out-of-centre locations because of the space needs of such large single-storey buildings and because of the policy of providing ground-level car parking. Superstores

Figure 7.9 *Metro Centre, Gateshead*

have been developed at a rather faster rate in France and West Germany than in Britain, but they are increasing in importance in Britain with the major retailing companies developing them in joint venture schemes.

Retailers in Britain, like Marks and Spencer, Texas Homecare, MFI and Comet have also developed retail warehouses. These are frequently purpose-built single-storey buildings, often strategically located near major radial roads, or in *retail parks*. Common facilities such as car parks can be shared between traders at these parks, or, more ambitiously, companies might combine to build a unit as a joint venture, like that of Tesco and Marks and Spencer at Cheshunt, Hertfordshire. The retail park is of recent origin in Britain, dating from 1982, but there are now 90 such parks with a total of 1 million m^2 floor space. Public utilities, like British Rail and British Coal, have been keen to see these developments on some of their derelict land.

Hypermarkets are typically at locations peripheral to towns. They have had a particularly important impact in West Germany and France. They are large stores, 5 000 m^2 or more, and sell a wide range of higher order goods as well as food and drink, with a split of around 20 per cent of durable goods sales and 60 per cent of foodstuffs, the balance being in clothes and petrol. The building of hypermarkets, as well as other types of out-of-town retailing, is often a contentious issue in Britain, with fears expressed about the adverse consequences to in-town traders.

Against these trends in decentralisation are *convenience stores* which have in-town locations. These are located in residential areas to appeal to pedestrian shoppers as well as car users. They provide a service to the community by opening 'all hours', and have their origin in the corner shops once common in British towns. Large convenience stores are often organised as chain groups by specialist companies, and others by partnership groups such as Spar, Mace and VG. A new feature is the interest taken by petrol companies in this type of operation. At their petrol forecourts they already have retail sites at which they can set up a convenience shop.

Changes in office location

In contrast to HQ functions, routine office work does not require a central location for operational efficiency. Offices performing these lower-level functions no longer have to agglomerate in central places. They can be placed elsewhere and linked together by communication networks (Chapter 8). Push factors such as the high cost of space, lack of room for expansion, high staff costs and congestion combine to make city centres less desirable for office location. In Britain, both private firms and central Government have relocated offices away from central London. Although offices were moved to peripheral regions, many moves were of relatively short distance to outer London boroughs, for example Croydon, Hounslow and Richmond, and to places in south-east England.

New patterns of office location are also being brought about by the economic growth of regions which are peripheral to traditional core regions. In the USA, service activity expanded faster in the sunbelt states than in the northern frostbelt ones between 1966 and 1977. Office location is also changing at an *intra-metropolitan* scale, with suburban office growth a common feature in countries such as the UK and the USA (Table 7.4). These changes give rise to

	Offices in CBD	Offices outside CBD	Percentage of total outside CBD	Percentage of offices under construction outside CBD
	(million sq m)			
New York	12	7	36	68
Chicago	9	6	39	46
Los Angeles	2	12	85	85
Washington	6	7	53	71
Dallas	3	8	73	77
Boston	3	5	62	56
San Francisco	3	2	33	60

Table 7.4 *Office location in selected cities of the USA, 1986*

Area includes offices under construction

new patterns of offices in the city, as the example for Dallas in Figure 7.10 shows. In Dallas the CBD retains substantial office blocks, but there are out-of-centre locations chosen in relation to the improved accessibility provided by new road developments.

ASSIGNMENTS

8 a. With the aid of Figure 7.9, comment on the layout of the Metro Centre, Gateshead.

   b. With the aid of an atlas, suggest how this development might have affected other shopping centres in the north-east.

9 With reference to Figure 7.10:

   a. describe the pattern of office location outside the CBD;

   b. how effective is the number of floors as an indication of office importance at a location?

   c. suggest two other ways of measuring office importance;

   d. to what extent are offices concentrated in the CBD?

   e. you are advising a mythical Dallas oil company on the merits of moving from old established offices in the CBD to a new office block on the outskirts. The Chairman of the company doesn't want to move. Write a short report to persuade him.

10 a. Explain why many offices have been moved from London to places in south-east England and even further from London.

   b. Examine the consequences of such moves.

11 a. For a town of your choice, describe recent changes in the location of shops and offices.

   b. To what extent do any of Figures 7.7 and 7.10 and Tables 7.3 and 7.4 illustrate your example?

RECREATION AND TOURISM

Many people in the DMEs devote much of their leisure time to the pursuit of recreation. *Recreation* involves a wide range of voluntary activities, including sport, hobbies, gardening and visiting places. If this recreation takes place at a distance from home so that an overnight stay is involved then the recreation becomes part of a *tourist activity*.

Both recreation and tourism have increased since the early 1960s. International tourism has increased more than tenfold, so that by 1985 the number of visitors moving from one country to another was more than 330 million per year. Tourism is one of the world's most important activities, with the leading tourist countries each earning in excess of US$5 000 million dollars in 1985. For some of the LDCs, tourist receipts are a most important source of foreign currency, while for regional economies tourism is a key industry in terms of employment.

Demand for recreation and tourism

Demand for tourist facilities and services comes principally from people in the DMEs. Three underlying factors – ability, mobility and motivation – can be said to promote demand for tourism. The ability of people to engage in recreation and travel stems from their prosperity. As already noted, many people in the DMEs have substantial disposable income to spend on luxury activities like recreation. Furthermore, changes in working conditions, with shorter periods at work and more paid holidays, mean that people have more leisure time.

Greater mobility, and with it easier access to places, has come from improvements in transport and from the availability of the car for personal transport. Travel abroad for many people has been brought within their means by the mass transport methods organised by coach companies, airlines and tour operators. Travel arrangements are easily made through travel agents, while tour operators promote holidays and provide cheap travel and accommodation through package holiday schemes.

For a majority of people, motivation is likely to be based on a need for recreation as a means of relieving the stresses of the normal working routine. For others, knowledge about other countries means that there is greater awareness and interest in different cultures and a keenness

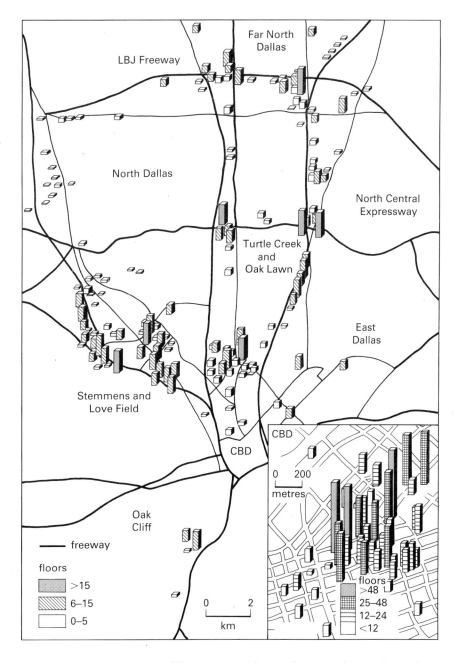

Figure 7.10 *The location of CBD and suburban office development in Dallas, 1979*

to experience them at first hand. These different motivations affect the type of demand for travel services. Mass travel arranged by tour operators might suit tourists interested in the three 'S's', sun, sand and sea, but other people might require special arrangements in order to explore unusual places and pursue specialist interests.

The resource base of recreation and tourism

People like to visit places because of particular features to be seen or experienced there. Combined, or individual, natural features of climate, scenery and wildlife strongly influence a person's choice of area. Many people seek places with warm climates and long periods of sunshine.

151

Figure 7.11 *The ski resort of Bormio, Lombardy, Italy*

Mediterranean areas are sought after by families in more northerly countries like West Germany, the UK and Scandinavia for these dependable conditions. For winter holidays, some people want cold conditions with plenty of snow in order to ski, hence the popularity of Alpine resorts (Fig. 7.11), but others, from both Europe and the US frost belt states and Canada, seek the warmth of venues like the Caribbean islands or Florida.

As noted in Chapter 1, landscapes of scenic quality, mountains, lakelands or coastlands are esteemed. These landform qualities might be linked with others, such as wildlife richness, in their appeal to people. Some African countries have tourist significance as a result of such combinations of features. Finally, the human environment offers a wide selection of attractions: historic buildings, the traditions and customs of the population, and the availability and quality of entertainment such as international arts festivals, and other recreational facilities.

The physical resources of tourism can be classified in a variety of ways. One classification by M. Clawson and J. Knetsch, 1966, relates the type of area to intensity of use. The least intensely used are the *resource-based* areas which are relatively remote and of high scenic quality such as Glacier Park in the USA or Le Parc des Ecrin in the French Alps. Some of these areas have unique landscape features, in effect being regarded as wilderness areas. Many countries have given protected status to designated areas of especially high quality, for example, as National Parks. *Intermediate resources* are more readily accessible to the user, although the boundary between these areas and the former ones is not exact. Examples in Britain are the Country Parks such as Frensham Common and Box Hill, Surrey, or the Lee Valley and Colne Valley Regional Parks. Intermediate resource areas are likely to offer a mix of recreational opportunities so that multiple uses such as camping, hiking, skiing and fishing take place in an area also used for agriculture or forestry. The final category is that of *user-orientated resources*. Here, there is intensive management of resources developed for mass use in the form of theme parks, amusement parks and sports grounds.

Tourist activity tends to concentrate selectively on places, so that even resource-based areas are put under great pressure. The large number of people visiting the National Parks in England and Wales has caused serious deterioration of the land at popular sites, where the physical capacity of the land is exceeded. Pathways and so called *honey-pot* sites are being seriously affected by erosion, as is clearly evident in parts of the Peak District, Lake District and Snowdonia. There is also loss of value from exceeding the *psychological capacity* of an area. This is when a person feels that those indefinable qualities at a place, its solitude and tranquillity, are lost because of the presence of too many other people. Figures for attendance at National Parks in the USA show that people find resource-based areas attractive. Visits made increased by 50 per cent in the period from 1970 to 1986 to reach 70 million, with 3 million visits made to each of the Grand Canyon and Yosemite National Parks in 1986.

Visits to the National Forests totalled 226 million visitor days, with 25 per cent of the visitors making use of camping facilities.

Tourists from the DMEs are attracted to the LDCs by a combination of factors: the scenery, climate, wildlife, cultural distinctiveness and beaches. Countries in Africa and Asia offer many of the first four features; the Caribbean countries the advantages of sunshine and sea. Kenya, amongst African countries, has developed a thriving tourist industry largely based on its National Parks and Nature Reserves (Fig. 7.12).

In Europe, there is heavy concentration on Alpine localities, as in Austria, France, Italy and Switzerland, and an accompanying intensive development of facilities for skiers in parti-

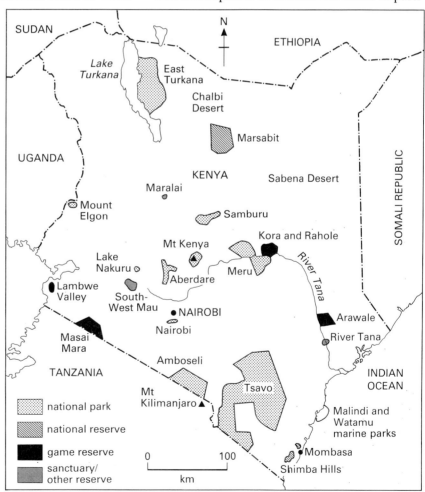

Figure 7.12 *National parks and nature reserves in Kenya*

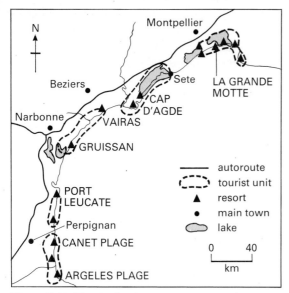

Figure 7.13 *Tourist developments in Languedoc-Roussillon*

cular. Mediterranean coastlands attract large numbers of visitors, and have become highly urbanised as a result. In France, tourist resorts in Languedoc-Roussillon are incorporated into broader regional development schemes (Fig. 7.13). The development of tourism in Spain in the 1950s and 1960s along the Costa Brava and parts of the Costa Blanca aimed at the mass tourist market resulted in the construction of many high-rise hotel and apartment blocks. Further south in Spain, along the Costa del Sol, holiday villages with their own sports facilities are a feature, with hotels along promenades and villas on the lower slopes of the hills rising behind the coast. The spread of villas and apartments across hillsides also characterises the Costa Brava, as Figure 7.14 shows.

International tourism

International tourism is completely dominated by the developed countries of Europe and North America. Sixty per cent of the world total of 330 000 million tourists in 1985 was accounted for by just ten of these countries. The concentration of tourist movement on Western Europe is illustrated in Figure 7.15.

This reflects the affluence of people in these countries and the nearness of countries to each other. West Germany, the Netherlands and Switzerland have a disproportionately large outward tourist movement relative to their populations, which simply reinforces the point made above: that people are prosperous and are conveniently near several other countries offering a wide range of tourist attractions. In contrast, fewer French people travel than might be expected from the population size of the country. A possible reason is that France has a great variety of both user- and resource-based resources and hence visits to other countries are less compelling. This is probably true of the USA also, although high incomes allow many of its people to travel extensively abroad.

Spain, France and Italy are popular destination countries, due to the attractions of the physical environment. In Spain's case, a further factor is the relatively low cost of holidaying there. The number of British holiday-makers going to Spain is also affected by the way in which tour operators focus attention on resorts on Spain's Mediterranean coastline and provide *package holidays* to hotels at these resorts.

USA travel patterns are again dominantly intra-regional; two-thirds of the destinations are in the Americas, mainly contrasting environments in the US, the Caribbean and Canada. The remaining third is to a wide-ranging set of destinations, especially within Europe, but increasingly in Asia.

One significant change in world tourism since 1965 has been the growth of tourists from Japan; at that time, only about 100 000 Japanese travelled abroad, but by 1990 the figure was around 4 million. Destinations in Asia are common, especially in South Korea, Singapore, Hong Kong, and, more recently, China. The premier destination, though, of Japanese travellers is the USA, which 1.5 million Japanese visited in 1985.

Tourism and the Less Developed Countries

Whereas in the DMEs there is a great deal of intra-regional travel, this is not so in the LDCs.

Figure 7.14 *The colonisation of hillsides by tourism: apartments sprawl across Punta Ifach, Costa Brava*

Figure 7.15 *International tourism, major source countries of visitors and their destination countries, 1985*

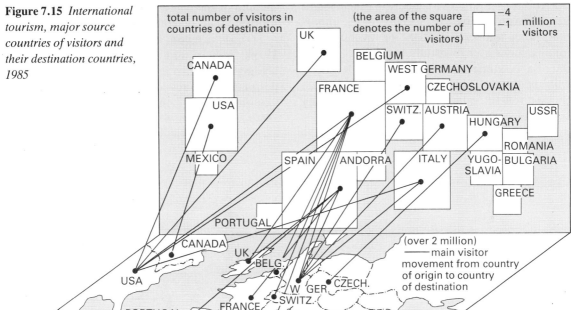

These countries depend on tourists from outside their own region, although this is a situation which is changing with the growth of tourism between Asian countries.

Problems arising from tourist development The extent to which the tourist industry benefits a country is a contested matter, and several negative effects are commonly identified. It is argued that one of the least desirable consequences is the effect on the moral standards of the host countries, in that along with tourist development, has come a growth in crime, prostitution and drugs. There is also a cultural impact, with a possibility that traditional cultures might succumb to habits and goods introduced by visitors, with the adoption of what has been termed a 'Coca Cola' society.

There is considerable environmental impact as a result of development of the necessary tourist infrastructure of new hotels, airports and roads. It is inevitable that this progress will displace traditional houses, shops and markets. There is also pressure on the natural environment. The setting aside of game parks in Kenya, Tanzania, Zambia and Zimbabwe, for example, has safeguarded animals. Unfortunately, there is evidence that tourists concentrate attention on certain species with the result that the normal behaviour of those animals is disrupted.

It is difficult to evaluate the economic balance sheet of tourism in LDCs, and again there are several negative factors. Tourist development has an *opportunity cost* because labour is removed from alternative activities which might be more productive, or socially more important, than tourism. It might be necessary to import goods and foodstuffs because local produce is insufficient or too unusual to satisfy tourists' needs. There could be overdependence on the tourist industry, leaving the economy vulnerable to changes in fashions in tourism.

Economic advantages of tourist development Set against these negative aspects is the contribution of tourism to employment and to the economy as a whole from foreign earnings. An obvious benefit to a country is employment: jobs are created in hotels, bars and restaurants, and also in supporting activities like transport and handicrafts. People employed in the tourist industry spend the money they earn and hence stimulate employment in other sectors of the economy. The limitations are that employment is seasonal and, because of the concentration into resort areas, benefits are not always widely spread through the rest of the economy. However, as international tourism is expected to grow in real terms at up to 5 per cent a year to the end of the century, the gains to LDCs from tourism could be considerable.

Tourist revenue in 1986 was between US $1 000 million and US $2 200 million in the leading Caribbean and south-east Asian tourist destination countries (Table 7.5). In the Caribbean (Fig. 7.16), the industry is geared to American tourists who comprised 60 per cent of

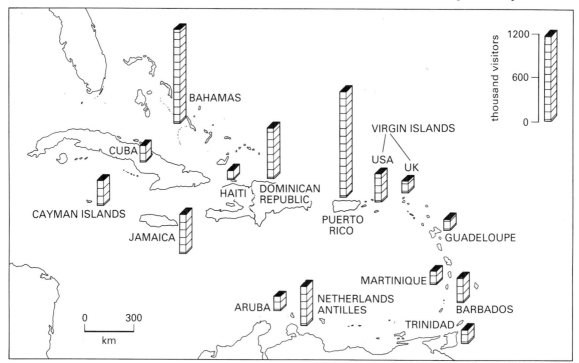

Figure 7.16 *Tourism in the Caribbean, 1985*

Asian	US$million	Caribbean	US$million
Singapore	2 080	Puerto Rico	660
Hong Kong	1 370	Bahamas	800
Thailand	1 160	Dominican R.	280
China	1 130	Jamaica	410
Taiwan	960	Neth. Antilles	220

Table 7.5 *Tourist receipts for selected LDCs, 1985*

tourist arrivals of 8 million in 1986, with favoured destinations in Puerto Rico, the Bahamas and the US Virgin Islands. The pleasant weather conditions between December and April, with temperatures around 25°C when the northern USA is freezing, coupled with other attractive features such as sandy beaches, have acted as magnets to visitors from the USA.

Although on small islands such as these, capital and goods to support the tourist industry have to be bought from outside, there are benefits from multiplier effects. This is especially the case if, over a period of time, local production and ownership of facilities such as hotels, cafes and car-hire firms increases. Recent studies of the Caribbean industry show that over 40 per cent of tourist expenditure is retained locally.

Tourists are attracted in large numbers to Asian countries such as Malaysia, Singapore, Hong Kong, Thailand and Japan (Fig. 7.17).

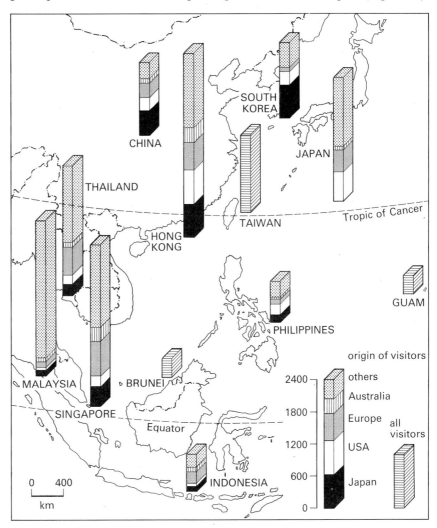

Figure 7.17 *Tourism in East Asia, 1985*

157

Figure 7.18 *Commercial development in Kenya: The Aberdare Country Club*

There is a considerable intra-regional movement as well as the large numbers coming from the USA and Europe. Stop-over visits to Singapore and Hong Kong are common by travellers from Europe en route to other destinations in the Pacific area.

Compared with Caribbean and Asian LDCs, most tropical African countries have relatively modest tourist industries, although their potential in terms of scenic resources is considerable. As noted earlier, Kenya has developed an important tourist industry, earning more from tourism in 1985 than from any single agricultural export. There were 500 000 visitors contributing $300 million to Kenya's economy. In general, East Africa has spectacular scenery to tempt the tourist: the Rift Valley, the lakes and volcanic mountains of Elgon and Kilimanjaro. As well as the grandeur of the landscape, there is a great variety of wildlife, with provision in the game parks for seeing some of the world's most impressive animals in managed, but natural, habitats (Fig. 7.18). Additionally, there is the development of coastal resorts like Diani Beach, whilst visitors are attracted to the expansive beaches such as those between Kilwa and Malindi.

SERVICE ACTIVITY AND THE ECONOMY OF MDCs

The previous chapter commented on the process of de-industrialisation, the shift of employment from manufacturing to services. All the major free-market industrial countries have experienced this shift. This means, of course, that employment in services is greater than any other sector, while the contribution of service industries to the volume of GNP has also increased since 1965.

How exactly do services contribute to the economy? Clearly these activities are key ones in certain regions and in metropolitan areas because of the employment created. Further, the service industry is a major source of *invisible earnings*, as shown by Table 7.6. This is the contribution made by selling services to people and companies in other countries. Such earnings come from tourism, and also from financial services such as banking, insurance and financial consultancy. Certain institutions help finance their activities from the sale of services, for example, universities selling education to foreign students and private hospitals selling medical care to foreign patients. Service activity, like manufacturing, can thus be wealth-creating for a country. However, it is interesting to note that despite a large service sector, the UK only managed to produce a GNP/capita of $10 556 in 1988, compared with the $23 616 in Japan and $18 923 in West Germany, both of which produced more manufactured goods than the UK.

Country	US$million
USA	21 660
UK	12 120
Switzerland	8 580
France	8 040
Spain	5 900
Austria	3 750
Singapore	2 960

Table 7.6 *Net external earnings from the service sector 'invisible earnings', 1985*

Are services, then, a satisfactory substitute for manufactures?

They may not be, simply because there is a continuing demand for goods. To an extent, this demand is actually generated by people carrying out more of their own service needs. They drive cars instead of relying on public transport and they carry out domestic tasks and a great deal of household repairs and improvements with the aid of machinery and equipment. Even when people engage in leisure time activities, they use a lot of equipment, for example, sports equipment, hi-fi units and television sets. Sophisticated products are increasingly demanded. If these goods are not made in Britain, they have to be imported and paid for with foreign currency. This means that Britain's exports of services will have to help pay for the goods that the people want but no longer manufacture.

ASSIGNMENTS

12 a. Identify the main factors affecting demand for recreation and tourism.

   b. For one factor, comment in more detail on how it affects demand.

13 Study Figure 7.15 and describe and account for the main patterns of tourist movement shown.

14 a. With reference to Figure 7.17, suggest why tourism has become important in these countries.

   b. For any four countries, comment on and explain the main origins of tourists.

15 a. Describe the environmental resources helping to stimulate tourist development along the Mediterranean coast of France.

   b. With the aid of Figure 7.13, comment on the distribution and the development of tourism in Languedoc-Roussillon, France.

16 a. To what extent is it necessary for a country to manufacture the goods that are demanded by people?

   b. Discuss the types of service activities in the UK that might contribute to export earnings.

Transport, Trade and Development

TRANSPORT

Transport and the economy

The sinews of the economic system are its transport and communications networks, along which flow goods and information. Reference to Chapter 1 and Figure 1.4 will remind you how the economy is organised and how its components are interconnected. Decisions made in one component are relayed to other parts of the system, resulting in transactions between them. The flows initiated, whether transport flows of tangibles such as people, commodities and manufactured goods, or communication flows of instruction and information, depend upon a network of linkages. The efficiency of the economy greatly depends upon the ability of the network to handle these transactions speedily and at low cost. Much effort is spent on improving transport methods and networks in order to increase economic efficiency.

Interaction between places

Transport serves several needs. It is essential for the movement of goods. People need transport to gain access to services such as medical, educational, recreational and financial services. Transport, therefore, enables *spatial interaction*, that is movement between places, by linking consumers and suppliers. According to E. L. Ullman, 1956, spatial interaction depends upon three conditions: *complementarity, intervening opportunity* and *transferability*. For interaction to occur a demand has to exist at one place and a supply at another. This is the idea of complementarity. It is not sufficient for the places to be different; one place must have what another

wants. Thus crude oil is moved over long distances from the Middle East in order to satisfy the needs of consumers in the USA, Japan and Europe. In return, there is a flow of manufactured goods from the industrialised countries to the Middle East. However, the volume of movement between places is reduced if new sources that are nearer consuming areas are used as alternative supplies. This is intervening opportunity; for example, North Sea oil sources affecting Middle East supplies to Europe.

Transferability depends on the cost of transport and varies from one type of good to another. High-value goods withstand the cost of transport more easily than low-value ones and can be sent over longer distances. Even so, as distance increases flow decreases, until the economic margin is reached and worthwhile transfer stops. No matter how strong complementarity is, there will be no movement if the cost of transfer is too great, that is to say when the friction of distance becomes too severe.

Over a period of time, of course, this margin is pushed outwards because technical improvements to transport bring about savings in the time and cost of transfer. The bulk carriage of commodities is a case in point. The scaling-up of vessels has so reduced unit costs of moving bulky materials like iron ore that distant sources, such as those in Australia, are feasible as supplies for Europe and Japan. Very roughly, the scaling-up of a bulk carrier or tanker from 50 000 dead weight tonnes (dwt) to 150 000 dwt halves the operating costs per tonne of cargo.

Predictions about the size of flows between two places can be made by applying the *gravity model*. The model given below predicts that the interaction between two places will increase in proportion to the product of the populations of the places but decrease as the distance between them increases. Expressed as a formula, the gravity model is:

$$I_{ij} = a \frac{P_i\,P_j}{d^b_{\ ij}}$$

where, I_{ij} is the interaction between places of populations P_i and P_j; d_{ij} is the distance between the places; a and b are constants.

Although population is a convenient measure of the attractive force between places, alternative measures can improve analysis. Population could be modified by weighting it by income per capita, or be replaced by GNP of the places, or by the number of retail establishments at the places. Distance is often squared to account for the distance decay effect, but it could be replaced by other measures such as cost or time.

The cost of transport

The cost of transport is closely related to the mode of transport as shown for road, rail and water in Figure 8.1. There are fixed or capital costs whatever the mode of transport. Capital has to be spent on equipment such as ships, railway waggons, road vehicles and aircraft; on the infrastructure of roads and rail track; on facilities at terminals, such as warehouses, offices and repair shops. The cost of using and maintaining these fixed assets, together with handling charges at depots, are shown as the *terminal costs* for each transport mode. The lines rising with distance on the graphs account for the operating, or *line haul*, costs. These costs are made up mainly of wage and fuel bills, and vary with the volume of traffic and the distance it is moved.

Terminal and line haul costs bear on the different transport modes with varying severity (Fig. 8.1). The terminal costs of road transport are comparatively low, but the cost of operating road haulage rises steeply with distance because the costs are spread over small loads. The reverse is true for water transport. In this case terminal costs are high, but operating costs per unit load rise less sharply than either rail or road transport. This is because greater economies of scale are possible with water transport and this leads to lower average costs. Rail transport has an intermediate cost structure with relatively high fixed costs, but with the lowest unit costs over middle distances. Although air transport is not shown in the figure, it should be noted that its fixed costs are very high as aircraft and airports represent large capital investments. Operating costs are also high on account of the high salaries paid to skilled staff and because of the large quantities of fuel consumed by jet-propelled aircraft. However, people and firms are willing to pay high prices for speed of movement. Airlines also provide the shortest routes across areas of rugged terrain which would be difficult to cross using land transport.

Note that all three curves (Fig. 8.1) are drawn to show a tapering effect, that is that costs rise more slowly as distance increases. This is because average fixed costs are lower for long hauls compared with short hauls. In reality this tapered effect is complicated by the charges, or freight rates, levied by transport firms. These freight rates, which depend on the type of goods carried and on competition, alter with distance in a series of steps, like the stage fares charged on buses. This can have an important locational effect because customers at a distance from the supply point pay less than if transport charges were levied strictly according

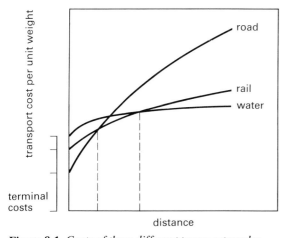

Figure 8.1 *Costs of three different transport modes*

to distance. The effect is to extend the supplier's market area.

Finally, where different modes of transport are used and there is a transfer of goods from one mode to another, intermediate locations at *transshipment* points can offer low total transport costs as shown in Figure 8.2. Note that in the figure different freight rate zones give rise to transport costs rising in steps. One of these stepped lines shows how the procurement cost of a raw material increases with distance from the source. The other line shows how the costs of delivering a product increase as distance from a market increases. The two costs added together at a place give the total cost of transporting a raw material to it and distributing products from it. At the transshipment point the savings on handling costs produce the lowest total transport costs, as shown for this example.

The cost of constructing the transport network

As road vehicles and rail trucks require roads or track to run on, the question of the best routes for the network arises. Two opposing objectives, described by W. Bunge in 1966, are at work here (Fig. 8.3). The *least-cost-to-user* objective provides a network which is completely connected so that no breaks of journey are required. The *least-cost-to-builder* motive keeps the total route length as short as possible so that the cost of engineering work is minimised. The links shown in the figure show a shorter pathway than one going through each place in turn. The connectivity of the two different networks can be measured by the β index. As shown in the figure, the higher of the two values indicates the greater connectivity of the user-benefit network. There are, of course, many other ways in which the five places might be connected.

In practice, where there is concentration of population and economic activity, a highly connected network is built over a period of time, with the *nodes*, points of interchange, located within the urban areas. This is a convenience to people and businesses. In open country, where places are spread apart, construction costs are

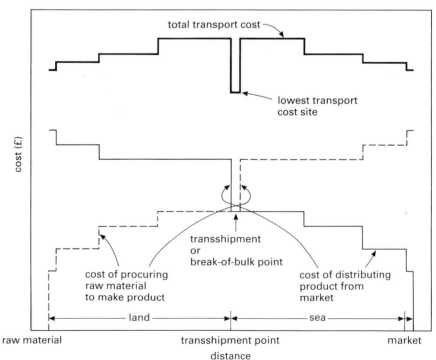

Figure 8.2 *Illustration of the transshipment point as a site of lowest transport costs (after Hoover)*

Figure 8.3 *Alternative network connections for five towns*

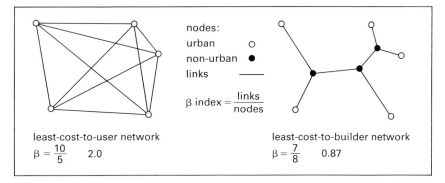

Figure 8.4 *Transport networks in the Amazon Basin*

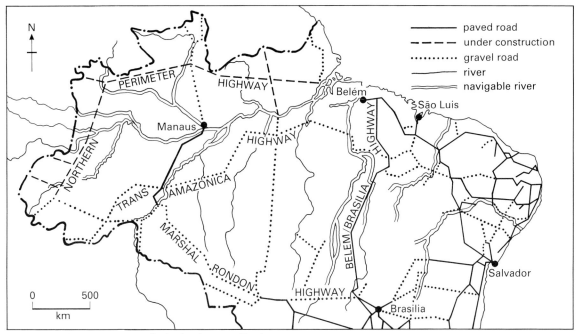

kept down by building a minimum of links. The building of simple straight-line links is frequently disrupted by economic opportunities along the way and by physical obstacles. Routes are diverted to take in places which can provide extra traffic. It might be necessary to avoid obstacles such as hills, lakes and marshes, assuming that building a way round the obstacle is cheaper than paying for extra engineering work to overcome it.

Political and social factors also influence the development of transport networks. The post-1944 building of a system of interstate highways in the USA was motivated by defence objec-

tives. More recently, the Brazilian government has promoted the building of highways in the Amazon basin (Fig. 8.4) with the aim of integrating remote regions there into the national economy.

The functions of different modes of transport

Rail transport Rail transport has the advantage of delivering bulk goods at low cost over intermediate distances, provided that the intensity of use is high enough to offset the relatively

Figure 8.5 *TGV, France*

high terminal costs. In some areas, especially rural areas where passenger density is low and there is little freight, these high costs have led to uneconomic services. Consequently, in a number of European countries, and particularly in the UK in the 1960s, rural areas have experienced cuts in rail services.

On inter-city routes, however, the railways are trying to win back custom by providing new fast services. In Britain and the USA, inter-metropolitan travel has been greatly improved in quality and travel time, and, as a result, has won back passengers. The introduction of high-speed trains in some countries has proved very successful, for example the New Tokaido Line along the Tokyo-Osaka corridor, Japan, and the TGV (Train de Grande Vitesse) (Fig. 8.5) services in France from Paris to Nice (Le Mistral) and to Lyons (Le Lyonnais). Of all EC countries, France has experienced a dramatic increase in passenger rail traffic, up by more than 40 per cent between 1970 and 1983. Once the Channel Tunnel is opened there will be potential for high speed links between London and Paris and hence for Britain to be connected with the high-speed rail network of the EC.

At a world scale, Figure 8.6 shows that a small number of countries account for most of the railway traffic. In some cases, this simply

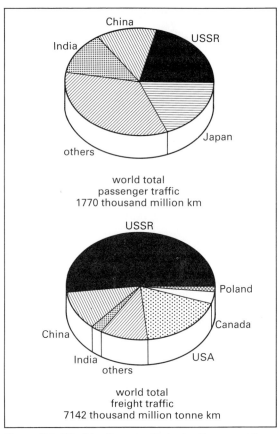

Figure 8.6 *World railway traffic by leading countries, 1985*

reflects a country's size and the long distances that passengers and freight are carried. Japan is included in the passenger traffic diagram on account of the great number of people commuting to work by train. The USSR's position in freight traffic is exceptional, but explained by the importance of heavy industry in the Soviet economy and the need to move bulky materials between widely separated resource and production locations.

Road transport   Compared with rail, road transport provides a very flexible service for a wide variety of light goods, including perishable and fragile goods. Short hauls are less costly than rail, but the use of larger vehicles on improved roads means that road haulage is able to compete strongly with railways even for intermediate distance traffic. Motorways in particular allow rapid inter-city movement, except that even on such roads there is frequently severe traffic congestion especially near

intersections which link to nearby cities. The building of orbital roads around cities has not, in fact, dealt successfully with problems of congestion as the case of the M25 around London shows (Fig. 8.7). Designed for a capacity of 85 000 vehicles per day, some sections of the M25 carry over 130 000 vehicles per day. Part of the problem is that the mere presence of the motorway has created use. Generally in Britain, demand for road space is rising faster than increases in road capacity.

Capacity problems are even more severe within urban areas. New York, Los Angeles, London, Paris, Tokyo and other cities commonly experience severe traffic congestion, and not just on roads in the centre, but in the suburbs as well. Thus it is becoming more desirable that alternatives to the car are provided for urban travel. This implies greater investment in public transit services, such as buses and underground and light railways. A service like the new computer-controlled London Dockland Light

Figure 8.7 *Traffic congestion on the M25 between junctions 30 and 31*

Figure 8.8 *The London Docklands light railway*

Figure 8.9 *Container handling facilities at Tilbury docks, Outer Thames*

Railway (Fig. 8.8) shows one way of popularising the railway for commuter travel.

Water transport Water transport is the most economic of the transport modes for the bulk carriage of materials over long distances. As noted earlier, the use of large vessels, especially of oil tankers and bulk mineral ore carriers, is economic, but it has also imposed limitations because of the draught of such ships. Ships of 200 000 dwt draw water of 20 metres or so and are restricted to deep-water ports and terminals. Deep water terminals at ports have been built to accommodate these large carriers, for example, at Europoort (Rotterdam) and Fos (Marseilles). Heavy industries of oil refining, chemical processing and iron- and steel-making have been attracted to these important transshipment locations, as noted in Chapters 5 and 6, and shown in Figure 5.17.

A technological change of major significance has been the introduction of containerisation (Fig. 8.9). This is the use of a standard size container in which cargo is packed by the dispatcher. Handled by special machinery, containers speed up loading and unloading and reduce handling costs. Ships of 40 000 dwt can be unloaded in 24 hours, allowing fast turn-

round. Such intensive use of large cargo ships means that one ship can do the work of 10 conventional ones. The impact on ports has been very great as fewer berths and a much smaller labour force are needed. The whole of the London wet-dock system has become redundant for cargo handling as a result. These changes have affected many ports in the European Community, with the result that a small number of ports account for most of the large container trade (Fig. 8.10). Three ports in France deal with 84 per cent of this trade and five in the UK handle 62 per cent.

For most countries, the role of canals for freight movement has long since dwindled in the face of competition from the railways, although some of the historic legacy of canalside industry remains. Rather than canals, it is navigable rivers such as the Rhine (Fig. 8.11), Seine, Volga-Don and Mississippi that are important for carrying bulk cargoes.

Pipelines Pipeline transport is to some extent a competitor to water transport, having some of the same characteristics of high fixed costs and low operating costs if used at high capacity. Pipelines of 5 million tonne per year capacity, for example, can be operated at half the cost of

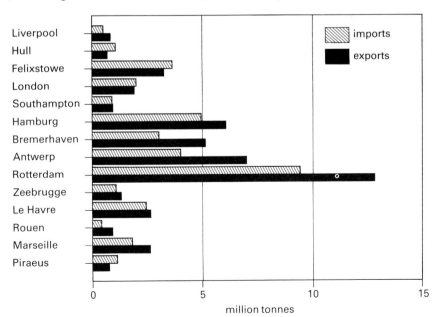

Figure 8.10 *Large container traffic at ports in the EC, 1985*

Figure 8.11 *Barges at Rhine Harbour, Basle*

barges for transporting oil over distances of around 1 000 km. Pipelines are largely restricted to the bulk movement of liquid products and play a special role in the petroleum industry by linking oilfields to ports in resource areas and oil terminals to refineries in market areas (Fig. 5.19). Pipelines are also significant as a means of gaining access to oil resources in remote areas as, for example, in Alaska and West Siberia.

Air transport Air transport is distinctively different from the other modes of transport discussed so far in that it is much faster and more costly. The use of larger and faster aircraft has stimulated demand for air transport since the early 1960s. This has led, in turn, to demand for more capacity at airports. These demands are in competition for expensive land relatively near to cities. So far as international air routes are concerned, there is a clear hierar-

Figure 8.12 *International passenger traffic at selected European airports, 1982 and 1986*

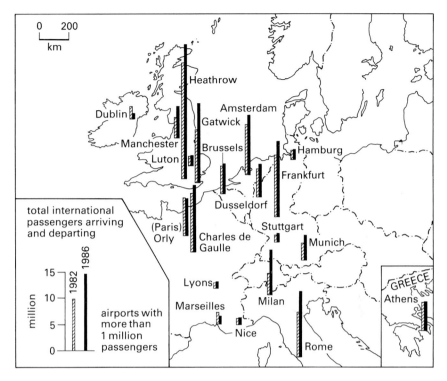

chical pattern focusing on countries with sizeable and wealthy populations. The principal routes are those across the Atlantic, between the USA and Europe, and those between European countries. As shown in Figure 8.12, international passenger traffic in the EC is concentrated at a small number of main airports. Internal domestic air travel is also significant in countries where long distances separate the principal cities as in the USSR, USA and Australia.

Spatial consequences of changing transport technology in MDCs

Improvements in transport aim to make the flows between places faster and less costly. They are a response to demands for easier accessibility. As a personal means of transport the motor car gives people much greater freedom of choice over where to live in relation to work place. This freedom has led to suburban expansion and to residential development in the urban/rural fringe and in rural villages. The car

is therefore an important force in the process of *counter-urbanisation*.

In the DMEs, widespread car ownership and improved road networks mean that in-town facilities of shops and offices, which used to have maximum accessibility, are now no more accessible than out-of-town places served by new highways as suggested in Figure 7.7. People are, therefore, setting up new patterns of movement when they visit these new locations. Generally, economic activity is encouraged to locate near to motorway intersections (Fig. 8.13). This is a photograph of the Aztec West development on the north-west outskirts of Bristol, close to junction 16 on the M5 and within 2 km of the M4/M5 interchange. The concept at a site like Aztec West is to provide attractive modern low-rise buildings for a mix of industrial, warehousing and office activities. The setting is landscaped and the community of workers served by on-site shops, restaurants and banks. Firms engaged in distribution are encouraged to set up regional delivery services at such strategic locations while small manu-

Figure 8.13 *The Aztec West site, Bristol*

facturing business are attracted because of the ease of access to other firms, suppliers and markets.

The economic impact of airports is often considerable. Airports are big employers, Heathrow for example having a workforce of some 55 000, but they also act as magnets for a range of light industrial activities. This is not only because firms set up to provide services for the airport, but also because some firms, in electronics especially, seek access to the fast transport services provided by the airline companies.

Highly significant changes are also occurring in communications. Telecommunications reduce economic distance by allowing instantaneous exchange of information between people. Computer networking allows data exchange and manipulation between individuals and businesses. Facsimile machines have a particular significance in that they give instant written communication between offices. As a result of these communication changes, it is feasible for people to work at home and be linked to a central office through a variety of information-technology systems, an arrangement referred to as *teleworking* or *telecomputing*. Communication changes are thus combining with road and rail transport improvements as the technologies enabling people to move out of cities.

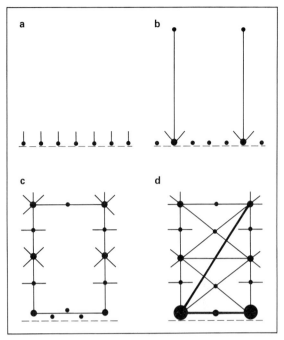

Figure 8.14 *Idealised sequence of a network development in a LDC*

Transport and economic development in LDCs

In many LDCs improvement of transport is seen as a necessary step towards economic development. Indeed, governments often give priority to transport as part of larger objectives of economic and social development. Unfortunately, serious barriers to these developments arise because existing levels of economic demand are often too low to stimulate and pay for transport improvements, yet without such change economic growth is hampered.

A model describing the evolution of a transport network is shown in Figure 8.14. The early stage is limited to trade at scattered ports, with limited communications inland. Then two ports come to predominate, and, from these, single lines of communication penetrate inland and some feeder lines emerge. Finally, after phases in which additions to the network are made, an interconnected system emerges, with some priority routes and some key centres acting as growth points.

This model has been applied to analyse transport development in Africa. Figure 8.15 gives an example for East Africa. Railways were constructed at the time of British colonial rule at the turn of the century. The intention was to link ports such as Mombasa and Dar es Salaam to the interior, and especially to the cash-crop producing areas in the White Highlands near Nairobi. However, despite this early start, the connectivity of the rail system in East Africa is low, with many areas unserved by rail and hence remaining isolated from the cash-crop economy supported by rail services. The final interconnected stage assumed in the model has not been achieved.

Transport developments in LDCs have often been paid for by foreign companies investing primarily in mineral exploitation and commercial agriculture. The rail transport serving the copper mining area of Zambia has already been commented on in Chapter 3. Other examples are the railway links built in association with the extension of coffee growing in the states of Parana and Rio Grande do Sul, Brazil, and in the tin mining and rubber plantation developments of Malaysia. India's rail network, which has a very long history of development, is used

Figure 8.15 *Railways development in East Africa*

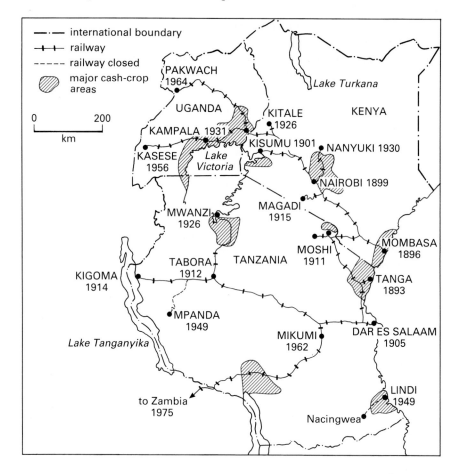

intensively for passenger movement as shown in Figure 8.6.

The modern trend in LDCs is to develop roads and truck transport as ways of connecting rural communities and linking them to wider market opportunities. There are high costs of maintenance in tropical countries where unsurfaced roads may be washed out, but the flexibility of truck transport compensates for the disruption. As mentioned earlier, some countries are building roads to help open peripheral regions. Ambitious schemes such as those for Amazonia (Fig. 8.4) have implications not only for Brazilian policies of integration but also for the rest of the world because of the accelerated deforestation they promote through clearance and settlement.

Although road transport improvements can help inter-regional contact, they do not neces-

sarily lead to a spread of economic activity to more remote regions. Indeed, for many LDCs the orientation of the economy towards primary commodity production often means that the produce of peripheral regions is simply sent out to coastal areas where the main port-related processing activities are located, for example, at ports such as Lagos, Tema and Dar es Salaam.

ASSIGNMENTS

---

1 a. Comment on the factors which affect complementarity between countries.

 b. What changes in technology have affected the use of road transport over the past twenty years?

 c. Describe the spatial consequences of the changes you noted in (b).

2 a. What is the difference between terminal costs and operating costs?

  b. Why are the transport cost curves, Figure 8.1, drawn to show decreasing charges with distance?

  c. Redraw Figure 8.1 to show the effect of a small decrease in railway transport costs.

  d. Comment on the effect of this on the two other transport modes.

3 a. For any one country shown in Figure 8.6, suggest the type of freight likely to be carried and comment on the role of the railway for freight movement.

  b. Comment on rail developments in the EC.

  c. Suggest why in France there is an increase in the amount of passenger traffic carried by the railways.

4 a. Give reasons for the role of airports as growth points for commercial and industrial development.

  b. Find out about, and write a brief report on the problems of choosing a site for a third London Airport.

5 For any one urban or rural area you know well, write a short account of its road traffic problems, and recommend how they might be solved.

6 a. With the aid of Figures 8.14 and 8.15, describe the evolution of the East African rail network.

  b. Comment on the extent to which the network has connectivity.

INTERNATIONAL TRADE

Why trade occurs

International trade is the exchange of commodities, goods and services between countries, reflecting, at its simplest, demand and supply differences between them. The capacity of a country to produce the goods demanded by its people depends upon the application of the factors of production as already discussed in Chapter 6. Countries differ in their *production efficiencies* because of variations in the use and quality of the factors, particularly those of capital and labour. One theory of trade suggests that countries with abundant labour supplies should make and export products which require a great deal of labour to manufacture them, and that countries well endowed with capital resources should produce those things which are *capital-intensive* to make.

A country benefits from exporting a commodity which it can make at lower relative costs and by importing one for which it has relatively higher costs. This is the principle of *comparative advantage* developed by David Ricardo in 1817. This principle still contributes usefully towards the explanation of why countries trade with each other and why they gain if they specialise their production.

Comparative advantage

To illustrate the principle, hypothetical data for two commodities are given for the UK and France in Table 8.1. For each unit of input used, farmers in the UK can produce either 50 tonnes of beef or 40 tonnes of wheat, or some combination of the two. France, with better climatic conditions, can produce more of each commodity. Acting independently, each country produces some of each commodity in order to satisfy home demand. If more of one commodity is wanted then less of the other is produced from the fixed resources available. The amount of the one given up is the *opportunity cost* of producing the other. This opportunity cost is the domestic exchange rate for the commodities. As shown in Table 8.1, in Britain 1 tonne of wheat has to be given up for each 1.25 tonnes of beef, while in France 1 tonne of wheat only buys 0.75 tonnes of beef. However, given that it is possible for France to produce just as much beef as Britain and still consume more than twice as much wheat, why should France trade with Britain?

This is simply because, disregarding transport costs, the French can buy 1.25 tonnes of beef in Britain for each tonne of wheat they export in exchange. This is a much better deal than they

Table 8.1 *Hypothetical production and exchange possibilities for two commodities in the UK and France*

	Output per unit input		Domestic exchange rate	Possible domestic consumption		Possible consumption after trade	
	Beef	Wheat	Beef/Wheat	Beef	Wheat	Beef	Wheat
	(tonnes)		(tonnes)	(tonnes)		(tonnes)	
UK	50	40	1.25	25	20	20	30
France	60	80	0.75	25	46.75	30	50

can get at home. Once the countries start to trade, farmers are encouraged to specialise, with those in the UK transferring resources from grain to livestock and those in France to wheat production. As a result there is greater total output, with resources used more efficiently as skills develop and as scale economies are applied. If the terms of trade were 1:1, the new consumption patterns might be as shown, with consumers in Britain giving up some beef to consume more of the scarce commodity, wheat. The French not only keep more wheat for home use, but also increase consumption of beef. The situation is that consumers in both countries gain satisfaction as they can buy extra quantities of the scarce goods.

Factors influencing trade patterns

Although comparative advantage helps to explain why countries trade, there are several factors which need to be considered for a fuller explanation. One obvious factor is that of transport costs. If countries are far apart, the prices of exchanged goods will be increased and demand reduced. Clearly, however, distance is not a bar to trade. This is because there is a positive encouragement of trade when there is complementarity between countries. As mentioned earlier, Europe needs crude oil which it obtains from the Middle East, whilst the Middle East wants manufactured goods from Europe. The resulting cross-trading amounted to $30 000 million in 1984.

Technological changes affect trade. New products create export opportunities for the innovative country, as they did for the USA in the early days of computers. If substitutes are introduced then both import and export relationships might change as has happened with the introduction of synthetic fibre and rubber. The natural rubber producers lost market share, whilst the manufacturing countries gained sales from improved products using these synthetics.

Trade is also strongly related to market opportunity, for example where a combination of people and wealth bring about a high purchasing power. Large and wealthy nations not only buy more, but they also buy more luxury items. The USA market is thus potentially very attractive to foreign export companies. The Jaguar Motor Company, for example, sold more cars in this market in 1987, 45 per cent of all the cars it exported, than in any other international market.

Because size of markets is important, it can be advantageous for countries to form large trading blocs, as for example the European Community. Such trading blocs are designed to give member states preferential access to the new combined market, whilst keeping competitors at bay by setting up quota restrictions and tariff barriers.

The pattern of international trade

The trade data given in Table 8.2 compare five leading trading MDCs with selected LDCs. The importance of the top five countries can be judged from the fact that in 1985 they accounted for 40 per cent of total *visible trade*. Visible trade is that of goods, the physical presence of which can be recorded as they leave one country and as they enter into another.

These five countries contrast with the next group, selected NICs, because of the different rates of growth of exports. In 1970 these NICs were relatively insignificant exporters, but since then their economic growth has been reflected in rapidly increasing trade links with other countries. Note that per capita export values vary considerably within the NICs: those of Hong Kong and Singapore are much higher than the MDCs, but the others are lower.

The last group is of five low-income LDCs. These countries have only a small share in world trade, and very low export values per capita. There are signs of a growth in exports, with annual growth at least matching those of the MDCs. However, these percentage changes are calculated from very low base figures and the low-income LDCs have a long way to go to catch up in terms of total value.

A final contrast should be noted from the table, namely trade in services such as banking, transport and tourism. The balance of trade in these so-called *invisibles* helps some MDCs to offset imbalances in goods. Of the NICs, only Singapore recorded a substantial surplus of invisible trade in 1985. In contrast, Mexico and

Brazil had large deficits of invisibles but both had sufficient positive balances in goods to cancel out the deficits on services.

Changing patterns of trade

Significant changes in the spatial pattern of world trading have occurred since the early 1970s. In 1970 there was about twice as much trans-Atlantic trade as trans-Pacific, but by 1986 trade flows across these two oceans were on similar scales. The USA, the world's largest trading country, now trades as much with Japan and Asia as it does with Europe, Africa and the Middle East.

A study of Figure 8.16 shows the great importance of the USA market for Japan, Hong Kong, South Korea, Singapore and Taiwan. Asian producers also have important cross-trading links with Japan, as well as varied trade between themselves. Note that trade with individual European countries is seldom large enough to chart at this scale, but the Community

	Imports	Exports	Goods balance	Annual average change	Exports per capita	Services balance
	$ thousand million			1970–83 per cent	$	$ million
USA	362	213	−148.5	7.9	890	21 700
W. Germany	159	185	25.3	8.2	3 032	−1 000
Japan	130	176	45.6	12.9	1 457	−5 200
UK	110	102	−8.4	9.7	1 802	12 100
France	108	101	−6.7	7.4	1 830	8 000
Brazil	14	24	10.3	14.2	176	−12 900
Mexico	14	22	8.2	27.6	283	−8 300
Hong Kong	31	30	−1.1	17.6	5 491	na
S. Korea	31	30	−0.8	21.7	735	−1 400
Singapore	26	23	−3.5	19.1	8 769	3 000
Bangladesh	2.8	1.0	−1.8	14.6	10	−400
India	15.0	8.3	−6.7	9.1	11	−1 100
Ghana	0.6	0.6	0.0	13.7	44	−300
Kenya	1.5	1.0	−0.5	10.0	44	0
Zambia	0.7	0.9	0.2	0.4	134	−400

Table 8.2 *World trade 1985 – selected country comparisons*

Figure 8.16 *Total imports and exports and trade between major trading partners for selected Asian countries, 1986*

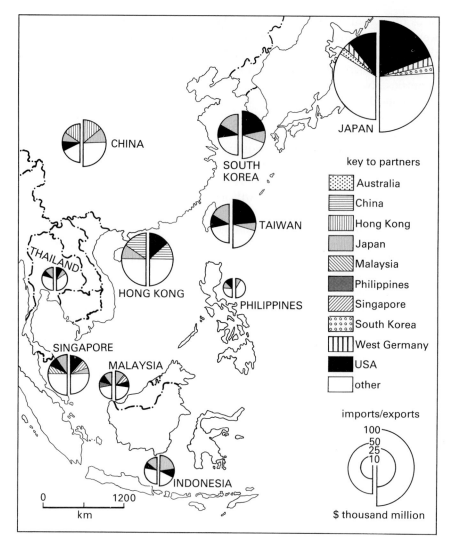

as a group is an important trading partner, and is the destination for over 10 per cent of the exports from each of the Asian NICs.

Broad changes in the pattern of world trade are explained in part by shifts in demand and supply relationships of the primary commodities. Demand for the agricultural produce of the LDCs has been affected by the increased ability of several European countries to satisfy domestic needs from home supplies. The value of the agricultural goods imported by Europe from the USA, South America and Africa has fallen since 1980, hence affecting trans-Atlantic movements. Even so, for African and South

American LDCs agricultural exports are still important, amounting to $7 000 million and $27 000 million respectively in 1984.

Japan's economic growth has meant that shipments of raw materials across the Pacific have increased considerably since 1970. Europe, though, remains an important market. On the supply side, the principal source zones are Australia, North America and south-east Asia. World trade in energy is dominated by oil. Reference back to Figure 4.5 shows the key role of the Middle East for supplies and the main movements to Japan and Europe.

The main explanation for shifts in trading

patterns, however, is the much faster rate of growth of trade in manufactured goods compared with agricultural or raw material commodities. Growth in manufactures has come from generally buoyant economic conditions which have enlarged demand for such goods. Trade in manufactured goods has been encouraged by reductions in tariffs agreed by countries who are parties to the General Agreement on Tariffs and Trade (GATT).

The most impressive geographical shifts in trade of manufactured goods over the period resulted from the industrial growth of Japan after 1960 and its escalating role as an exporter of manufactured goods. Between 1960 and 1980, Japan's share of world manufactured exports rose by 6 per cent to 14 per cent, the USA's share fell slightly, and the UK's from 11 per cent to 5 per cent. More recently, the industrialisation of the NICs, with their export-driven economies, has brought further change. The consequences of these changes to the general direction of trade in manufactured goods are shown for selected countries and regions in Figure 8.17. Japan, North America and Western Europe dominate the world scene as source areas. They send their products to wide-flung

markets across the world. Japan's strong links across the Pacific to other Asian countries and to North America are clearly apparent. For North America the most important market area is Western Europe, but other substantial flows are to Latin America, Asia and Japan. Careful inspection of Figure 8.17 reveals that North America receives more incoming manufactures from its trading partners, with the exception of those in Latin America, than it sends out. The most important destination for Western Europe's manufactured goods in 1984 was North America, with other major flows to Comecon and to Middle East countries.

As a result of the grouping of countries, the intra-trading that takes place between countries is concealed in Figure 8.17. This intra-trading is in fact a large part of total international trade. By far the largest amount of such intra-trading is that between West European countries; this amounted to $335 000 million in 1984, with over 60 per cent of this accounted for by the European Community. Figure 8.18 shows the extent of intra-trading between seven of the Community countries. West Germany's commanding position and balance of exports with its trading partners shows clearly on the chart.

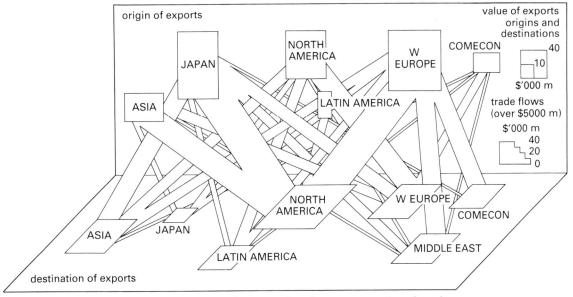

Figure 8.17 *Manufacturing trade transactions between selected country groupings, by value ($ thousand million)*

Figure 8.18 *Trade between major trading partners of the EC, 1987*

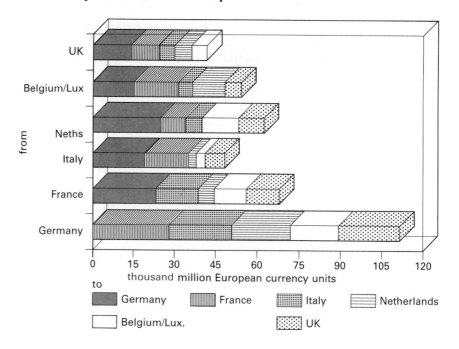

ECONOMIC DEVELOPMENT ISSUES

Dependency and the LDCs

ASSIGNMENTS

7 a. What factors are likely to affect the volume and type of trade between two countries?
   b. For NICs and low-income LDCs, comment on and explain the differences in their export trade.

8 a. With the aid of Table 8.1, find:
      (i) what level of wheat production is possible given beef output of 15 tonnes.
      (ii) what would be the new pattern of trade if the exchange rate was 1 tonne of beef to 1.25 tonnes of wheat?
   b. Give reasons why a country, despite the benefits arising from free trade, might decide to produce as wide a range of goods as possible from home resources.

9 a. With the aid of Figure 8.18, describe and account for trade between EC members.
   b. Comment on the trade opportunities between Western Europe and Eastern Europe.

10 Examine the reasons for the development of trans-Pacific trade and the relative decline of trans-Atlantic trade.

Although industrialisation has enabled a small number of LDCs to export manufactured goods, for many others there is still reliance on the export of primary products. For these countries, the difference in value between exported products and imported manufactured goods makes it difficult for them to earn enough to pay for the purchase of the tools, machinery and fertilisers needed to improve agricultural production, let alone provide a surplus for capital investment into industry. The situation has worsened since the early 1970s because prices of primary commodities have fallen in real terms from their high values at this time (Fig. 8.19). These trade difficulties, together with social problems arising from inadequate provision of housing, education and health-care, led LDC members of the United Nations to set out a declaration of needs in 1974 aiming for the creation of a *New International Economic Order* (NIEO).

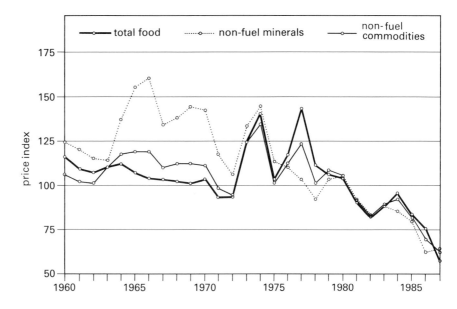

Figure 8.19 *Commodity indices at constant 1980 index of 100*

A New International Economic Order

The LDCs' objectives include improved trading relationships, industrialisation, economic aid and development, and social change. Trade remains a key issue given the importance of markets in the *North* (the MDCs) to countries of the *South* (the LDCs). The North influences not only the South's access to these markets, but also the production of the commodities themselves. For agricultural products, this influence can be traced back to the colonial systems of the 18th and 19th centuries and the setting up of plantations for cash crop production as in the Caribbean, West and Central Africa and Asia for crops like sugar cane, coffee, cocoa, tea and rubber. Production of such export crops is still a significant source of income for many LDCs.

However, where there is over-concentration on a few commodities, LDCs are vulnerable to fluctuations in world commodity markets. Several African countries are dependent on just a single commodity (Fig. 8.20). Oil or minerals dominate the export earnings of Mauritania, Nigeria, Gabon and Zambia, whilst Uganda, Ruanda and Ghana are heavily dependent on coffee or cocoa. Such narrow export possibilities hinder economic development because of

fluctuations in output and income. Attempts by the United Nations to stabilize commodity prices have been largely unsuccessful.

One way in which the LDCs have attempted to reduce their dependence on the markets in the MDCs has been to increase trade amongst themselves by setting up trading blocs. Many problems stand in the way of success for these blocs. Market opportunities are limited within such groups because access is restricted in the absence of adequate transport. Also, there is often a lack of complementarity between countries, as is shown for example by countries in the Central American Common Market (CACM). Costa Rica and Honduras both depend heavily on fruit exports while Guatemala, El Salvador and Nicaragua all export coffee. As they produce similar products there is little incentive to trade with each other.

Apart from help with trade, LDCs need financial help for schemes of economic development. As discussed in Chapter 6, many TNCs have invested in selected LDCs, as for example in their search for low-cost labour in Asian countries. Increasingly, however, the transnational banks in the MDCs have become concerned about making loans because of the risks involved. Much debt has accumulated amongst

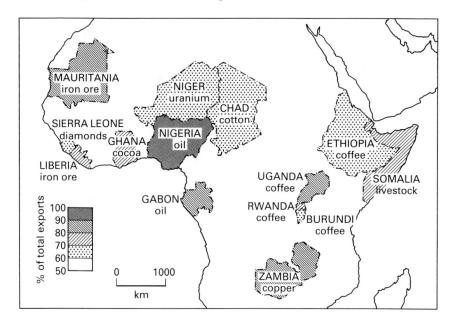

Figure 8.20 *African countries dependent on single commodity exports, 1981*

LDCs, particularly in those that were industrialising at a fast rate in the 1970s. The two greatest world debtors, Brazil and Mexico, owed $212 000 million in 1985, i.e. 20 per cent of the total world debt.

For low-income countries, debt is an even more difficult problem, and aid is essential simply to fight against poverty and starvation. Aid in excess of $1 000 million was given annually in the mid-1980s to each of Egypt, India and Bangladesh.

In order to catch up with the MDCs, many LDCs are seeking greater access to the North's technology by pressing for the transfer of industry. The reasons for basing economic development on industrialisation were discussed in Chapter 6. That the process can succeed is shown by South Korea and Taiwan, where export earnings produced surpluses of $10 000 million each in 1988. Unfortunately the situation for many LDCs is that industrial momentum is insufficient for self-propelled economic growth.

Finally, there are problems of high levels of unemployment in many LDCs. This is partly the result of the high birth rates of the late 1960s, so that the labour force is now growing much faster than jobs can be created. Lack of

employment opportunity is associated with a range of social and economic ills. In rural areas there is surplus labour, forcing a migration, especially of young people, to the cities in a search for work. It is logical that people should seek work in cities because manufacturing in the LDCs is heavily concentrated in them. Policies of import substitution and export industrialisation have led to ports and the largest cities becoming the principal markets and manufacturing bases. However, far too many people congregate in the cities for the number of jobs available, with many newcomers drifting to the shanty towns where they compound the problems of concentrated joblessness and overcrowding.

DIVERGENCE IN THE WORLD ECONOMY

Fast economic growth characterised the western industrial countries in the 1960s, but this growth was interrupted by the oil crisis of the 1970s, when economic recession accompanied sharply increased costs of manufacturing. Relationships between countries as manufac-

180

turers have greatly altered in the 1980s, especially between Asian producers and the DMEs. Partly as a consequence of the intense competition, the older industrial regions in the DMEs have experienced industrial contraction. Their relative decline is also the result of a failure to attract or develop new industry, which has gone instead to preferred sunbelt locations.

There are also changes in the organisation, ownership and location of manufacturing arising from the investment strategies of the TNCs, as already discussed in Chapter 6. Investment in Europe by USA and Japanese firms has risen in the run up to full Community integration in 1992. By 1990, Britain will almost certainly have the greatest number of Japanese manufacturing plants in the EC (Fig. 8.21), with large investment by Nissan, Toyota and Honda in motor manufacturing. This investment will bring jobs to Newcastle, Derby and Shotton, but also intensify competition in the European car markets.

Market opportunities are occurring elsewhere. The Asian countries are shifting towards greater consumption of goods and there is the great potential of market expansion in China. These shifting relationships between Occident and Orient are thus of major global significance. Many LDCs, unfortunately, look like being left out of the expanding opportunities.

ECONOMIC ACTIVITY AND THE ENVIRONMENT

In Chapter 1 it was argued that resource depletion of the kind predicted in the Club of Rome model was unlikely. Indeed, concern about resource depletion has faded for the reasons discussed in Chapters 2 and 3. Replacing this concern is the issue of pollution. There is now widespread debate about global environmental degradation, particularly that arising from atmospheric pollution and tropical forest clearance. That there is universal concern about these issues is because the associated warming of the atmosphere, the *greenhouse effect*, has planetary consequences as opposed to the localised effects of pollution from industrial waste.

Pollution caused by specific industries and affecting nearby areas, as for example that shown in Figure 8.22, can be dealt with in a variety of ways. A straightforward economic way is by imposing taxes on the polluters. It would be possible to set a level of tax that would make it more costly for firms to carry on discharging pollutants than to pay for the processing plant to treat them. Thus firms would find it more economic to take preventive action.

How, though, can the monumental task of protecting the global environment be achieved?

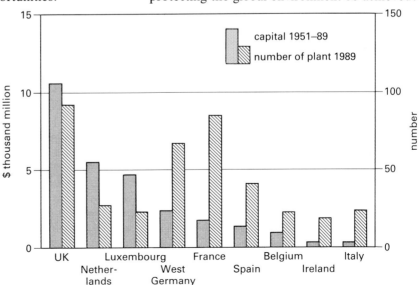

Figure 8.21 *Japanese investment in nine EC member countries*

Figure 8.22 *Pollution from industrial plant at Teesside, North-East England*

Attempts to limit pollution of the atmosphere by controlling the use of ozone-damaging products like the chloro-fluoro-carbons (CFCs) used in aerosols and as refrigerants makes sense, even though there are resource implications in using less effective alternatives. Trying to restrict other types of pollutants, for example carbon dioxide and sulphur dioxide gases, and smoke emissions from coal fired power stations, is more difficult, partly because of the scale of the activity. Technically, control over sulphur dioxide and smoke particles is feasible, if costly, as noted in Chapter 5. An alternative solution is to use fuels other than coal. But oil and natural gas are fossil fuels, and all fossil fuels when burnt emit carbon dioxide, the gas that contributes most to the greenhouse effect. Nuclear power stations do not give rise to CO_2, but reliance on this power source causes grave concern because radioactive wastes are produced. Renewable energy sources are environmentally attractive because of the absence of associated pollutants, but these resources are not of the magnitude, nor always in the right market locations, to be sufficient replacements for fossil fuels at least in the short and medium terms.

Curbing economic growth might be a route to reducing pollution. It is unlikely, however, that an economic system based on zero growth would appeal to a majority of people in the advanced nations, accustomed as they are to high standards of living based on the mass consumption of goods including carbon monoxide producing goods like cars. For LDCs, a zero growth option would deny them an opportunity to catch up with the MDCs.

It makes more sense to opt for a policy of *sustainable economic growth* in the world economies. This means shifting production methods away from those based on high inputs of primary commodities. It also implies some slowing down in the rate of demand by practising conservation methods. As suggested earlier, one way to cut the output of the gases which contribute to global warming is to reduce electricity generation from power stations which use fossil fuels. The benefits of such reduction would be considerable given that 65 per cent of the greenhouse effect is associated with energy use. Greater energy efficiency could help by slowing down demand for energy without necessarily inhibiting economic growth. Energy efficiency along with conservation could be used as the routes to reduced energy production and hence to environmental protection. Even so, pollution would still occur.

Nations will have to deal with the continuing pollution that inevitably results from economic activities. Like industrial production, pollution is international in scope. Consequently, if one country introduces environmentally friendly methods, then all countries benefit. Clearly a major challenge to the world-wide adoption of environmental protection and counter-pollution methods will be for nations to reach agreement about a code of conduct. Evidence of co-operation between nations is to be seen in the way the United Nations is gaining support for its sponsored programmes and conferences. The Montreal Protocol, 1989, included a de-claration by 27 countries to halve CFC use by the end of the century. The idea of an 'Inter-national Green Cross Code' was proposed at the Moscow Conference, 1990, as a way of helping countries in ecological distress. How-ever, caution was expressed at the Washington Conference, 1990, in the statement that there is

a need to couple environmental action with economic feasibility. Will there be sufficient ingenuity and resolve amongst nations at the turn of the century to protect the atmosphere and environments such as the 'last wilderness', Antarctica?

ASSIGNMENTS

11 a. Why is it that many LDCs rely on the produc-tion and export of primary commodities?

   b. Comment on the problems associated with such dependence.

12 a. What are less developed countries seeking in the New International Economic Order?

   b. Comment on the interdependence between LDCs and MDCs.

13 a. Why is there such concern about the pollution of the global environment?

   b. What action can be taken to limit the effects of industrial pollution?

   c. To what extent is a sustainable economic growth policy feasible?

Figure 8.23 *The Signy Island scientific base in Antarctica; a scene in the short Summer showing the break up of sea ice*

Glossary

Accessibility
The ease with which economic activities are interconnected, or a place is reached from other places. Route convergence at a place.

Agglomeration economies
Savings made by a firm, and external to it, by clustering along with other firms. Costs of obtaining services are reduced. Exchange between firms gives rise to benefits from linkages.

Approximate conversion factors
One tonne of crude oil equals:

1.5	tonnes of coal
1.111	thousand cubic metres of natural gas
12	thousand kWh of electricity
10	million kilocalories
7.33	barrels of crude oil
1164	litres of crude oil

One million tonnes of crude oil per year:
20 000 barrels of crude oil per day

Backwash effect
Withdrawal of resources, labour and capital from a peripheral region, leading to a concentration of wealth in a core region at the expense of the periphery.

Bid rent
The amount a person or firm is willing to pay to occupy a parcel of land at a particular distance from a centre or market.

Capital goods
Equipment, machines and tools made by a firm and used to manufacture further goods.

Central place
A settlement which serves its surrounding area by providing goods and services.

Command economy
An economy operated by centrally organised decision-making which controls production and exchange.

Comparative advantage
A principle which states that a region will produce those goods for which it has the best combination of the factors of production, leading to specialisation, especially in agriculture.

Complementarity
The principle that interaction between places depends upon a demand and supply relationship between them.

Consumer goods
Goods in a finished form that can be used immediately by the domestic purchaser. As durable goods they include items like electrical appliances and furniture; as non-durables, food and drink.

Cumulative causation
The progressive economic success of a region compared with other regions because of its ability to attract capital, labour services and innovation. The conceptual argument in Gunnar Myrdal's model.

De-industrialisation
The decline of the relative importance of manufacturing in an economy.

Economic rent
In agricultural geography, the surplus return from land in one use rather than another. Calculated from the total revenue received less the costs of production and transport.

Factors of production
The essential requirements of capital, land and labour needed to bring about productive activity.

Footloose industry
An industry which does not require any specific kind of location.

Gross Domestic Product (GDP)
The total output of the domestic economy produced within a time period.

Gross National Product (GNP)
GDP plus net income from abroad, i.e. income earned from investments overseas less payments made to foreign countries.

Intervening opportunity
The notion that the attractive force of a distant place is adversely affected by nearer opportunities.

Linkage
Connections between firms involving the flow of materials, goods and services, i.e. manufacturers sending components to assembly firms.

Market economy
An economy in which most of the output is for exchange with decisions taken by individual firms and consumers. The market serves as the clearing system where goods and services are exchanged for money.

Multiplier effect
An initial investment which sets off a succession of smaller transactions in the economy, causing a chain reaction of further growth (positive effect) or decline (negative effect).

Non-renewable resource
Use of which depletes the finite stock which is not being replaced and hence threatens the future use. Also referred to as finite, fund or stock resource.

Oil equivalent
A measure of energy in which fuels with different calorific values are standardised against oil. Because large quantities are often involved, million tonnes of oil equivalent (mtoe) are commonly used.

Range of a good
The distance people are willing to travel to a place to purchase goods or services.

Renewable resource
Can be consumed without limiting future use provided that net renewal in a time period is not exceeded; also flow or continuous resource.

Spread effect
The spread of economic growth from a prosperous core region to poorer peripheral regions.

Sustainable yield
A quantity which can be taken from a renewable resource in perpetuity.

Threshold population
The minimum number of people needed to support retail or service activity at a central place.

Transferability
The ease with which a commodity can be transported, i.e. low transport cost compared with a good's value.

Transnational Company (TNC)
A company with operations in more than one country and often with activities on a global scale.

Transshipment point
A place where a commodity is transferred from one transport mode to another. Frequently, commodities are made up into smaller consignments during transshipment, hence the term break-of-bulk.

Value added
The value added to production inputs by the manufacturing process.

Additional Reading

GENERAL REFERENCES

Texts which cover a range of relevant topics are:

Cole J. P. (1983) *Geography of World Affairs*, Butterworths, London.

Haggett P. (1983) *Geography A Modern Synthesis*, Harper and Row, New York.

Knox P. and Agnew J. (1989) *The Geography of the World Economy*, Arnold, London.

Simmon I. G. (1981) *The Ecology of Natural Resources*, Edward Arnold, London.

For a useful appraisal of models and theories in Geography see:

Bradford M. G. and Kent W. A. (1977) *Human Geography Theories and their Application*. Oxford University Press, Oxford.

CHAPTER 1
ECONOMIC SYSTEMS AND RESOURCES

For a review of changes in communist countries in Eastern Europe see This Changing World, 1990, *Geography*, 75, 239–277

Selective reading from the following is recommended:

Hodder B. W. and Lee R. (1974) *Economic Geography*, Methuen, London, (Chapters 1 to 6).

Fernie J. and Pitkethly A. S. (1985) *Resources Environment and Policy*, Harper and Row, London. (Chapters 1 and 2).

Barke M. and O'Hare G. (1984) *The Third World*, Oliver & Boyd, Edinburgh. (Chapter 1).

Cole J. P. (1987) *Development and Under-development*, Methuen, London. (Chapters 1 and 2).

References in the text:

Malthus T. (1872) *An essay on the principle of population*, London. Reprinted in Blunden J. et al. (1979) Fundamentals of Human Geography: A Reader, Harper and Row, London.

Meadows D. H. (1972) *The Limits to Growth*, Pan Books.

Myrdal G. (1957) *Economic Theory and Under-developed Regions*, Duckworth, London.

Rostow, W. W. (1966) *The Stages of Economic Growth*, Cambridge University Press, Cambridge.

CHAPTER 2
NON-FUEL RENEWABLE RESOURCES

Descriptions and assessments of Von Thunen's land use analysis can be found in:

Chisholm M. (1962) *Rural Settlement and Land Use*, Hutchinson, London.

Morgan W. B. (1973) The Doctrine of the Rings, *Geography*, 58, 301–312.

For further development of the concept of economic rent and of economic and ecological aspects of input/output analysis in agriculture see:

Found W. C. (1971) *A Theoretical Approach to Rural Land Use Patterns*, Edward Arnold, London.

Simmons I. G. (1980) Ecological-Functional Approaches to Agriculture in Geographical Contexts, *Geography*, 65, 305–316.

For discussion of aspects of agriculture see:

Barke M. and O'Hare G. (1984) *The Third World*, Oliver & Boyd, Edinburgh. (Chapters 4 and 5).

Senior M. (1979) *The Tropical World*, Longman, London. (Chapters 8 to 13).

Pierce J.T. (1990) *The Food Resource*, Longman, London.

Farmer B.H. (1977) *The Green Revolution*, Macmillan, London.

Rigg J. (1989) The Green Revolution and Equity, *Geography*, 74, 144–150.

Simpson E.S. (1980) Plantations: Benefit or Burden? *Geographical Magazine*, 112, (Analysis 1–3).

Bowler I.R. (1986) Intensification, Concentration and Specialisation in Agriculture: the case of the European Community, *Geography*, 71, 14–24.

On water and forest resources, see:

Fernie J. and Pitkethly A.S. (1985) *Resources Environment and Policy*, Harper and Row, London.

Sewell W.R.D. (1974) Water Across the American Continent, *Geographical Magazine*, 96, 472–479.

Wilcock D., Birch B.P. and Cantor L.M. (1974) Changing Attitudes to Water Resource Development in California, *Geography*, 61, 127–136.

Mather A.S. (1987) Recent Trends in Forest Resources, *Geography*, 72, 1–15.

References in the text:

Prothero R.M. (1957) Land Use at Soba, Zaria Province, Northern Nigeria, *Economic Geography*, 33, 72–86.

Griffin E. (1973) Testing the Von Thunen Theory in Uruguay. *Geographical Review*, 53, 500–516.

Rutherford J. (1966) *New Viewpoints in Economic Geography*, Martindale Press, Sydney.

CHAPTER 3
MINERALS AND MINING ACTIVITIES

Blunden J. (1985) *Mineral Resources and their Management*, Longman, London.

Fernie J. and Pitkethly A.S. (1985) *Resources Environment and Policy*, Harper and Row, London. (Chapter 11).

Hay I. (1976) A Simple Location Theory for Mining Activity. *Geography*, 61, 65–76.

Manners G. (1981) Our Planet's Resources, *Geographical Journal*, 147, 1–22.

Prestwich R. (1975) America's Dependence on the World's Metal Resources, Shifts in Import Emphases, *Institute of British Geographers Transactions*, 64, 97–118.

Warren K. (1973) *Mineral Resources*. Penguin Books, Harmondsworth.

Senior M. (1979) *The Tropical World*, Longman, London, (Chapter 14).

Soussan J. (1988) *Primary Resources and Energy in the Third World*. Routledge, London. (Part I).

Spooner D. (1981) *Mining and Regional Development*, Oxford University Press, Oxford.

CHAPTER 4
ENERGY, THE ECONOMY AND RENEWABLE ENERGY RESOURCES

Foley G. (1987) *The Energy Question*, Penguin Books, Harmondsworth, Middlesex. (Chapter 9).

Schumacher D. (1985) *Energy: Crisis or Opportunity*, Macmillan, London. (Chapters 6 to 9).

Soussan J. (1988) *Primary Resources and Energy in the Third World*, Routledge, London. (Part II).

CHAPTER 5
NON-RENEWABLE ENERGY RESOURCES AND THE POWER INDUSTRIES

Foley G. (1987) *The Energy Question*, Penguin Books, Harmondsworth, Middlesex. (Chapters 5 to 8).

Odell P.R. (1986) *Oil and World Power*, Penguin Books, Harmondsworth, Middlesex.

Mounfield P.R. (1985) Nuclear Power in Western Europe, *Geography*, 70, 315–327.

Soussan J. (1988) *Primary Resources and Energy in the Third World*. Routledge, London. (Part II).

Schumacher D. (1985) *Energy: Crisis or Opportunity*. Macmillan, London. (Chapters 2 to 5).

Davis J. F. (1981) Shifts in US Coal Production: Trends and Implications, *Geography*, 66, 304–309.

Department of Energy (1989) *Development of the Oil and Gas Resources of the United Kingdom*, HMSO, London.

International Energy Agency (1982) *world Energy Outlook*, Organisation for Economic Co-operation and Development, Paris.

CHAPTER 6
MANUFACTURING ACTIVITIES

For reading on the theories and models of industrial location:

Bale J. (1981) *The Location of Manufacturing Industry*, Oliver and Boyd, Edinburgh.

Chapman K. and Walker D. (1987) *Industrial Location*, Basil Blackwell, Oxford.

Lloyd P. E. and Dicken P. (1977) *Location in Space*, Harper and Row, London.

The important topic of industrial change is covered at world and UK scales by:

Dicken P. (1986) *Global Shift: Industrial Change in a Turbulent World,* Harper and Row, London.

Kemp T. (1983) *Industrialisation in the Non-Western World*, Longman, London.

Lever W. F. (ed.) (1987) *Industrial change in the United Kingdom*, Longman.

References in the text:

Smith D. M. (1971) *Industrial Location*, J. Wiley, New York.

Kennelly R. A. (1968) *The Location of the Mexican Steel Industry*. In Smith R. H. T., Taaffe E. J., King L. J. (eds) Readings in Economic Geography, Rand McNally, Chicago. 126–157.

Hoover E. (1948) *The Location of Economic Activity*, McGraw Hill, New York.

Martin R. Rowthorn B. (1986) *The Geography of De-Industrialisation*, Macmillan, London.

Myrdal G. (1957) *Economic Theory and Underdeveloped Regions*, Duckworth, London.

Valavanis S. (1968) Lösch on Location in Smith R. H. T., Taaffe E. J., King L. J. (eds) Readings in Economic Geography, Rand McNally, Chicago.

CHAPTER 7
SERVICE ACTIVITIES

Daniels P. W. (1982) *Service Industries: Growth and Location*, Cambridge University Press, Cambridge.

Davies R. L. (1976) *Marketing Geography*, Methuen, London.

Bird J. H. and Witherick M. E. (1986) Marks and Spencer: the Geography of an Image, *Geography*, 71, 305–319.

Price D. G. and Blair A. M. (1989) *The Changing Geography of the Service Sector*, Bellhaven Press, London.

Pearce D. (1987) *Tourism Today*, Longman, London.

Murphy P. (1985) *Tourism: A Community Approach*, Methuen, London.

Lea J. (1988) *Tourism and Development in the Third World*, Routledge, London.

References in the text:

Christaller W. translated by Baskin C. W. (1966) *Central Places in Southern Germany*, Prentice Hall.

M Clawson and J Knetsch (1966) *The Economics of Outdoor Recreation*, John Hopkins University Press, Baltimore.

CHAPTER 8
TRANSPORT, TRADE AND DEVELOPMENT

For a discussion of the first two themes of this chapter see:

Barke M. (1986) *Transport and Trade*, Oliver & Boyd, Edinburgh.

Reading about world development and interdependency between countries is recommended from:

Brandt W. (1980) *North-South: A Programme for Survival*, Pan Books, London.

Cole J. P. (1987) *Development and Underdevelopment: A Profile of the Third World*, Methuen, London. (Chapters 4 and 5).

Dicken P. (1986) *Global Shift: Industrial Change in a Turbulent World*, Harper and Row, London. (Chapter 12).

Gilbert A. (1985) *An Unequal World: the Links between Rich and Poor Nations*, Macmillan, London.

For a survey of the significant environmental issues affecting people see:

Slater F. (ed.) (1986) *People and Environments: Issues and Enquiries*, Collins Educational, London.

References in the text:

Bunge W. (1966) *Theoretical Geography*, Lund Studies in Geography Series Cl, Royal University of Lund.

Ullman, E. J. (1956) *The Role of Transportation and the Bases for Interaction*, in Thomas W. L. Man's Role in Changing the Face of the Earth, University of Chicago Press.

STATISTICAL AND OTHER SOURCES

Keeping up to date in Economic Geography is a challenge. Some useful, relatively inexpensive data sources are:

United Nations (annual) *World Statistics in Brief*, United Nations, New York. (Available from HMSO).

Eurostat (annual) *Basic Statistics of the Community*, Office for Official Publications of the European Communities, Luxembourg. (Available from HMSO).

British Petroleum Company plc (annual) *BP Statistical Review of World Energy*, BP International Ltd, London. (Also available as an IBM-compatible diskette).

The following statistical sources include useful comment on selected topics:

World Resources Institute (annual) *World Resources*, International Institute for Environment and Development, Basic Books, New York.

The International Bank for Reconstruction and Development/The World Bank (annual) *World Development Report*, Oxford University Press, Oxford/New York.

Other statistical sources:

United Nations (Annual) *Statistical Yearbook*, United Nations, New York. (Available from HMSO).

The Economist Publications Limited (1987) *The World in Figures*, Hodder and Stoughton, Sevenoaks, Kent.

British Geological Survey (1988) *World Mineral Statistics 1982–86*, British Geological Survey, Keyworth, Nottingham.

World and country maps and statistics on selected topics by countries are available on diskettes for IBM compatible, Nimbus and Archimedes machines from:

PC Globe, Applied Knowledge Ltd., George Street, Halifax

You can also keep up to date by reading articles in journals. The following are suggested as particularly relevant:

Geography, Journal of the Geographical Association, Sheffield.

Geographical Magazine, The Monthly Magazine of the Royal Geographical Society, London.

Geography Review, Philip Allan Publishers Ltd., Oxford.

The Economist, The Economist Newspaper Ltd., London.

Index